Mapping AsiaTown Cleveland

In the series *Asian American History and Culture,*
edited by Cathy Schlund-Vials, Shelley Sang-Hee Lee, and Rick Bonus.
Founding editor, Sucheng Chan; editors emeriti, David Palumbo-Liu,
Michael Omi, K. Scott Wong, and Linda Trinh Võ.

A list of additional titles in this series appears at the back of this book.

REBECCA JO KINNEY

Mapping AsiaTown Cleveland

Race and Redevelopment in the Rust Belt

TEMPLE UNIVERSITY PRESS
Philadelphia • *Rome* • *Tokyo*

TEMPLE UNIVERSITY PRESS
Philadelphia, Pennsylvania 19122
tupress.temple.edu

Library of Congress Cataloging-in-Publication Data

Names: Kinney, Rebecca J., 1979– author.
Title: Mapping AsiaTown Cleveland : race and redevelopment in the Rust Belt
   / Rebecca Jo Kinney.
Other titles: Race and redevelopment in the Rust Belt | Asian American
   history and culture.
Description: Philadelphia : Temple University Press, 2025. | Series: Asian
   American history and culture | Includes bibliographical references and
   index. | Summary: "Cleveland's AsiaTown presents a unique opportunity to
   analyze the role of regional racial formation in the community
   development of an Asian American urban center in a midsize Rust Belt
   city, underscoring the contextual and mutable understanding of place"—
   Provided by publisher.
Identifiers: LCCN 2024053868 (print) | LCCN 2024053869 (ebook) | ISBN
   9781439924754 (cloth) | ISBN 9781439924761 (paperback) | ISBN
   9781439924778 (pdf)
Subjects: LCSH: Asian American neighborhoods—Ohio—Cleveland—History. |
   Asian Americans—Ohio—Cleveland—History. | Asian
   Americans—Ohio—Cleveland—Social conditions. | Community
   development—Ohio—Cleveland. | AsiaTown (Cleveland, Ohio)—History.
Classification: LCC F499.C66 A23 2025 (print) | LCC F499.C66 (ebook) |
   DDC 305.8951077/132—dc23/eng/20250212
LC record available at https://lccn.loc.gov/2024053868
LC ebook record available at https://lccn.loc.gov/2024053869

The manufacturer's authorized representative in the EU for product safety is
Temple University Rome, Via di San Sebastianello, 16, 00187 Rome RM, Italy
(https://rome.temple.edu/).
tempress@temple.edu

Printed in the United States of America

9 8 7 6 5 4 3 2 1

Contents

List of Figures

Acknowledgments

This book is first and foremost about Cleveland and the Asian American Clevelanders who have called the city "home" over the decades. These are their stories that are carried here, and I offer my deep gratitude to all of the people who have graciously shared their memories, time, and experiences with me over the years and whose names appear throughout the pages of this book. Thank you! I acknowledge Joyce Huang and Karis Tzeng for facilitating introductions, inviting me in, and also working with my students over the years. Thank you to Philip McFee for creating beautiful AsiaTown illustrations and permission to reproduce "Festival" for the book cover.

This project on Asian American community development in the Rust Belt is one that I've been thinking about before I even knew I was thinking about it. There are at least five distinct origins to the questions at its core that trace back decades. First: My early childhood years regularly eating with my family at an American Chinese restaurant in a metro Detroit strip mall. This restaurant was the one place in my life where I regularly engaged with racial mirrors and whose staff treated my sister and I with such kindness and care, as they would "secretly" slip each of us a wax paper packet of almond cookies and a wink at the end of every meal. Second: As an undergrad, I took an urban planning class on "Race and the City," which opened up a space to find answers and ask endless questions. Although we did not engage with Asian American placemaking, we did read June Manning Thomas's *Redevelopment and Race: Planning a Finer City in Postwar Detroit*, which influenced greatly what would become my first book and to which this second book pays homage in its title. Third: In the early 2000s, I worked for Asian Neighborhood Design in San Francisco, where I first encountered Asian American community development. Thank you to Grant Din, Delynda DeLeon, Steve Suzuki, and countless colleagues and community members for teaching me about the joys, tensions, struggles, and successes of community development from the ground up. Fourth: My MA thesis on redevelopment and renewal in San Diego's Asian Pacific Thematic Historic District, where many of the ideas that are developed in this book first began as kernels. Thank you to Lisa Sun-Hee Park, Roberto Alvarez, and Natalia Molina for your engagement with that project. Fifth: In 2016, after learning of my interest in Rust Belt Chinatowns, Harrod Suarez sent me an article about Cleveland's Night Market, and so this specific project began.

The years I have worked on this project have been full of the beauty and heartbreak of life. I am lucky that my list of travel companions is long, and I am grateful to have this space to formally acknowledge their support.

As I move into "mid-career," I realize how fortunate I am to have relationships that now span decades with Natalia Molina and Lisa Sun-Hee Park who have served as advisers in every step of this career. Thank you to Natalia Molina for continuing to serve as my academic "godmother." Thank you to Lisa Sun-Hee Park for your candor and support from my very first conference paper all the way to today.

Throughout this process, I've relied on the wisdom of so many colleagues, and I appreciate Margi Dewar and Mark Souther for each taking time to share their expertise, generally, and on Cleveland, specifically, at the early stages of this project. I am grateful for conversations along the way about work and so much more with: Long Bui, Josen Diaz, Andrew Herscher, AJ Kim, Joo Ok Kim, Kit Myers, Yumi Pak, Kong Pha, Tom Sarmiento, Harrod Suarez, Theo Verinakis, and Oliver Wang. Thank you to Harrod Suarez for first introducing me to AsiaTown and the "Cleveland Crew." Harrod, Natasha, Freed, and Viplav, thank you for making every research trip full of food, fun, and laughter. The worst part about this project concluding is that I don't get to see you as often. At Bowling Green State University, I thank Nicole Jackson, Starr Keyes, Clayton Rosati, and Jolie Sheffer for their friendship and Jeff Brown, Radhika Gajjala, Lisa Hanasono, Tim Messer-Kruse, Luis Moreno, Angela Nelson, Susana Peña, Sarah Rainey-Smithback, Andy Schocket, Rob Sloan, and Kim Stanley for being wonderful colleagues. Amy Davidson and Rebekah Patterson, thank you both for your everyday magic. Vera Lux, thank you for your census wizardry. Thank you to Trinidad Linares for excellent research assistance at the very beginning of this project.

I am grateful for the questions and comments I've received from audiences over the years at conferences and invited talks at Ewha Womans University, University of California San Diego, Sogang University, Wayne State University, Virginia Tech, University of Wisconsin, University of Michigan, Stanford University, University of Cincinnati, and Carnegie Mellon University. These were productive and constructive venues to take ideas off the page and into the world. Thank you to the National Endowment for the Humanities "Mapping, Text, and Travel" 2016 Summer Institute, where this project formally began as a kernel of conversation with this fantastic group. I am grateful to the BGSU Building Strength Grant, the Stoddard and O'Neill Endowment, and the Institute for Society and Culture for their financial and institutional support of the project.

This book is all the better for the readers I've been fortunate to have over the years. I appreciate each of you for struggling with me through drafts and offering brilliant insights, kindness, and sharp critique to help keep me going. Thank you to: Mariola Alvarez, William Daniels, Rachel Kravetz, Emily Merrill, Tamara Nopper, Clayton Rosati, Jolie Sheffer, and Harrod Suarez for reading and commenting at various stages of the project. Thank you to: Thomas Xavier Sarmiento, M. Bianet Castellanos, and Christopher Perreira, the guest editors of the "Unsettling Global Midwests" special issue of the *American Studies* journal, for their comments on a prior version of Chapter 5.

I have found such a lovely home for this book at Temple University Press and the Asian American History and Culture series. Thank you to series editors, Cathy Schlund-Vials and Rick Bonus for their support of the work and for helping place it with wonderful reviewers. Thank you to the editors, reviewers, and Temple University Press Board for incisive critique and genuine support for the project throughout the process. Shaun Vigil has been great to work with throughout the process, and I appreciate our conversations and his guidance along the way. The entire TUP team has been a delight to work with, and I am looking forward to getting this book out into the world!

I am so grateful for friends that are family and family that are friends. I would not have been able to complete this book (or let's be honest, function) without the support and friendship of spectacular people who share laughter, tears, and everything in between, with good humor, amazing hugs, and delicious food and drink. Thank you for sharing in this life with me, I am so grateful for you: Jan and Jesse Adler, Mariola Alvarez, Angela Ball, Hana Crisp, Jerry Glowzinski, Colleen Hilton, Jungin Hwang, Tania Jabour, Angela Kong, Karin Lim, Martha Luna, Jenny Na, Josh Rice, Killy Scheer, John Shelsta, Marta Sierra, the extended Guanco-Atkinson-Mayo crew. Merci beaucoup à la famille Guibert pour votre gentillesse. Rupal Shah, thank you for always supporting me and for being living proof that you can share life in a continuous series of fifteen-minute phone calls, sprinkled in with visits. I am so grateful for you. Thank you to the yoga teachers and communities that served as homes in Detroit, metro Detroit, San Diego, and Seoul throughout the life-cycle of this book: Yoganic Flow, Citizen, Namaste, Ginseng, and 요가 필드.

Thank you to Amanda, André, Archer, and Cresslin Guanco for your love, support, and bringing dessert and deep belly laughs to every situation. I do not know what I would do without you, the refuge of your home filled with Mr. T., *Supermarket Stakeout*, and the best snacks ever, and the joy you bring to my life. Although my mom, Darlene Hall, left this world as this project was just beginning, I carry her wit, wisdom, and unfailing belief in me everywhere I go. My biggest thank you of all is to Thomas Guibert for being my teammate and partner on this epic journey of life that has taken us here and there and everywhere in between. Thank you for showing up every day to share in the silly, the scary, and the delicious. I am so thankful for that first 맛없는 삼겹살 and all the 맛있는 막걸리 that has followed. 너무 사랑해!

Mapping AsiaTown Cleveland

1

Mapping AsiaTown

Race, Space, and Placekeeping in the Urban Midwest

Clevelanders speeding along the East Side's east–west arteries, which connect the downtown neighborhoods to the suburb of Cleveland Heights, are used to seeing the many one- to four-story brick mixed-used light industrial buildings, pockets of commercial strips, and patches of blight that dot the landscape. On a particular stretch just east of downtown, passersby may take note of the red-and-gold wayfinding signs that say "AsiaTown." Or they may see the faux Chinese–style entrance to Asia Plaza, replete with red-painted columns supporting a green-tiled roof that gently slopes upward in the style of historic Chinese temples, welcoming visitors to the shopping center. They might make note of a similar red, green, and gold motif alongside Chinese script on the prominent Payne Commons sign announcing a strip mall that houses the businesses: Koko Bakery, Han Chinese Kabob, and Map of Thailand. Although Cleveland, Ohio, is not a location that most people associate with Asian American place, a multigenerational panethnic community of Asian Americans are living, working, making place, and building community in the Cleveland "AsiaTown" neighborhood.

The geographic locations of the residential and commercial center of the Cleveland Chinese American community, specifically, and the Asian American community, more broadly, have shifted throughout the past 150 years. These movements often were a result of the legacy of white supremacist urban development, which prioritized policies of urban renewal that willfully deemed places where immigrants and communities of color make and call home "slums," "ghettos," and "blighted areas" as readily available for demolition and destruction to make way for modernization and "clean up campaigns" and "ideal" locations to place expressways. This history of forced re-moval and community demolition of Cleveland's Chinatown communities make it similar to many Chinese American communities across the country. However, the duration of Cleveland's Chinatown, as a still active presence in the central city, is different from the fates of its Rust Belt peers, like De-troit, Pittsburgh, and St. Louis, that were forced to relocate and disperse in the face of twentieth-century policies of urban renewal.

Cleveland's AsiaTown, understudied and, in fact, largely unknown even within the region itself, presents a unique opportunity to analyze the devel-opment of an Asian American urban center in a city that is primarily under-stood via a Black-white racial binary. The central place of this study is the city of Cleveland, generally, and the city's East Side neighborhood of AsiaTown, specifically. In Cleveland, a place most often studied through a prism of Black-white racial segregation and the lens of postindustrial decline,[1] Asian Amer-ican community life is frequently invisible. Rather than considering this ap-proach as a "one off" study of Asian American community formation, I posit a study of Asian American community formation in Cleveland as an ideal loca-tion to examine the interconnectivity between the local understanding of race, place, and belonging, in relationship to larger national narratives. By turning toward Cleveland, a midsize postindustrial city in the urban Midwest, we can center the place-based experience of Asian Americans in Cleveland through the framework that Wendy Cheng describes as "regional racial formation,"[2] the "place-specific processes of racial formation, in which locally accepted racial orders and hierarchies complicate and sometimes challenge hegemon-ic ideologies and facile notions of race."[3] Part of the underlying argument herein is to understand that Asian American experience in Cleveland is both intertwined with and also unique from Asian American racial formation writ large, which is often defined through the regional historical narrative and ex-perience of Asian Americans on the coasts. Cheng's turn toward the regional enables a way to understand that hegemonic notions of race and region are part of the project of racial formation, showing that a regional focus both com-plicates and reveals the processes of racial formation. *Mapping AsiaTown Cleveland: Race and Redevelopment in the Rust Belt* is invested in weaving together the specific regional history of Cleveland as a key to unlocking sto-ries of transnational, national, and local Asian American placemaking.

The Midwest Turn: Regional Racial Formation in Asian American Studies

Since the late twentieth-century, scholars have made repeated calls to geo-graphically reimagine the field of Asian American Studies and center communities beyond the typical focus of the West and East Coasts. In the very first issue of the *Journal of Asian American Studies* in 1998, Stephen Sumida's "East of California: Points of Origin in Asian American Studies" signaled the ways in which studies of Asian Americans in the South[4] or the Midwest[5] are presumed to be "regional portraits, whereas studies of the West Coast are assumed to be not regional but unbounded, central, and broadly paradigmatic."[6] A decade later, Erika Lee weighed in with her own call to center the Midwest in Asian American Studies to illuminate new issues as it also "challenges some of the field's key assumptions and paradigms."[7] By picking up the prior calls of Stephen Sumida and Erika Lee to look "East of California," I argue that a turn toward the Midwest enables us to see the regionality of Asian American life, the constructions of Asian Americans in American racial discourse, *and* the field of Asian American Studies.[8] The idea of the "Midwest" itself is one that is predicated on the settler colonial narrative of manifest destiny that already imagines the geographic determinism of the United States. And, instead of suggesting the studies of communities and Asian American life in a city like Cleveland are parochial or provincial, I argue herein that they provide new pathways of connections and understandings of both the national and the regional context of mappings and routes of knowledge that include and exceed the "typical" narrative of Asian immigration to California or large urban centers.

A spatial turn to the Midwest, generally, and the Rust Belt, specifically, in Asian American Studies is a literal call to see other pathways of knowing. A turn toward the industrial Midwest illuminates the ways in which differentially situated economic development, inter- and intraracial relationships, and cultural contexts yield a regionally specific understanding of Asian American life and culture. Thus, a regional turn offers a way of understanding that it is not only what happens on the coasts that informs the Midwest but what happens in the Midwest has its own specific contexts, which, in turn, informs what happens on the coasts. Indeed, some of the key nodal points of twentieth-century Asian American life and history emerge from a literal location in the Midwest: Japanese American resettlement during World War II, Southeast Asian resettlement during and after the Vietnam War, the relocation of tens of thousands of Korean people through transnational adoption, the murder of Vincent Chin, and the rise of the national justice movement that followed. These examples reveal the ways in which Asian American life in the United States has been governed by both legal policies that prioritize the dislocation of families and communities through forced movements and the everyday and structural violence of anti-Asian racism. Crucially, the presumed absence and invisibility of Asian Americans in these Midwestern communities is one of the many ways that forms of violence persist. Indeed, it is the context of regional racial formation that, for the most part, centers the Rust

Belt along a Black-white binary and suggests that Asian Americans are absent from the urban Midwest.

As a result of differing regional realities, Chinese migrants, for example, first migrated to places in the Midwest like Cleveland in the late nineteenth century. It is commonly accepted that "the Chinese who settled in Cleveland came from other urban areas . . . seeking relief from the intense anti-Chinese hostility on the West Coast and trying to find new economic opportunities."[9] This pattern of migration aligns with other Chinese communities that developed in places like Chicago and St. Louis in the late nineteenth and early twentieth centuries.[10] While not without racial animosity, in the urban Midwest, there was a measure of relief from the anti-Chinese legislation and physical violence and attacks to person and property that communities on the West Coast faced.[11] This reality of differential regional racial formations is also the reason that a Japanese American community emerged in Cleveland in the 1940s (see Chapter 2).

In some ways places like San Francisco and Cleveland can serve as a mirror to understand how regional narratives about race differently impacted the community formation of Asian Americans and African Americans.[12] For example, urban historians contend that, for the most part, U.S. cities did not experience hard lines of racial segregation until about the 1910s.[13] The notable exception to this time frame is San Francisco's Chinatown, which Charlotte Brooks argues was, by the 1870s, "the first segregated neighborhood in America,"[14] making the Chinese the first ethnic group to be simultaneously barred from immigration and residentially segregated. During this same time in Cleveland, African Americans had a relatively high level of social and residential integration. Kenneth Kusmer's canonical *A Ghetto Takes Shape: Black Cleveland, 1870–1930* shows how Cleveland's Black-white color line sedimented in the period *after* Black people from the South began moving northward after the Civil War. Kusmer argues that, prior to 1870, there was a sense in which Black Clevelanders were "almost" equal.[15] Kusmer notes that this integration of Black and immigrant communities, was, in fact, "probably quite similar to that of most other cities," arguing that "the pattern of life in nineteenth-century urban America was usually not amenable to the formation of ghettos, either black or immigrant," generally, given that the "high geographic mobility of urban workers, the rapid growth of many cities, unpredictable patterns of land use, and the need for people of all classes to live fairly close to their place of employment made the strict residential separation of any one group or class difficult."[16] This was also the case for the early Chinese community that "settled in an area along Lakeside and St. Clair Avenues on Ontario Street," near Public Square, the historic and contemporary plaza in the center of Cleveland's downtown.[17]

A regional comparison of racial formation reveals that, while segregation comes later to the urban Midwest and north, the situation on the West Coast is different. Brooks traces the segregation of the Chinese in San Francisco to the nineteenth century while also contending Kusmer's point that, "before 1910, most African Americans in Northern cities lived in integrated neighborhoods, although often in spatial proximity to other black households."[18] Because of the smaller population of Asian Americans in cities like Cleveland, these places proved to be a reprieve from the segregation and racial terror of the West Coast and spurred movement of some Chinese in the late nineteenth and early twentieth century (see Chapter 3).

A Brief History of Cleveland: Rise and Decline

The land known by many, since 1796, as Cleveland is a homeland of the Erie, Kaskaskia, and Mississauga peoples, drawn to the area by the Cuyahoga River and Lake Erie.[19] Settler colonization, a spatialization of white supremacy, undergirds the history of the United States, including Cleveland. Under the auspices of "manifest destiny" the United States, a settler state, colonized Indigenous land through violence and the forced relocation of Indigenous peoples, resulting in an entirely new spatial rendering of the United States as a nation-state that encompassed the landmass from "sea to shining sea." Like Indigenous peoples, white settlers were drawn to the land in the Great Lakes region for its access to Lake Erie. Beginning with the Greenville Treaty of 1795, throughout the 1800s, a series of treaties eventually ceded much of what is now known as Ohio to the United States, and most Indigenous tribes were forcibly relocated to reservations west of the Mississippi River. Much of this takeover of land was based on a rendering of Indigenous stewards of place as ill-suited to cultivate and tend the land in the model of capitalist production, ultimately creating a geographic and ideological narrative that displaced and expelled Indigenous nations based on narratives of power and difference.[20]

After the completion of the Ohio and Erie Canal in 1832 the port city of Cleveland emerged as a major nodal point connecting the waterways from the Atlantic Ocean to the Mississippi River. These waterways were the transportation highways of the mid-nineteenth century, and Cleveland was poised as a major hub on this national network. This prime location enabled what some called "the Cleveland system of manufacturing, in which factories no longer had to be located right next to mines or other sources of raw materials, but could take advantage of water transport to move heavy cargo and finished goods long distances."[21] As the city boomed as a major shipping hub, extraction industries like steel and oil set up home in Cleveland to be close to the waterways, including John D. Rockefeller's Standard Oil. In this context, Cleveland grew and drew populations of immigrants and migrants throughout the late nineteenth and early twentieth centuries. As Roxanne Dunbar-Ortiz argues, many of these machinations are made invisible in narrative and in rhetoric. Indeed, the founding of the United States relies not only on the myth of "manifest destiny" but on the twinned myth of "nation of immigrants."[22]

Cleveland, like its counterparts across the industrializing Midwest, saw its overall population boom in the years from 1870 to 1950, as immigrants from abroad moved to the city directly (until 1924) or as a result of secondary migration, and Black and white migrants from the South made their way to the industrializing north. Cleveland's location as a port city at the mouth of the Cuyahoga River and a point of connection between the Atlantic Ocean and the Upper Great Lakes, served then, as now, as an important shipping port. Cleveland continued its role as a major shipping node with the arrival of the railroads. David Stradling and Richard Stradling note that the population grew by 850,000 people from 1860 to 1940 as the city and its industrialists "built a complex economy around oil refining, chemical manufacturing, and steel production."[23] As home to the notable American industrial giants, "Standard Oil, American Ship Building, the Sherwin-Williams Paint Company, and Republic Steel," Cleveland's industries built Cleveland and beyond. Yet, they quip that "Cleveland was built in a hurry and dismantled even more quickly."[24]

Cleveland's population grew along with the industries. As the industries grew, the rich grew richer. As these industrialists were building their fortunes on the extraction of resources and the labor of the working classes, they opted to move to areas outlying the center city. For example, in the mid-nineteenth century, the primary residential area of Cleveland's elite, "Millionaire's Row" was located along Euclid Avenue between East 22nd and East 55th, the present-day East Side neighborhood of MidTown (see Chapter 4). However, "by 1900 the growth of industry and population had rendered these areas less attractive as they were hemmed in by dense immigrant and working class districts, and were adjacent to the noise and dirt of Cleveland's major industrial areas."[25] The "most prestigious" location for the elites, up through the 1920s, was in the East Side Wade Park allotment, where the estates had restrictive covenants that limited the sale of property to nonwhite persons.[26]

However, by the mid-twentieth century, many of these stately homes on the East Side, in the neighborhoods in the Hough and Glenville areas, would be divided up into multifamily apartments to house the many migrants who arrived to work in the World War II "arsenal of democracy" boom economy (see Chapter 2). These primarily white neighborhoods transformed into mostly Black neighborhoods by the 1960s, flipping a pattern of stark racial segregation of white to Black. It is during this time period of the mid-twentieth century that Japanese Americans also came to Cleveland's East Side, integrating both white and Black neighborhoods as neither white nor Black neighbors (see Chapter 2).

In Cleveland, the imprint of anti-Black racism reverberated through the fabric of the city. Much of the twentieth-century population exodus was fueled by white residents who moved into newly built and racially exclusive suburbs and bedroom communities. From the first recorded census, in 1830, through the 1940 census, Cleveland's white residents represented 90 percent or more of the population. This percentage share continually drops in each census beginning in 1950. White residents were 83.7 percent of the population in 1950 and 71.1 percent of the population in 1960. And, following the Hough Uprising of 1966, Cleveland's rebellion by Black residents protesting racial inequity in the "long hot summers" of the 1960s, the 1970 census counts 61.1 percent of Cleveland's residents as white. By 1990, the city was 49.5 percent white, halved from the 1830 census count that showed 99.1 percent of Cleveland's residents as white. Where did all the white people go? And, the answer, as in cities across the United States, is not that far, a short drive along a state or federally funded road or highway to a racially segregated white suburb.

Metropolitan Cleveland paralleled the national program to subsidize whiteness in the form of racially exclusive suburbanization, and, like their counterparts across the country, many white Clevelanders left for the suburbs. For example, Westlake, an affluent suburb twelve miles west of downtown, experienced an explosive population growth that reveals the inverse of the City of Cleveland's decline. In 1950, Westlake had 4,912 residents and the 1960 census counted 12,906, an increase of 162.7 percent.[27] In one of the most infamous cases of attempted housing integration in the metro Cleveland area, Reverend John R. Compton, a Black minister, purchased a home in Westlake in September 1966. The previous white owners moved out on September 23, and the house was firebombed on September 24.[28] On two consecutive days, the *New York Times* reported on the firebombing and stated, "Westlake, has no Negroes among its 15,000 residents."[29] The *New York Times* also reported that, although insurance appraisers estimated the value of the ranch-style house to be between $10,000 and $15,000, Reverend Compton paid $23,250 for the house, significantly above its valuation.[30] The case itself, including the 60 percent plus price gouging on the part of the white seller, is notable not because of its exceptionality but because of its mundane continuance in a long line of other such cases around the urban north, stretching from the 1925 widely publicized case of Dr. Ossian Sweet in Detroit[31] up through the present day.[32]

Cleveland experienced demographic shifts similar to its Rust Belt counterparts. For example, the population of Cleveland peaked in the 1950 census when it was the seventh largest city in the country with 914,808 residents. In the subsequent seventy years, much like other Rust Belt cities, the reported population has declined in each decennial census. The 2020 census counted 372,624 people.[33] Cleveland, like cities across the country, followed typical patterns of growth in the late nineteenth and early twentieth centuries and then population loss as state-subsidized programs of white property accumulation underwrote suburbanization and freeway building. These overall structures of growth and decline also shaped the lives of Cleveland's Chinese and Asian American communities. Yet, what is notable is that Cleveland's Asian American community, like the Black community, has grown in the inverse pattern of white Clevelanders, steadily increasing in population beginning in the 1940s.

Welcome to AsiaTown Cleveland

As scholars of critical race studies and geography have long argued, the racialization of space is linked to the project of white supremacy itself. Or, literally, as George Lipsitz shows, "racism takes place."[34] Ruth Wilson Gilmore argues that geography is a manifestation of the "fatal couplings of power and difference," which produces "race as a condition of existence and as a category of analysis, because the territoriality of power is a key to understanding racism."[35] Indeed, as activists, scholars, and lay people have long shown, racism is spatialized in multiple ways.[36]

Cleveland has been home to a Chinese community since at least the 1880s; the 1880 census recorded twenty-six residents born in China.[37] Cleveland and other cities in the industrial Midwest were places of secondary migration for Chinese immigrants. As Huping Ling shows in *Chinese Chicago*, most of the initial immigration of Chinese to the United States occurred in 1849–1882 with approximately three hundred thousand immigrants. Many of these immigrants had California as their initial destination. Although most Chinese immigrants remained in California, Ling outlines a history that begins in the 1860s of a small but continual out-migration from California to points in the U.S. interior. Ling suggests that this occurred because of two primary factors: first, the virulently racist anti-Chinese movement that operated through both racially targeted legal discrimination (Foreign Miners Tax, Laundry Tax, etc.) and acts of physical intimidation "that subjected immigrants and their businesses to violent physical attacks and abuse," and, second, at the completion of the transcontinental railroad, in 1869, many Chinese found themselves out of a job. As Ling notes, "During the last stage of construction of the Central Pacific Railroad, Chinese constituted 90% of the workforce of twelve thousand men."[38] Many of those who left rode the rails that they had built and departed for places in the Midwest and the South.[39] The English language archive does not reveal why some of these earliest Chinese migrants settled in Cleveland, but they were but one ethnic immigrant group among many who chose Cleveland as the place to call home.

The earliest North American "Chinatowns" were often constructed to segregate those that were deemed "different" from white Americans. Chinatowns were rarely monoethnic and pointed instead to places where Chinese, other Asian immigrants, other people of color, and poor people lived and worked. Kay Anderson's foundational text links "The Idea of Chinatown"[40] to the racial logics of presumed difference coproduced in popular narrative and legislation that in turn served to rationalize the ghettoization of Vancouver's Chinese community into a Chinese quarter. Nayan Shah's canonical work on San Francisco's Chinatown shows how the spaces of Chinatown were cocreated alongside discourses about Chinese and Asian bodies as vectors of disease, thereby rationalizing the ghettoization of Asian bodies as part of the public health discourse.[41] And Jan Lin argues that the changing historical stages of U.S. capitalism create conditions that prioritize the shifting policies of containment, removal, and renewal of ethnic communities[42] that we see play out in the case of Cleveland's AsiaTown as well.

Cleveland's first historic Chinatown was located near Public Square. As Emily Aronson and Robert Kent show, there was simultaneously a second primarily residential Chinatown in the early 1900s that was approximately two miles east of this downtown location (see Figure 1.1). The two communities together accounted for a population of 330 people of Asian descent in Cleveland in the 1920 census.[43] The small downtown community experienced its first instance of dispersal when urban renewal policies razed the neighborhood for downtown civic center development in the 1920s. By 1930, the Asian population in Cleveland nearly doubled to 649 people[44] as the community began a slow transition from the downtown Chinatown to the Rockwell Avenue Chinatown as more and more buildings of the historic Chinatown were targeted for demolition. The anchor to the Rockwell Avenue Chinatown was the forced movement of the On Leong Merchants Association from Ontario Street to Rockwell Avenue as their building became slated for demolition.[45] Aronson and Kent note that two more Chinatown buildings were marked for demolition in 1929, as they occupied the planned site of the new parcel post building, and, by the 1930s, there were no further traces of this first historic Chinatown.[46]

While Cleveland's first historic Chinatown faced demolition earlier than its Rust Belt counterparts, it was a bellwether for other cities.[47] In Cleveland, like these other cities, the relocated Chinatown often was smaller in size and population and did not necessarily "take off." The movement ushered in a relocation both within the city and, at this time, to China, as a number of Chinese Americans were return migrating to China (see Chapter 3).[48] This

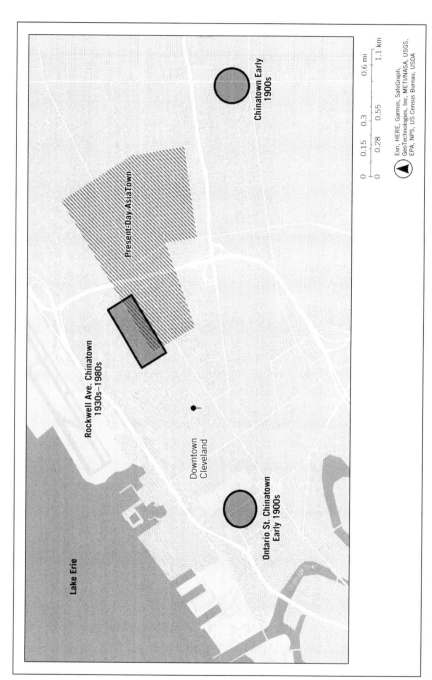

Figure 1.1 Cleveland's historic Chinatown locations. *(Map by MidTown Cleveland Inc.)*

is the part of relocation that is understudied—the ways in which forced movement severs the ties of communities, that, even if businesses, associations, and people can relocate, the community is forever changed. Yet, Cleveland's Chinese community rebuilt, and, by 1937, the Rockwell Avenue Chinatown was firmly established with businesses, ethnic associations, restaurants, grocery stores, and residences.[49] By 1940, the Chinese and Japanese population in Cleveland had declined to 377.[50] Notably, the 1950 census reveals an explosive growth in the Asian population to 1,499 due to the relocation of Japanese Americans incarcerated during World War II concentration camps throughout the Midwest (see Chapter 2).[51]

In the face of the overall population decline of Cleveland, and the postindustrial decline of the city as a whole, in the 1980s, the Rockwell Avenue Chinatown was in decline, and, by the early 2000s, consisted of only about one block, including a restaurant and the On Leong Merchants Association. In contrast, the "AsiaTown" area further east was growing during this same time. The reasons for the decline of the Rockwell Avenue Chinatown are multiple and overlap with the "urban crisis" and general decline of industrial cities in the latter half of the twentieth century.[52] In Cleveland's Rockwell Avenue Chinatown, specifically, part of the decline can be traced to the building of the Inner Belt Freeway (I-90) in the 1950s, part of a trend of demolition and freeway building as Chinatowns across the country experienced similar challenges and threats.[53] First, the freeway itself served as a physical border to the Rockwell Avenue Chinatown and stymied any potential growth. Second, as an outcome of the easy access to the freeway, the surrounding neighborhood increasingly turned over to commercial and wholesale development during the 1960s. This type of development eroded the residential feel of the neighborhood as light industry began to encroach on the available residential space. And third, like in cities across the country, the freeways provided an easy and efficient route for non-Black residents, including Asian Americans, to depart to the suburbs.

Across the country, and in Rust Belt cities like Cleveland in particular, the move to suburbanization that began in the post–World War II period accelerated throughout the late twentieth century. Asian American suburbanization began as early as the 1940s as Chinese Americans began to make their way from the late nineteenth- and early twentieth-century urban Chinatowns to the suburbs.[54] In some cases these movements were tacitly accepted and, in others, vehemently opposed.[55] Although not immune to racism, the Chinese community in Cleveland was not held as strictly to the Black-white color line, and, in many cases, Chinese Americans were able to move into primarily white suburban communities. As Chinese Americans, and other Asian Americans, moved to the suburbs so too did businesses and restaurants. Nationally, in 1990, 54 percent of Asians resided in the suburbs and 46 percent resided in the city of the one hundred largest metropolitan areas. By 2010, that trend for suburbanization continued with 62 percent of Asians residing in the suburbs of the one hundred largest metropolitan areas.[56] This increasing residential suburbanization resulted in the increasing suburbanization of Asian businesses and services as well. In greater Cleveland, the suburbanization of Asian Americans has concentrated in a handful of suburbs. Although the state population of Ohio is only 2.9 percent Asian, four Cleveland suburbs have Asian populations of greater than 10 percent: Pepper Pike (15.6 percent), Solon (15.2 percent), Beachwood (13.2 percent), and Middleburg Heights (10.3 percent).[57] And, from 2010 to 2020, five Cuyahoga County communities had an over 90 percent increase in the population of Asian residents: Hunting Valley (171.4 percent), Walton Hills (142.9 percent), Warrensville Heights (126.5 percent), Lyndhurst (96.0 percent), and Pepper Pike (94.5 percent).[58]

Asian American suburbanization occurs alongside a shifting discourse of Asian American urban space, what Ellen Wu points to as the discursive "deghettoization" of Chinatown in the period between the end of World War II and through the 1960s. Wu argues that through "discourses and deeds intended to reconfigure popular impressions of its residents and their surroundings" by Chinatown stakeholders, "social scientists, policy makers, and ordinary Americans," Asian American space became a location of possibility rather than stigma.[59] In this time period, the shifting discourse of Asian American space parallels the perpetuation of the model minority discourse in national popular media. The model minority paradigm, generated by white news media, emerges primarily as a way of disciplining both Asian Americans and African Americans. The myth emerges as a series of articles and news features touting the successes of young Asian Americans, moving, as one article goes to show, from the confines of the Japanese incarceration camps to the campuses of elite universities like Harvard and Stanford in the matter of a generation. This representation is a striking juxtaposition to the simultaneous portrayals of young Black men that are heating up the streets of cities across the country during the long hot summers of the 1960s, protesting segregated conditions, ghettoization, and the inequity of Black life in America.[60]

As part of the spatialization of the model minority myth, Yoonmee Chang shows how Chinatowns are reconceptualized as "enclaves," *not* "ghettos," which is part of the racialization project of anti-Black racism. Chang states:

> "Ethnic enclave" is broadly synonymous with "cultural community."
> Rejecting the negative connotations of "ghetto," "ethnic enclave" redefines racially segregated spaces of Asian American class inequity into productive communities infused with and driven by ethnic culture. "Ethnic enclave" constructs spaces like Chinatown as unique

repositories of Asian culture, an esteemed and valuable culture that is and should be productively cultivated, and that engenders and organizes meaningful and rewarding social relations.[61]

In effect, the notion of ethnic enclave is a spatial rendering of the model minority myth that both disavows inequities in Asian American communities and sets up a narrative of Black "ghetto" and Asian "enclave," both perniciously engaged in the project of linking culture to life conditions. It suggests that the racialized ideas of "immigrant hard work" and "cultures of poverty" produce differing life conditions.[62] What both of these spatial narratives occlude, however, is the way the logics of whiteness structure white places as invisible and "normal" and spaces inhabited by people of color as locations of orientalist and anti-Black fantasy.

Although many Asian Americans in Cleveland have moved to the suburbs, and the Rockwell Avenue Chinatown has shrunk, to this day it still maintains its current size of about one block. By the 1970s, new immigrants began to move to the other side of the freeway, just east of the Rockwell Avenue Chinatown (see Chapter 3). Businesses, restaurants, and stores began to develop along the main avenues from E. 30th to E. 55th Streets, the area currently known as AsiaTown. AsiaTown is located on Cleveland's near East Side midway between downtown and the closest inner ring suburb of Cleveland Heights, which lies just east of Cleveland's city borders. As discussed previously, the current iteration of AsiaTown is at least the third distinct Chinatown in Cleveland. A Cleveland Asian American community history published in 1977 identified a loose configuration of shops, restaurants, groceries, and community spaces in the geographic area of E. 30th to E. 55th Streets between Payne and Superior, the area that would become the footprint of AsiaTown, as discussed in Chapter 3.

The name "AsiaTown" gestures toward both an attempt at inclusive pan-ethnicity and also the ongoing conflation of "Asian" and "Chinese" being interchangeable in the United States. And, throughout the long history of Asians in America, there has been the case of misrecognition of Chinese for Japanese, Japanese for Chinese, and other cases of ethnic lumping based on race.[63] Notably here, the name "AsiaTown" was a creation intended to present a more inclusive neighborhood name, yet the neighborhood is still majority Chinese both in demographics and in business representation, as discussed in Chapter 4. Therefore, this panethnic naming has an effect of continuing to maintain the legacy of Chinese as a stand in for all Asians and Asians as all Chinese and flatten the distinction between ethnic groups, even as it also serves as a form of naming to join common economic and cultural interests. These compromises of naming and representation ring true to and echo the earlier history of the political rise of the term "Asian American" in the 1960s, as a political act of solidarity with and across ethnic communities of color in the United States.[64] This tension between panethnic inclusivity and conflation of diverse ethnic groups is one of the through lines of this book.

The case of AsiaTown Cleveland is unique not only because it defies the typical classification of Asian American commercial spaces but because of its continued presence and growth throughout the height of urban decline in the city, generally, and the Rust Belt, at large. Chapter 2 highlights the historical time period when Cleveland, like its "arsenal of democracy" peers, reached peak population. In the decades that followed, Cleveland's population as a whole decreased from a U.S. census high of 914,818 in 1950 and has steadily decreased every consecutive decade to 372,624 in 2020.[65] The steepest census decline occurred from 1970 to 1980, with a population decrease of 24 percent from 750,903 in 1970 to 573,822 in 1980.[66] Yet, Cleveland's Asian American population demographics are, in many ways, opposite of Cleveland's as a whole. Although, given the imprecise and flawed ways the U.S. census has enumerated race over time,[67] these numbers should be seen as a snapshot rather than a precise accounting. The grouping of "Asian" is even more complicated because this category is hard to track, as Yến Lê Espiritu and Michael Omi show in "Who Are You Calling Asian?"[68] In 1950, the Cleveland "Asian" population was 1,499 and, by 1970, 1,852.[69] While the general Cleveland population as a whole declined by 24 percent between 1970 and 1980, the Asian population increased by 82.7 percent to 3,384. A number of factors contributed to this increase: the fallout of the Vietnam War and its impact on increasing numbers of Southeast Asians migrating to the United States, the expanding population of U.S.-born Asian Americans, and increased immigration from Asia after 1965. Throughout the past four decades, Cleveland's Asian population has grown at a modest but steady clip. By 2020, the Asian population of Cleveland was 10,517.[70]

Placekeeping as Resistance: Articulating History and Place in the Shadow of Neoliberal Multiculturalism

In general, the history of Asian American places, from Chinatowns across the country to the holding and detainment center on Angel Island and the concentration camps of World War II, reveals that most Asian American places, historically, were created as spaces of exclusion from white society alongside narratives about Asians being, as what Mae Ngai terms, "Impossible Subjects," or as Yên Lê Espiritu suggests as "differentially included" into U.S. culture and society. Both scholars point to the ways in which Asian Americans as laboring bodies and working subjects have been long desired, but that full social, legal, and economic inclusion into the nation-state have been clearly demarcated through legislation and social policies that limited the extent of that inclusion.[71]

Yet, the case study of Cleveland shows how Asian Americans have not just been acted upon; they have built lives in these spaces, forming social groups and building communities. In this way, this focus on Cleveland's AsiaTown broadens the conversation on place-based studies of Asian American communities to include the Rust Belt as a location where Asian ethnic groups have built commercial districts and neighborhoods. Scholars have previously focused on place-based studies that trace the development of diasporic Vietnamese communities in Orange County, Boston, and San Diego,[72] the South Asian community in Muncie, Indiana,[73] the Asian American experience in the segregated South,[74] the Cambodian community in New York,[75] and numerous studies that focus on Asian American groups in the greater Los Angeles region.[76]

In contemporary urban development, Asian American places like Chinatowns are sometimes utilized spatially to signify "how the yellow peril became the model minority."[77] By building on Jodi Melamed's conception of neoliberal multiculturalism, wherein anti-racism becomes incorporated into the official discourse through the rhetoric of multiculturalism and diversity,[78] we might begin to delve further into what this idea of "model minority" might mean spatially in the larger discourse of neoliberal multiculturalism. For example, as discussed previously, Asian American place was initially created as a location to separate and spatially exclude Asians from larger zones of the city for purposes of housing and commerce; a spatial manifestation of cultural and legal sentiments seeking to bar and exclude Asians from immigration, citizenship, and American life. However, Melamed's work on neoliberal multiculturalism points to moments in the mythology of the American nation-state where racial *inclusion* into the project of the U.S. nation-state becomes paramount in order to keep its mythos alive. And this is the moment where we begin to see the ways in which the multicultural neighborhoods built through structures of exclusion become an "asset" in an inclusive narrative of urban redevelopment in America.

Asian American "placemakers,"[79] business owners, Asian American developers, Asian American community members, and artists who serve as spatial and community anchors of development, have long served the AsiaTown community. However, more recently, the support for the development of the neighborhood and events like the Cleveland Asian Festival (CAF; see Chapter 5) has included broader community members, politicians, community development corporations (CDCs), and the City of Cleveland, more generally. Much of the outside support comes as a gesture toward multiculturalism and the idea that "Chinatowns" are, in the twenty-first century, desirable tourist destinations to showcase a city's global diversity. Yet, these spaces are born of and through exclusion. It is this tension that permeates the contemporary context for development. Asian American placemakers continue to fight to develop their communities, and the contemporary context of ethnic-based redevelopment demands at least a partial buy-in to diversity discourse.

One way to think about these multiple use values of space is by distinguishing between "placemaking" and "placekeeping." "Placemaking" is the concept most commonplace in urban development and planning as a shorthand for "creating" or "defining" place. The term "placemaking" which originated in the 1960s, is used by corporations and city governments, nonprofits, and neighborhood development groups alike. It is everywhere. The redeployment of placemaking in the 2000s, centered around the ideas of "activating" space, creating walkable neighborhoods and street-level energy, with new cafés and downtown lofts bent on attracting the generation of young white professionals who return-migrated to cities their grandparents and parents had abandoned for the suburbs, makes sense in the longer trajectory of creating spaces in the service of capitalism. In this way, it echoes narratives that have come before, the desire to "make place productive," which echoes the Lockean cultivation of the land, making it commodifiable and useful.[80] Historically, placemaking was seen "as a reaction to a perceived loss of a sense of 'place' amid the architectural dystopia of the urban renewal era."[81] It makes sense that the emergence of the idea begins with the loss of place, as urban renewal gutted neighborhoods and communities to build freeways, municipal buildings, and surface parking lots in cities like Cleveland.

"Placekeeping" is different. Rather than making place following the destruction of what once was, placekeeping is focused on keeping place that already is. A term coined by Detroit activist Jenny Lee,[82] the notion of placekeeping suggests that places have been and are long held. Rather than a nod toward simply preserving buildings or creating place, it is about keeping the memories, stories, and present of the neighborhood alive as well, about keeping a place and supporting the roots and growth rather than the displacement, demolition, destruction, and rebirth.[83] Joyce Huang, the director of planning and placemaking at the MidTown Cleveland Inc. CDC (MTC),[84] reflecting on the relationship of placekeeping to communities of color, in particular, describes:

> So, in that book about Philly's Chinatown, the author talks about *placekeeping*.[85] Which, I love the definition of it. It's basically about spatial justice, about the history of a place, so it's slightly different from placemaking, because placemaking kind of assumes that there is nothing there before and you have to create place. Whereas placekeeping is for communities of color, I think that's going to be the big project.[86]

And this is the work for Asian American placemakers in Cleveland, to find balance between the histories of racism bound up in the community histories of place: the resettlement of incarcerated Japanese Americans, the growth of communities in the face of urban renewal, presumed invisibility, alongside the hypervisibility of diversity discourse. In the end, Cleveland placemakers and the proponents of neoliberal multicultural diversity both want a thriving Asian American commercial and residential neighborhood.

And it is into this complex space where Asian American placemakers have both the opportunity and the challenge to amplify, make, and keep place for their communities. Those representing the community must seek a delicate balance between community-led development, which creates economic- and ethnic-based place that appeals to an in-group, while simultaneously relying on an appeal to neoliberal multiculturalism to gain broader public support through grants, funding, and tourism (see Chapters 4 and 5). This dance requires an enormous amount of agility, underscoring the contextual and mutable nature of place. Throughout the book, the tensions, challenges, and successes are palpable as community members define, engage, shape, and keep Asian American place.

Method and Researcher Subjectivity

At its most simple formation, this book is a story of Cleveland told by Asian American Clevelanders who lived and engaged with the city from 1943 to 2023. While it does not claim to be a sweeping eighty-year history of the city, or even the Asian American community, it does tell a history of the experiences of Asian Americans in a Midwestern city in the mid-twentieth and early twenty-first centuries. With Cleveland often overlooked in histories of both the Rust Belt and Asian America, *Mapping AsiaTown Cleveland: Race and Redevelopment in the Rust Belt* aims to knit together the multiple histories of Asian Americans, within the changing context of Cleveland's own story as it "managed decline in 'the best location in the nation,'"[87] as an act of placekeeping.

These histories of place were told to me by a variety of narrators: in person, through oral histories, in the pages of newspapers, and in government documents. These stories were enhanced by the sensory experiences—sounds, tastes, energy—of spending time in AsiaTown as an actively engaged visitor. I was first introduced to AsiaTown through a Filipinx friend from California who relocated to Cleveland. They knew of my research interests in Midwestern Asian America and invited me to attend the "AsiaTown Night Market"[88] in Cleveland in August 2016. After this first weekend visit, I returned to AsiaTown approximately every two to three months for visits ranging from two to ten days between August 2016 and March 2019. During this time, I was living approximately three hours away. In the beginning, I would plan my visits around an event taking place in the community—Lunar New Year, Night Market, Cleveland Asian Festival (CAF)—but, as time went on, and I began to be invited to take part in the community planning efforts, I would plan my research trips around quarterly AsiaTown Advisory Committee (ATAC) meetings. ATAC began formally in 2017 as an advisory board of multiethnic community members, volunteers, and residents initiated by an urban planner in the Midtown CDC (see Chapter 4). Each research visit was notable for the ease by which I was able to meet people and make connections in AsiaTown and in Cleveland's planning and development circle more broadly. Cleveland, with a 2019 census estimated population of approximately 381,000 people, has a rather tight-knit planning community.[89] And Cleveland's Asian American community, with a population of 9,906, representing approximately 2.6 percent of Cleveland's overall population, is even more intertwined.[90]

Since the fall of 2016, I have been involved in a variety of ways as both a participant and an observer in AsiaTown: attending community meetings, attending and participating in meetings of ATAC, attending the CAF multiple times and serving as a volunteer for the festival in 2018 and 2023. Additionally, during this time, I interviewed twenty-three community stakeholders, some multiple times, in conversations that lasted anywhere from forty-five minutes to two hours. After the spring of 2019, while I was unable to meet regularly in person with the advisory committee or travel to Cleveland, I remained active on email and in meetings remotely when at all possible. During the fall of 2020, my Introduction to Asian American Studies class, which met remotely,[91] partnered with the AsiaTown community and engaged in community-led research projects. I made follow-up visits to Cleveland in September 2022 and May 2023. In addition, I spent time at the Western Reserve Historical Society archives, seeking out the recorded history of Asian Americans in Cleveland, which, unsurprisingly, was rather sparse. For Chapter 2, the Densho Digital Archive was an invaluable resource of oral histories and images that tell the stories of Japanese resettlement to Cleveland.

As an Asian American professor at a rural state university, approximately two hours west of Cleveland, I entered this community as an outsider. However, as a transnationally and transracially adopted Korean person who grew up three hours away in metro Detroit, I brought with me the shared experiences of being "the only" or one of a handful of Asian people in cities that are cleaved by a Black-white binary of race relations. In the Midwest, this shared understanding of growing up outside of one of the populous Asian American communities in California, Atlanta, New York, New Jersey, or Chicago, served as a point of entry and often resulted in a warm and friendly welcome when I would enter spaces, even as an outsider.[92] I fully believe that, in a community with a larger population of Asian Americans, it would have been more difficult to make connections. Additionally, because the community is very interested in drawing in larger community participation, they are welcoming to newcomers and people joining the work as volunteers. So, while I am not an insider to this community, I do believe that my subject position has enabled access and understanding of the work the community is undertaking. Throughout this process, I would clearly and consistently name my position as both *not* a Clevelander and a researcher. However, as I discuss further in Chapter 5, at times my position as an Asian American person at community events was interpellated by outsiders that I was a member of the community.

Mapping the Book

The continued survival of Cleveland's urban Chinatown place it with more famous and large-scale urban Chinatowns like those in New York, Chicago, and San Francisco, except, of course, Cleveland's Asian population is miniscule in comparison to these places.[93] This book seeks, on one hand, to trace the multiple and fragmented histories of Cleveland's Asian American communities from the early twentieth century to the early 2020s in order to partially account for how and why there is currently an Asian American commercial and residential district in the middle of Cleveland's East Side. Yet, *Mapping AsiaTown Cleveland* is not a comprehensive community history. Rather, it is intended to trace particular social and historical contexts that produce a contemporary articulation of Asian American life. In the pages that follow, I build the analysis of the tensions and joys of Asian American place-keeping in Cleveland. In each chapter, I continue to provide context for the work of regional racial formation alongside the primary sources that reveal the ways in which Asian American life emerges within and exceeds these racial logics.

In Chapter 2, I center the histories of Japanese Americans, the most populous Asian ethnic group to call Cleveland home during the period of the city's industrial rise. From 1942 to 1946 an estimated 3,000–3,500 Japanese Americans who were incarcerated during World War II resettled in Cleveland. When they arrived in Cleveland, they made home and built community at places like the Cleveland Hostel and the Erie Hotel Annex on the East Side. Cleveland, like the West Coast cities from which Japanese Americans were forcibly removed, was amid a racial and social transformation of its own. Chapter 2 illuminates very clearly the regional context of systems of white supremacy. We can see that the "Japanese problem" of the West Coast was a "solution" of sorts to a labor shortage in the Midwest and a growing counterpoint to the "Negro problem" of the urban North. This chapter highlights the experiences of Japanese American resettlers in the racially changing East Side neighborhood of Hough, where they were making home and building community alongside their fellow migrants, Black and white Southerners, weaving together the history of resettlement with the history of the neighborhood that would erupt in a rebellion during the "long hot summers" of the 1960s.

In Chapter 3, I trace the historical formation of contemporary AsiaTown in and through key community businesses—restaurants, food distributors, and grocery stores—as essential community placemakers. I situate the narratives of three Chinese Americans whose differing life experiences span three generations from the 1960s to the late 2010s. Their histories and affiliations with food distribution, groceries, and restaurants reveal that place-keeping through food is both a means of survival and a way to build community.

Chapter 4 shows how the formal creation of the AsiaTown Advisory Committee became a central point to grow the organizing capacity of AsiaTown. While this group of people had gathered in various formations over the years as the community leaders and the initiators for community events and development, this was the first time that a Community Development Corporation (CDC) had specifically and on an ongoing basis called in a group to be part of the planning process. Cleveland has a nationally recognized model of CDC planning, which is directly rooted in community responses to anti-Black racism in housing and community development that the 1966 Hough Rebellion revealed to the nation. Chapter 4 focuses specifically on this context as present-day AsiaTown lies at the intersection of three distinct CDC districts. This "in betweenness" means that for much of its history AsiaTown was not well represented in terms of planning and only since 2017 have members of the Asian American community been on the board or staff of any of the CDCs. The chapter tracks the shifts that led to the hiring of the city's first Asian American planner at MTC. Although AsiaTown organizing was only a small percentage of her workload, due to the already active network of community leaders and volunteers, this opening provided an inroad into structural representation, key to creating a climate for change, and began to bridge the gap between community, CDC, and city planning. The questions of earlier generations of Asian American activists and community leaders are raised and examined anew in this chapter: How do Asian Americans mobilize and represent themselves to and for the Asian American community and the Cleveland community at large?

In Chapter 5, I analyze the Cleveland Asian Festival (CAF), the annual signature event of the community as a scenario that presents, represents, reinforces, and unsettles Asian American racial scripts. By examining the festival as both location and performance of Asian American place, we can understand how the pervasive racial scripts—Asians as good immigrants and the exotic other—continue to circulate, even as the festival works to unsettle anti-Asian discrimination. The CAF reveals the complex work of putting on a festival that does the work of both celebrating community and Asian American placemaking within the overall spatial logics of white supremacy that developed ethnic neighborhoods in the first place. The CAF, an example of community-led placemaking, simultaneously reinforces and complicates the racial narratives of Asian Americans and Asian place.

Finally, in the Conclusion, I turn to the 2020 "Imagine AsiaTown Visioning Report" and link this process of community imagination to the history of a young Japanese American resettler moving to Cleveland in 1945. By tying together these two moments, seventy-five years apart, I aim not to wrap up a narrative with a tidy conclusion—rather, these two points in time are joined to invite readers to imagine possibility in the face of uncertainty, just as the narrators throughout the book have done. By centering a long history of making place and keeping history and keeping place and making history, we can see how communities continue to build for the present and the future.

2

Wartime Resettlement to the "Arsenal of Democracy"

Japanese American Neighbors and
the Cleveland Color Line

Cleveland it was really, it was a nice place to be. We were
married in '45 and we were there 'til '48. It was about time
we, cause my home was Los Angeles.

—Yasu Koyamatsu Momii[1]

In October 1943, the same month she turned twenty-two, Yasu Koyamatsu
Momii arrived in Cleveland from the Gila River Concentration[2] Camp in
Arizona. Yasu recalls that some of her friends had begun leaving Gila River
for indefinite leaves as early as March 1943. Before the war, Yasu, the youngest of four children, had lived in Los Angeles with her parents.[3] During the
war, under Executive Order No. 9066, they were forced to relocate first to
the Santa Anita Assembly Center and then to Gila River in Arizona. She recalls that, when she left Arizona bound for a job as a domestic, there were
job openings in Cleveland and Detroit, "But I went to Cleveland because my
brother had gone before me to school,[4] so he was there." Yasu's choice to move
to Cleveland represented a common pattern in resettlement, people often
chose a city or region where a family member had already moved.

The Cleveland that Yasu arrived at in 1943 was in full "arsenal of democracy" production mode; its factories retooled for war production. Yasu was
among the thousands of people that moved to industrial cities for opportunities in growing economies. Cities across the industrial Midwest reached
peak population during this time: Cleveland growing from 878,336 in 1940
to 914,800 by the 1950 census. Part of Cleveland's population rise comprises
an estimated 3,000–3,500 Japanese Americans who moved to Cleveland from
1942 to 1946 as part of the war resettlement program moving Japanese Americans first from the West Coast exclusion zone to government camps and then,
in some cases, to cities and towns in the interior for employment and educa-

tion. Japanese American communities in Cleveland and throughout the Midwest and East Coast grew as a direct result of the War Relocation Authority's (WRA) forcible removal and subsequent resettlement.[5] This evacuation achieved a main goal of the U.S. government: according to the WRA's director Dillon S. Myer, "One of the agency's chief accomplishments was the resettling of 'more than 50,000 Japanese all across the United States.'"[6]

In Cleveland, and in cities throughout the industrial Midwest, the shift to wartime production and the numerous workers required to people these jobs resulted in massive population movement and an increasing number of people who needed housing in already tight housing markets. In the case of Japanese American resettlers, as a way to combat the housing shortage, the Cleveland Resettlement Committee (CRC) elected to open a hostel for Japanese American resettlers in June 1943 in a former fraternity house at 2429 Prospect Avenue on Cleveland's East Side.[7] Cities throughout the Midwest and East Coast were opening hostels like the one in Cleveland that were created specifically to serve Japanese Americans who were leaving the concentration camps. In the two-plus years that the Cleveland Hostel was in existence, it "provided temporary housing for almost 850 resettlers, most of them single men and women."[8] In addition to housing, the hostel served as a gathering place for resettlers in a strange new city. Given that most of those leaving the camps, in 1943 and early 1944, were primarily single Nisei (American-born generation) in their late teens and early twenties seeking employment opportunities, the hostel and the other rooming house–type arrangements available were conducive to fostering networks and making friendships.

For Yasu Momii, the Cleveland Hostel was an important place during her time in the city. The hostel served not only as a temporary residence upon arrival but as a place where the Japanese community new to Cleveland would meet, make, and sustain connections. And it even became her workplace. After six months of working as a domestic at a home in Cleveland Heights, Yasu quit and took a job working as a cook at the Cleveland Hostel, where she worked until the hostel closed in July 1945. Yasu remembers that

> the hostel was a really nice gathering place where people would come, especially weekends if they had lived there at one time, or even if they hadn't. It was a meeting place, and we played bridge and chatted, and some people met their dates. . . . It was very active during the early days. It was a lot of fun.[9]

While it might seem strange to describe the hostel, in the context of resettlement as a whole, as a place of "fun," it was, at times, just that for Yasu. Indeed, it was in Cleveland at the hostel, shortly after she arrived in 1943, that Yasu met the person that she would marry in 1945.[10]

The hostel and the various other rooming houses established for Japanese Americans were not only spaces for community gathering as seen in Figure 2.1 but also a hub of information where people learned of jobs and housing opportunities. Isao East Oshima located his job repairing patterns and his living accommodations through the WRA.[11] He remembers, "That's how I ended up in that hotel, Erie Hotel annex, which was on the edge of downtown Cleveland. And there were, they had many *Niseis* from various camps. I don't recall anybody from Topaz." Isao and some of the guys from the Erie Hotel "moved over to the frat house, which was further out in a residential neighborhood, which was kind of a nice place to stay." Isao, who was born and raised in the East Bay, recalls not only the experience of getting to know other young men from Arizona and other places but also their camaraderie. After work, he and the other guys "went to the movies, went out and ate, went to, Cleveland had a Major League ball club, so we went to see the Major League baseball games. First time in a Major League game there." And he and his friends, young men in their late teens and early twenties, also

Figure 2.1 Harold S. Fistere (*far right*), Cleveland WRA area relocation supervisor, with a group of West Coast evacuees in the Cleveland Hostel operated by the American Home Baptist Mission Society, Cleveland, Ohio. (*left to right*) Mrs. Franzen and Dick Kurihara of the Manzanar Relocation Center and Glendale, California; Larry Takai of Sacramento, California, and Tule Lake; Rev. Shunji Nishi of Los Angeles, California; Miss Lois Uchida of Los Angeles and Heart Mountain; Max Franzen, manager of the hostel; and Mrs. Peggy Tanji of Oakland, California, and Topaz. (*January 1944. Courtesy of UC Berkeley Bancroft Library.*)

met up with young women. Isao was twenty-two when he resettled in Cleveland, and he remembered that "some of the guys knew some of the *Nisei* women in town, and they used to get dates with them. And then one of the guys got me a blind date one day. . . . That was about that, one time deal." These types of lively social interactions were commonplace at Japanese American rooming houses and the Cleveland Hostel (see Figure 2.2).

As more resettlers like Yasu and Isao moved to Cleveland, they found housing in the East Side Hough neighborhood. As is discussed later, the Hough neighborhood was growing exponentially during the war as a destination for not only Japanese resettlers but Black and white Southern migrants as well. The neighborhood was stretched to capacity as houses and apartments were subdivided and families and friends doubled up in rooms and apartments. However, WRA officials "were concerned that too many resettlers were moving in the Hough area, thus 'congregating' in ways that might herald the emergence of a Cleveland Little Tokyo, a situation opposed at every turn."[12] In response to this government concern, it is reported that "the hostel staff promoted wide residential distribution, encouraging resettlers not to be 'huddled' together."[13]

Figure 2.2 On their way to a picture show are Jimmie Okura, from Jerome and Wilmington, California, and Jean Ikeguchi, from Jerome and Harbor City, California, shown leaving the Co-op House in Cleveland where sixteen Issei and Nisei reside and eat together in a community kitchen. Going into the house on a visit are Mr. and Mrs. Joe Kanda, formerly of Poston and Los Angeles, California. *(Cleveland, Ohio. January 1944. Courtesy of UC Berkeley Bancroft Library.)*

In this chapter, I focus on the Japanese Americans who moved to Cleveland from 1942 to 1946 as a direct result of the U.S. government's policy of mass evacuation, incarceration, and relocation. It is well accepted that the program of mass evacuation and incarceration was one part of a strategy to intentionally break up Japanese communities. During the previous decades, despite state and federal laws barring citizenship and ownership of property and the sometimes hostile behavior from their non-Japanese neighbors, *Nihonmachi* (Japantowns) had formed throughout the West Coast.[14] At the time, these Japantowns were looked upon with suspicion, for the congregating and concentration of people of Japanese ethnicity, a self-fulfilling prophecy of housing segregation—housing options limited by de facto or de jure segregation, which, in turn, created racial ghettos. This chapter highlights the regional racial formation that transmuted Japanese Americans from a group of potential spies and saboteurs[15] who must be excluded from the West Coast to neighbors in places like Cleveland. In this chapter, I show how regional racial formation operates in the context of Cleveland's peak growth as an "arsenal of democracy" city and the ways in which Japanese American migrants begin to be constructed through the lens of "not white" and also "not black" and instead, "model citizen." In 1941, on the West Coast, Japanese Americans were evacuated under an order by the secretary of war, but, by 1943, in Cleveland, the WRA was working with the local press to shift the image of Japanese Americans from "enemy" to "model citizen," as I show in the chapter.

Although much has been written about Japanese incarceration in the eighty years since the enactment of Executive Order No. 9066, and the program of resettlement to the Midwest and East Coast, generally, as part of the narrative arc of Japanese American forced removal, incarceration, and return to the West Coast, relatively little scholarship has focused on the geographically specific experiences of relocation to places like Cleveland.[16] This chapter focuses in very closely on Cleveland, the third most popular destination for resettlement from the camps from 1942 to 1946. Yasu Momii and Isao East Oshima are but two of the approximately 3,000–3,500 people who relocated to Cleveland.

While the growth of the Japanese population by 3,000–3,500 might seem miniscule, when considered in the context of 1940 population numbers, it represents an increase from 18 individuals of Japanese descent counted in the 1940 census to the 1,078 counted in the 1950 census.[17] Since the census is a decennial enumerator, the estimated 3,000–3,500 Japanese Americans who relocated between 1943 and 1946 is not fully visible here. However, even without the accounting for the resettler population peak, the Japanese population in Cleveland increased by 5,888.89 percent between the 1940 census and the 1950 census. By comparison, the white population shrunk. The Black[18] population grew significantly by over sixty thousand people, a 74.64 percent population increase from 1940 to 1950. In Cleveland, like every city in the urban North, the shifting demographics of the 1940s ushered in a radically different social landscape by 1950.

From West Coast to Concentration Camp to Cleveland: Transmuting an Enemy Alien to a Model Citizen

Part of the process of relocation was a transmutation of Japanese Americans from their "threat" on the West Coast, into a vital part of the wartime economy in places like the Great Lakes region.[19] Almost as soon as the program of evacuation started, there was opposition, based not only on human rights but on farmers needing workers to maintain, grow, and harvest crops, and "military officials who planned to keep Japanese Americans confined for the entire war soon encountered vocal opposition from farmers desperate for labor."[20] Mere months into the program of incarceration, "the WRA allowed 10,000 internees to leave the camps temporarily in mid-1942 to harvest sugar beets in the intermountain West."[21] These initial temporary work release programs, where farmers recruited incarcerees for paid labor, laid the groundwork for more permanent work resettlement programs. By the fall of 1942, the WRA created a system for granting indefinite leave from the camps to locations in the Midwest and East Coast if incarcerees were enrolling in school or could show proof that they were leaving to take a job. They were required to apply for leave and register their address and location with the U.S. government.

In January 1943, the WRA opened field offices in the Midwest and East Coast to accelerate the indefinite leave of Japanese incarcerees from camps as a solution to two major problems that faced the war economy: first, the national labor shortage, and, second, the shortsightedness involved in incarcerating and maintaining small cities of thousands of people in the middle of rural regions that lacked the infrastructure to support the population of the camps.[22] The WRA's Cleveland District and the Great Lakes Area Resettlement Office opened in Cleveland on January 16, 1943.[23] The Cleveland-based office housed both the Northern Ohio-Cleveland district office, which was "responsible for a single city and its environs" and the Great Lakes Area field office. The Great Lakes Area territory included "the states of Michigan (excluding the upper peninsula), Ohio, Kentucky, West Virginia, western part of Pennsylvania and western part of New York State (up to and including Buffalo)." The area itself had six district offices: "1 Michigan District-Detroit, 2

Northern Ohio District-Cleveland, 3 Central Ohio District-Columbus, 4 Southern Ohio District-Cincinnati, 5 Western New York District-Buffalo, 6 Western Pennsylvania District-Pittsburgh."[24]

Although the WRA office was charged with facilitating resettlement, concerned citizens in Cleveland, in December 1942, decided "to form a committee, staffed by volunteers, to help resettle evacuees."[25] This committee, the Cleveland Resettlement Committee for Japanese Americans (CRC) began its work in early 1943. The WRA and CRC worked together to address the goal of Japanese resettlement in the Cleveland region, and "it was decided that the WRA would be primarily responsible for employment and the CRC for housing, the latter task far more difficult in a situation in which workers were streaming into the city to take defense jobs."[26]

The WRA placed Japanese resettlers into jobs throughout the city of Cleveland. By January 1946, the WRA records of agency-facilitated placements indicated "there are over 400 different firms and plants (exclusive of domestic and agriculture) where evacuees are employed."[27] In addition, the final report noted, "Since resettlers have become increasingly more self-reliant, some jobs were not cleared through WRA and an accurate record of their occupational spread is difficult to ascertain."[28] The final report includes a lengthy and somewhat random list of the types of jobs and places of employment:

> Hospitals, garages, body and fender, servicemen, hotels and restaurants, cooks, bakers, and bus boys, bakeries, accountants, clerks, typists, draftsmen, tool and die makers, welders, lathe operators, garment manufacturing (has been largest for women in the office and factory), cleaning, dyeing, pressers, dental technicians, watchmakers, shoe repair, photographers, darkroom men, beauty operators, window trimmers, truck drivers, shipping clerks, federal civil service jobs, welfare agencies, nursery school teachers, dieticians and doctors.[29]

This wide-ranging list, which does not include domestic and agriculture, the two jobs most often available to resettlers initially, does create a portrait of a wide variety of sectors and opportunities. This wide range also represents the fact that these were likely similar jobs and occupations that many Japanese Americans and nationals held along the West Coast prior to mass incarceration.

The earliest resettlers could not leave unless they showed proof of an offer of employment or education. Those who "chose" life "on the outside" of camp, even if it could only be realized by assuming an identity as a worker or a student, and in a place as foreign as Cleveland, took the leap. And those who did worked and studied hard, knowing full well that this "freedom," no matter how limited, could be temporary, as they were "free" at the pleasure of the WRA, an entity that had already proved itself to be capricious and irrational. Isao East Oshima left Topaz for Cleveland at the age of twenty-two in May 1943.[30] Isao was born in Berkeley, California, on April 20, 1921, the eldest of eight children.[31] In January 1943, only three or four months after arriving at Topaz, his sister May left camp on a work release for a job as a domestic in St. Paul, Minnesota. A few weeks later his sister Yuri joined May in St. Paul working as a domestic. By May 1943, Isao decided to leave camp, with a job waiting for him at a foundry in Cleveland and temporary housing at the Erie Hotel annex, both facilitated by the WRA.

In Cleveland, Isao East Oshima entered into a highly segregated workplace, as he remembered, "The foundry was primarily African American." This was in keeping with labor practices at the time where Black men worked the hottest, hardest, and dirtiest jobs, like the foundry. And, Isao, not a Black man but also not a white man, was hired from Topaz to work in the foundry. However, he remembers from when he reported to the foundry, "When they saw me, they said I was too small for the job." The employer decided to keep Isao on despite his being "too small for the job" in the foundry, and he was reassigned. He became an apprentice, and his job was to repair patterns: "When they got all nicked up, we try to fix 'em up and then they'll use it again instead of trying to make a new pattern, we just fixed the old ones. But I never did get a chance to learn how to make patterns, 'cause the patternmaker was never around." While Isao was busy on the job, this labor was less physically taxing in comparison to the work he described as "the heavy work in the foundry where they shoveled sand. . . . They were shoveling sand all day long."[32]

Although Isao was at the job for only four months, he was quick to learn the racial hierarchy of his Cleveland workplace. In the patterns department where he was an apprentice, "They were all Caucasians in that department, no African Americans. . . . The maintenance department was the same thing. Maintenance department was all Caucasians, and I think they had three *Niseis* but no African Americans there. . . . African Americans were primarily the heavy work in the foundry. And they had about ten percent white people, but that was it. They must have had, oh, 125 or 150 employees in the company there."[33] This brief portrait of Isao's factory experience aligns with the racial hierarchy of labor in the industrial North during World War II.[34] While not white, Nisei were sometimes able to work in departments that were not open to Black workers.

And, it is here, in this context of resettlement, in the competition for jobs and alongside other recent migrants, that the Japanese resettlers moved from "alien labor"[35] to "model worker" on the line, in the factories and in office buildings of cities like Cleveland. Notably, because of the ways that Asian populations had been configured on the West Coast as "cheap" and "dispensable" labor, they were faced with regional practices of targeted anti-Asian structural racism and discrimination in jobs, housing, education, property ownership, and citizenship. The irony was that, because of the ultimate act of racism and discrimination by the U.S. government in the form of incarceration, Japanese Americans were now resettling into the Midwest and East Coast where the racial climate was different.

For example, the Los Angeles Teamsters Union "which had maintained segregated locals of Japanese American produce and retail workers before the war, sought early to bar returned evacuees from these fields," upon the reopening of the West Coast exclusion zone in 1945.[36] Yet, at that same time period, the Congress of Industrial Organizations (CIO) in Chicago and United Auto Workers (UAW) in Detroit sought to organize Japanese Americans into labor organizations and the Detroit UAW went so far as to hire a Nisei organizer.[37] At the same time, Black workers were actively barred from joining labor unions throughout the urban Midwest region.[38]

Although Japanese Americans were clearly not white, in many of the "arsenal of democracy" cities that Japanese Americans were resettled to, they also experienced less discrimination in employment in comparison to the West Coast climate and also in regard to their Black peers in the Midwest. It is in this social and economic context that the WRA's public relations praise (discussed later in the chapter) of Japanese Americans as "hard workers" and "loyal" Americans citizens comes to light. The WRA began to highlight the successes and integration of Japanese resettlers in order to create good will for Japanese Americans among white Clevelanders. However, given the simultaneous and much more numerous migration of Black Americans, this conspicuous praise of Japanese American migrants created a contrast between the representation of Japanese American migrants and Black American migrants to Cleveland. In the cities and workplaces of the Midwest and East Coast that many resettlers moved into, these were also often towns and jobs that were destinations during the 1940s by African Americans who were migrating to cities like Cleveland in record numbers. In effect, the Japanese resettlers were competing for both jobs and housing with African Americans. Both groups were not white and composed of many newly arrived migrants.

Japanese American Neighbors: Changing Racial Demographics of the Hough Neighborhood

In the "arsenal of democracy cities" throughout the urban Midwest, the available housing stock was nearly nonexistent, and what was available was often old and dilapidated. Like other migrants to Cleveland, and especially migrants of color, Japanese American resettlers during the war faced limited availability of housing stock in a crowded market. And, for the Japanese that were relocating to Cleveland, "The majority of people settled in the Hough area, around 79th and Hough Avenues. During this period, the area was principally white, various European ethnics, and a few blacks."[39] Japanese resettlers were but one ethnic group of people that fueled the enormous population growth in the Hough neighborhood from the 1940s to the 1960s, peaking with the 1950 census.

The Hough neighborhood lies immediately east of the area of present-day AsiaTown and west of University Circle (see Figure 4.1).[40] Hough originally developed as an East Side streetcar suburb for the middle and upper class in the 1870s. After World War II, Hough became a bellwether neighborhood of overcrowding, rapid racial transition, segregation, and urban renewal, which eventually took root throughout the city of Cleveland.[41] By the early 1940s, Hough's wealthier white residents had already moved further east to University Heights and Cleveland Heights, and Hough was a neighborhood of working-class and immigrant white people. At the beginning of World War II, "Hough developed into a densely settled district of some forty thousand mostly white residents."[42] By 1966, the neighborhood gained national notoriety as the epicenter of Cleveland's urban rebellion during the long hot summers of racial unrest of the 1960s. During the intervening years of the 1940s and 1950s, the neighborhood grew with returning GIs of all races, Japanese resettlers, Puerto Rican migrants, and Black and white Southerners seeking jobs and housing in Cleveland. In Hough, the stately homes of Cleveland's wealthiest nineteenth-century families continued to be parceled into rooming houses and apartments.[43]

To say the neighborhood grew rapidly is an understatement; the population doubled between 1940 and 1955. In 1940, approximately forty thousand residents lived in Hough, in 1950, nearly sixty-six thousand residents lived there, and, by 1955, the population had grown to over eighty-two thousand.[44] This change was notable enough that, in 1957, Hough was the focus of a team of sociologists who argued, "The most pronounced change in the population of Hough since 1940 has been in racial composition."[45] In 1940, about 1 percent of the population was nonwhite.[46] And, by 1965, on the eve of the 1966 Hough Rebellion, the population was 87.9 percent Black.[47]

Both the population growth of Hough and the racial project of housing segregation in the Hough neighborhood from 1940 to 1965 were like many neighborhoods in Northern urban cities at the time. The underlying force of systemic racism created conditions of urban renewal, lack of new housing being built in the city, and the forced ghettoization of nonwhite residents. Racially exclusive housing for white people in the suburbs was being built at a pace unmatched by housing in the cities.[48] The existing housing stock was old and dilapidated. According to the 1950 census, "Many dwellings in the

Hough Area had no private bath, no running water, or were dilapidated, or a combination of two or more of these conditions."[49] Even though the housing stock was old, it was still in high demand in the years during World War II. As migrants moved to the city to fill jobs in the rapidly growing economy, a crucial difference for Japanese American resettlers is that, because of the forced evacuation from the West Coast, they, unlike their African American peers, received modest governmental assistance in locating and securing housing from both the WRA and the CRC.

The CRC housing committee, operated without much public outreach or promotion, instead working with realtors and relying on existing connections and social networks. While the CRC wrote individual letters to realtors to inquire after available rental properties, there were no public appeals for housing assistance, "even when (in mid-1945) the shortages were most acute or when specific problems had to be faced (e.g., the refusal of a development built with war housing funds to rent to Nisei)."[50] Even as the CRC attempted to steer clear of stoking local anger over resettlement by avoiding public appeals for rental housing, the severe housing shortage was a hot-button issue in Cleveland. In 1945, the Cleveland Real Estate Board pitted Japanese resettlers against returning World War II veterans. They "sent telegrams to Ohio's senators and area members of Congress complaining about the number of Japanese moving to Cleveland. The Board claimed that efforts to find homes for vets 'were being defeated to some extent by the unfortunate insistence of the . . . WRA who are seeking living accommodations for immigrant Japanese.' Veterans, the telegram says, should always receive priority for housing."[51] The Real Estate Board in effect was doing the work here to ensure that Ohio's legislators understood that, by veterans, they were concerned most primarily with white veterans. It is well documented that throughout the country veterans of color frequently received no preferential treatment in rental housing and were largely excluded from FHA veteran-specific home-buying loans due to racial covenants that enshrined whiteness as a key criteria for homeownership. Although the WRA had the sole charge to focus on the resettlement program of Japanese Americans, in 1945, George Trundle, the chairman of the CRC, wrote to Dillon Myer, the director of the WRA, urging him to keep the WRA office open after the war in order to solve the "Negro problem" in housing. Cleveland, Trundle noted, "has a notoriously bad reputation on housing Negroes."[52] But, the WRA was focused on the "Japanese problem," not the "Negro problem."

Japanese Resettlers Stretch the Color Line

Yae Wada first arrived in Cleveland at the age of twenty-four after she and her infant daughter traveled by train from Topaz to Cleveland to join her husband in a hotel that had been configured into a rooming house. Shortly thereafter Yae recalled that the WRA assisted the family of three by offering an apartment, "on the borderline of the white and Black area," in a mansion that was converted into apartments for families with children. Their apartment "was one that used to be a ballroom, so we had a beautiful hardwood floor ballroom, and a small narrow kitchen, a small little bedroom." Yae Wada was born November 3, 1919, in Berkeley, California, the youngest of two daughters born to Japanese immigrants.[53] In the spring of 1942, when mandatory evacuation occurred, Yae was married and running a beauty shop in Oakland. She relocated with her husband and father to Tanforan, where she suffered a miscarriage. In September, they were moved again to Topaz. Yae's husband was a machinist and left camp for a job in Cleveland shortly after their daughter was born in 1943. Because Yae and the baby were too sick to travel when her husband left, Yae and her daughter made the trip to Cleveland months later.

The experience of being incarcerated and her interactions at Tanforan and Topaz with white personnel, doctors, and camp administrators created in Yae a fear and mistrust of other people. However, as she recalled in an oral history interview over seventy years later, her chance encounters on her trip to Cleveland, and her early days in the city began to restore her faith in people. Despite the evidence of the prior years, she found kindness and goodness in strangers. She described in detail her train journey to Cleveland, starting as she boarded the train:

> I had my baby, I had her diapers, I had my clothes, and I had a bucket with five bottles of milk in it. I was having a hard—and the baby, I was trying to carry her on the train. And the person that helped me was this porter, this black porter. And the black porters, the way they make their money is by helping customers, and they get the tip, that's how they make their money. But he was grand to me, and he was going to help me, and I had to say, "No, thank you." And he kind of insisted because he knew I needed help, and I said, "I don't have money to tip you." And he said, "That's okay, that's okay," so he helped me to get on the train.

Even as Yae and the porter both knew that train porters earned their salary not from the rail company, but from tips, and that Yae had nothing to pay, and, therefore, this man would not earn any money from Yae during the two-day journey from Utah to Cleveland, this man assisted her. Not only that, once the train journey began, this man told Yae:

> "I have an empty room," he said, "Nobody's going to use this room until we get to Cleveland, Ohio." And I said, "Well, that's where I'm

getting off," and he said, "Yes." So he said he'd let me use the room. And I said, "I can't pay for it," he said, "That's okay." And after we got into the room, he offered to heat up the bottle for the baby. He said, "I have children." He said, "I know what you're going through, I have children." He was the first person that helped me.[54]

Yae Wada was ninety-nine years old at the time she recalled this memory. In nearly one hundred years of life she recalls with clarity both the nearly two years of nonstop assault—the harrowing experience of evacuation, movement to the temporary assembly center at Tanforan, and then to Topaz concentration camp, and the man on the train, "He was the first person that helped me."

Shortly after moving into the ballroom apartment, Yae remembers her family informally sharing their apartment with boys who were leaving camp and had no place to sleep. "They ended up at my place, first just to meet with other friends, and when I found out that they had no place to sleep that night, then we invited them to stay." Yae and her husband became their own mini-hostel, offering these young men places to sleep on bedrolls on the ballroom floor. Although Yae and her family and these young men had very little, they shared what they had. Yae recalls, "The way they paid their share of the rent was they would go some place and they would buy, like, two carrots or one onion, one or two potatoes, that was all they could afford to give me. That's why we had stew every other night."[55] It is in this context that Yae became an older sister and wife and mother to a household of people.

The years of forced removal and incarceration took their toll. Yae recalls that when she first arrived in Cleveland, she was "scared to go outside because I thought that people were going to throw rocks at us, and I didn't want them to hit the baby." Even though Yae was scared to be outside among strangers, it fell upon her to grocery shop and prepare meals for her family and their roomers. After arriving in Cleveland, she had a food ration book but did not know how to use it, as these were not part of life in camp. She recalls:

> There was a meat market that was on the black side [of the neighborhood]. And when I went there, there was a row of men that were sitting against the wall, and they all stopped talking. They were friends, they were all talking, and they all stopped talking and stared at me. They had never seen a Japanese before. And I went up to this meat market place, and this man was obviously the owner there. And I told him I just came out of camp, and I said, "Somebody gave me this stamp, and I have only a limited amount of money, and I don't know

how to use the stamp," and I had six people at that time that I had to feed. "Can you show me how to use it?" And he showed me how to use the stamps, he's the one that taught me, why it would be a good idea to buy hamburger. Because you can do so much with it, do more like make hamburger, make spaghetti, make meatloaf, and do a lot with hamburger if you learned how to cook, and that was the cheapest meat, but it was still good meat. So he helped me, he was real patient, and he's the one that helped me.[56]

They lived in Cleveland for two years. Yae's second daughter was born in Cleveland. After the war ended and they had saved enough money for the train journey, they returned to Berkeley. But Yae remembers and was heartened by the people that helped her in Cleveland, "And so this black butcher, this porter, after you meet nice people like that, I had a little more faith in people."[57] Into this context, Japanese Americans relocating to places like Cleveland experienced the firsthand kindness of neighbors.

Yae and Isao became very attuned to the regional racial formation that permeated the West Coast as anti-Asian racism in the form of "Alien Land Laws" and mass evacuation and incarceration and the urban Midwest as anti-Black racism in the form of residential and employment segregation. The particularity of the resettlement of Japanese Americans into cities like Chicago and Cleveland, which were experiencing rapid population growth, left Japanese Americans in a strange place as neither white nor Black. In Chicago, for example, "as members of a racial minority, Japanese Americans in the city enjoyed only limited social, residential, and employment opportunities. White people would work but not live beside them. But because they were not black, the Nisei escaped the worst of Chicago racism."[58] For Japanese Americans in Cleveland, there were instances where they were able to break into spaces that had previously been "whites only." And, the Japanese Americans arriving as a result of relocation from concentration camps were clearly not white. Even if the racial hierarchy of the urban Midwest placed them as not Black, the national structures of anti-immigrant nativism had identified them as a racial other.

Black people, white people, and Japanese American people moving to Cleveland faced a lack of quality housing. Racism exacerbated this condition for Black and Japanese migrants. Yet, the CRC was formed to resettle Japanese Americans. And, because of this, they worked to secure housing and jobs for those moving to Cleveland from the camps. This was very different from the context into which Black Americans were moving. Yet, there was not an appointed resettlement committee working in conjunction with a civilian government agency to aid in the resettlement of Black Americans.

Japanese Americans in Black and White:
The Resettlement PR Machine

On Sunday, May 30, 1943, an article titled, "Nation Still Tops to U.S.-Japanese: Couple Here Proud of Record in Aiding the War Effort" ran on page 6-A[59] of the *Cleveland Plain Dealer*. This article introduces Private Taro Katayama and his wife, Mrs. Yuki Katayama, newly arrived in Cleveland. The article features a photo (Figure 2.3) and a brief introduction to, "Two American Citizens of Japanese ancestry." The unnamed reporter describes the meeting with this couple "in the office of Harold S. Fistere, supervisor of the United States Relocation Authority in Cleveland," as one where Private Katayama, "with a degree of quiet pride," described the patriotism of the couple and their families. Private Katayama said, "Every eligible male in her family either is in the army, has volunteered, is awaiting induction or has been rejected for physical causes. The same is true of my family." This familial pledge of American loyalty is underscored by the reason that the Katayamas are in Cleveland: Mrs. Yuki Katayama is working as a secretary for the Cleveland WRA. The reporter informs readers that the Katayamas "cheerfully discussed the experience, turns of fortune and sacrifices they have gone through since the army moved them and many others of their derivation from the Pacific Coast." The article also apprises readers of their biographies of jobs and education before the war and states that the couple met "in the Japanese relocation center" in Topaz, Utah. The article outlines that Mrs. Katayama arrived in Cleveland in pursuit of secretarial work and that Private Katayama is visiting his wife in Cleveland on a brief military leave. In the short piece, key turns of phrase—"no trace of prejudice," "cheerful," "proud," "married," "college graduate," "army"—paint a portrait of the Katayamas as model citizens.

The accompanying image (Figure 2.3) is adorned with a caption beginning with the all caps announcement, "TWO AMERICAN CITIZENS of Japanese ancestry, Pvt. Taro Katayama and his wife, Mrs. Yuki Katayama, now sojourning in Cleveland, have cheerfully met the sacrifices the war has imposed on them," completes the story of this young couple. Even with the grainy texture of now-digitized newsprint, the message is easy to decode. Taro, handsomely wearing his U.S. military uniform is effortlessly perched on the corner of the desk where Yuki sits in front of a typewriter. They gaze at one another with adoring smiles. The image is composed rather like a film still from a Hollywood movie about an office romance from the era. Taro Katayama, playing the role of the leading man, costumed in military uniform, sheet of paper in hand, stopping by the desk of the image's ingenue, Yuki Katayama. For her part, Yuki appears as if she was disrupted midwork, not even taking her hands from the keyboard of the typewriter as she pauses to gaze warmly up at Taro. The composition of the image with the type-

TWO AMERICAN CITIZENS of Japanese ancestry, Pvt. Taro Katayama and his wife, Mrs. Yuki Katayama, now sojourning in Cleveland, have cheerfully met the sacrifices the war has imposed upon them.

Figure 2.3 Photo from article, "Nation Still Tops to U.S. Japanese," *Cleveland Plain Dealer*, May 30, 1943.

writer in the middle foreground and the Katayamas on the edges, each wearing a wartime "uniform" of sorts, suggests that they have been cast to play the role of a "hardworking" young couple in love, who also just happen to be Japanese American. This tableau is created not for the couple but for the readers of the *Cleveland Plain Dealer* who gaze upon this couple gazing at one another.

The carefully composed image visually echoes all that is unsaid or un-spoken between the couple and the reader gazing upon them. The empty space between the Katayamas, which represents nearly one-third of the image, is an unintended visual signifier of all the unseen forces that have brought Yuki and Taro to Cleveland. The space represents the inherent contradictions that, on one hand, so forcefully emphasize the Katayamas' pleasant dispositions alongside their incarceration in Utah. The gap between them, at the center of the image, serves as a reminder of the spaces that are omitted from their Sunday feature, those that the reporter refers to as the "turns of fortune and sacrifice" that befell them "since the army moved them and many other of their derivation from the Pacific Coast."[60] It is notable that Taro Katayama was a writer and a journalist,[61] and, given Taro's work in journalism, he was certainly aware of the role of their feature article in the Sunday paper.

By the time Yuki appeared in the *Cleveland Plain Dealer* article in May 1943, she had spent the prior thirteen to fourteen months incarcerated by her government—first at a racetrack about twenty miles from her home in Oak-land, California, to a concentration camp in central Utah, where she wed her husband, before relocating to Cleveland, Ohio, where she was working as a secretary for the WRA office in Cleveland. The WRA itself was responsible for the circumstances that led Yuki, now Mrs. Katayama, to her appearance in the Sunday *Cleveland Plain Dealer*, at nearly every possible level of cul-pability—from evacuation to incarceration to subsequent resettlement in Cleveland.

Mrs. Yuki Katayama was born Yuki Shiozawa on December 4, 1916, in Oakland, California.[62] Yuki was one of seven American-born children to her parents, Japanese immigrants.[63] Like most Japanese American residents of the Bay Area, Yuki, her parents, and her siblings were evacuated first to Tan-foran Assembly Center on the site of the Tanforan Racetrack in San Bruno, California, in the spring of 1942 when Yuki was twenty-five. At this assem-bly center and others throughout the West Coast, the housing for horses and racetracks was converted into holding centers that housed Japanese Ameri-cans and nationals.[64]

Yuki and her family spent about four months at Tanforan, departing for Topaz concentration camp in Delta, Utah, after it opened on September 11, 1942. The Topaz population record book reveals that the Shiozawa family arrived on September 22, 1942, after a two-day train journey from Tanforan to Topaz. As the Shiozawas were in the midst of their upheaval, perhaps in their months at Tanforan or in their early weeks at Topaz, Yuki met Taro Ka-tayama, a Utah-born college graduate who was working as a journalist in San Francisco at the time of the mandatory evacuation. Although we do not know the circumstances of the Katayamas' meeting, because they were the first couple to wed at Topaz Concentration Camp, we do know of their nuptials.

The Katayamas' feature in the *Cleveland Plain Dealer* is not the first time Yuki and Taro appeared in print as a couple. The *Topaz Times*, the paper produced by and for the incarcerees in the Topaz Concentration Camp, featured the Katayamas' wedding on page two of the November 17, 1942, issue. Sandwiched in between the end of a story soliciting teachers for the schools in the camp and an announcement about the upcoming Four-Day Festival in honor of Thanksgiving, there appears the news of the marriage of Yuki Shiozawa and Taro Katayama. Their nuptials were reported as the "First Wedding Held" (Figure 2.4) at Topaz, noting that "in the midst of swirling snowfall, Topaz' [*sic*] first nuptial rites were held Sunday in the Protestant Church, Roe [*sic*] 22. Yuki Shiozawa, 25, and Taro Katayama, 28, were married by Rev. Joseph Tsukamoto in a simple wedding ceremony witnessed by close friends and relatives."[65]

FIRST WEDDING HELD

By Alex Yorichi

In the midst of swirling snowfall, Topaz' first nuptial rites were held Sunday in the Protestant church, Roc 22.

Yuki Shiozawa, 25, and Taro Katayama, 28, were married by Rev. Joseph Tsukamoto in a simple wedding ceremony witnessed by close friends and relatives.

Before the wedding ceremony musical selections were presented by Mary Ikeda at the organ, and later by Goro Suzuki, cousin of the bride, who sang "At Dawning."

The bride's father, Tetsushiro Shiozawa, gave the bride away, while Jerry Katayama, brother of the benedict, was the best man. The brother is the JACL executive secretary of the Salt Lake chapter.

The bride, with a "Victory" pompadour hairdress, wore a wine-colored velveteen dress and accessories with 1 strand of pearls. She wore an orchid corsage rounded off with white bouvardias. The benedict wore a navy blue tailored suit.

Prior to evacuation the bride was a Civil Service stenographer in the Alameda County Charities Commission in Oakland. The bridegroom, formerly of Salt Lake City, is a graduate of the University of Utah, and was working on a San Francisco paper before the evacuation. He was also the editor of the Tanforan Totalizer. They are "at home" in 36-12-A until Thursday.

Figure 2.4 Text of article, "First Wedding Held," *Topaz Times*, November 17, 1942, p. 2.

When the *Cleveland Plain Dealer* interviewed the Katayamas in May 1943, Yuki (Shiozawa) Katayama was a secretary to the area supervisor of the WRA Great Lakes Area office in Cleveland. Yuki was one of eighteen thousand Nisei to leave the WRA camps permanently for destinations throughout the Midwest and East Coast by the end of 1943.[66] By the time she departed Utah for Cleveland in May 1943, it was less than a year after she was forced to leave her home in Oakland, California, and she had been at Topaz for less than six months. Although the "choice" to leave camp could not really be construed as a freely made choice, the option for the newlywed Yuki to leave camp for Cleveland—a place as unfamiliar and foreign as Delta, Utah—represented an opportunity beyond the small and limited life of camp.

Yuki worked at the WRA from May 1943 until the office closed in 1946, receiving at least two promotions in this time. By March 1946, when the Great Lakes Area WRA office issued its final report, it listed in its personnel overview, "Yuki S. Katayama, Administrative Assistant, started in WRA as a clerk, became the secretary to the Area Supervisor and was promoted to this position."[67] From the employee listing of thirty-one named individuals, Yuki is one of only two people with a recognizably Japanese name and one of eight people gendered as a woman.[68] What this must have been like for her, we will never know. But to be in an office charged with the sole purpose of the relocation of Japanese Americans from WRA camps to the Midwest as the only identifiably Japanese American woman privy to meetings and conversations deciding this fate must have been weighty indeed. However, although Yuki is the only identifiably named Japanese American woman employee in the report, the final report states, "The clerical and stenographic staff in the Area was filled almost entirely with Nisei girls."[69] This underscores that while the race and gender of the other Japanese American women in the office relegated them to a nameless secretary pool, Yuki was an exception to this anonymity. Yet, the other Japanese American women employees were asked to be visible in other outward-facing roles. In the final report of the Great Lakes office, a note about the "Nisei girls," the aforementioned "clerical and stenographic staff," suggests that their work was essential to the relocation effort,

> A great deal of the success of [the] WRA was due to the high caliber of service they gave. Not only were the District and Area offices able to secure first class assistance of this kind, but in addition, many of the girls were important in the public relations field, making talks to church and professional groups and generally proving [the] soundness of the Relocation Program by virtue of their own acceptability.[70]

It is not clear here if this work of "public relations" is a job that was part of their official office duties, if it is something that they volunteered to do, or if it is something that they were asked to do by the WRA office. We may never know who these "girls" were, how many worked at the office, or what their experiences were. Yet, we know that they were integral not only as labor "doing" the work of the office but also "performing" the work of respectability and Americanness in their appearances outside of the office.

The story in the *Cleveland Plain Dealer* praising Yuki and her husband Taro for their work and patriotism in the war effort, was one of numerous stories about the patriotism of Japanese American citizens that appeared in newspapers across the country. The story about the Katayamas was planted as part of the PR machine of the Great Lakes WRA. The Great Lakes Area Final Report, outlined a clear strategy for harnessing media to make the case that Japanese Americans were not only nonthreatening but American. The report states, "From the very beginning it was realized that associations Japanese Americans had with the easily recognizable and accepted aspects of contemporary American life were the items to stress in public relations work." To this end the PR team stressed things like membership in religious and community organizations that would be familiar to readers, "Girl Scouts, Boy Scouts, the Y.M.C.A., the Y.W.C.A., P.T.A., the company bowling team, labor unions, college clubs were emphasized." It was part of that work in creating a discourse that Japanese Americans are just like other (white) Americans. Additionally, part of the strategy also included stressing other attributes, such as "their personal cleanliness, strong family ties, pride in their home, all similarities with other Americans, civil rights, democratic ideals, and above all their loyalty and patriotism to [the] U.S. were factors which were used most when speaking to the press, radio, various groups and other media in this Area."[71] In fact, the list pulled directly from this final report suggests that the PR teams in these early WRA relocation offices specifically laid the groundwork for the model minority myth, with the Japanese resettlers forming the first examples of what these "model Americans" are, the best, most idealized community members, families, and citizens. This was a 180-degree turn from the discourses that resulted in the incarceration of Japanese Americans initially.

Making Home: Postwar Cleveland and Beyond

On December 17, 1944, all relocation orders were revoked, and the exclusion areas that were in place since early 1942 were rescinded, effective January 2, 1945.[72] When West Coast exclusion areas reopened on January 2, 1945, plans were put into motion to hasten resettlement and empty the camps. While about thirty-six thousand of those initially incarcerated left camps for work, education, or to enlist in the military in January 1945, there remained in camp about seventy-five thousand people.[73] Wide-ranging experiences and reports of violence along the West Coast resulted in about one-third of those still in camp opting to resettle in the Midwest and East Coast, even though the West Coast was "reopened."[74] In Cleveland, during 1945 and 1946, Japanese Americans continued to arrive. For example, "February 1946 shows a whopping net loss (18 arrive, 177 depart), March (the last month for which official figures are available) shows a gain (39 arrive, 18 depart)."[75] By December 1945, all camps except for Tule Lake were closed.[76] Once more, in a massive feat of mobilization, the government moved thousands of people in mere months. The Great Lakes War Relocation office closed in the spring of 1946, and later that same year the WRA itself shut down, and the remaining work became part of the "War Agency Liquidation Unit."

By 1946, Cleveland's Japanese American community had formed social groups such as "Les Debonaires, Nisei Fellowship, Keen Tyme, and the Young Buddhist Association. Many social activities were held in the First Methodist Church at 30th and Euclid." Also, the Matsuya Company "was supplying the community with the indispensable commodities of rice and, on weekends, noodles and fresh fish at 81st and Hough."[77] And, in 1946, the Cleveland chapter of the Japanese American Citizens' League (JACL) started. The Cleveland JACL "picked up locally where most of its members had left off in prewar California. The majority of its activities were social, but the group also engaged in some community service activities and supported the legislative program of the National J.A.C.L. The primary emphasis of the Cleveland Chapter in these early years, however, were installation dinners, balls, recognition affairs for the Issei, and seasonal parties."[78]

These early years of community organizing had a heavy emphasis on social events, and recognition events often seemed to be performing a dual role of community building and also outreach to the wider Cleveland community, frequently inviting "Caucasian dignitaries. . . . Some old time J.A.C.L. officers have indicated that this was done for public relations reasons. Some Nisei have reported that they were unsure of their standing in the larger community at this time."[79] Many in Cleveland's Japanese American community were bent on being "model citizens." And, in the wake of forced incarceration, this strategy makes sense: settle in, build a community, try and move past the war years, do not draw attention. Part of the strategy for survival, both individual and it seems community-wide, was to "move on" in the face of discrimination. While it was reported that "many Nisei have also faced employment discrimination in Cleveland" it was "of a much more subtle type than that experienced in prewar California. Typically, the Japanese did not react overtly to these slights, but simply moved on to where they were 'wanted.' In comparison with their prewar experience on the Pacific Coast, most Nisei report that their experience in Cleveland have been much less discriminatory."[80] Because of the fact that Cleveland was "less discriminatory," in comparison to the West Coast, many stayed for years after the war, some set-tling permanently.

Part of settling in seemed to rely on the community remaining some-what apolitical. For example, JACL held a home buyers' clinic in 1952, which, despite the racial climate, never discussed fair housing and discrimination.[81] The community worked to raise funds to purchase a building to serve as a temple, and, by 1955, they had raised the money to purchase a building on East 81st Street, "a rather ordinary looking house in the Hough area."[82] In 1960, the community was partially successful in establishing a Japanese lan-guage school. However, "in the early 1960s, many members felt frightened in the Hough area and were reluctant to attend services" and "during the 'Hough Riots' the Temple was fire-bombed. The Temple continued to be desecrated by vandalism. . . . In the late 1960s the remaining members decided to move the Temple to East 214th and Euclid Avenue."[83]

The Japanese Temple was not the only facility to move. In the wake of white flight and the declining tax base, basic services, and overall conditions in the Hough neighborhood, specifically, and the central city, more generally, many Japanese Americans moved out of the central city. By the mid-1970s, Japanese Americans had "widely scattered throughout the greater Cleveland area in middle-class suburbs such as Euclid, Parma, Wickliffe, and Cleve-land Heights. In part, migration from the central city has resulted from the prosperity enjoyed by the Nisei and Sansei. Desiring newer and better housing with the proverbial bigger yard, they have faithfully pursued the American dream."[84] And, like their fellow white Clevelanders, many Japanese Ameri-cans left the central city when and if it was possible. Although the whites-only suburban color line was more porous for Japanese American families than Black families, as evidenced by the suburbanization of the community, many Nisei in Cleveland experienced housing discrimination, as "a number were told by realtors that neighbors had voiced objections to their moving into the area. Many were 'steered' by agents. Most Japanese acquiesced in the face of such discrimination, and there is no available evidence to suggest that anyone attempted to contest such racist action."[85]

Even as some Japanese Americans decided to make their way in Cleve-land, still others opted to return to the West Coast. "By 1950, the Japanese population of Cleveland was 1,078 (of the county 1,189), according to U.S. Census figures, clearly a large drop from what may have been a high of 3,500."[86] And, the community continued to contract, as people "returned to their families, jobs, and the familiar locales of California. Farmers and nurs-erymen, desiring to reestablish themselves in their chosen work, were espe-cially prominent among the returnees. The pull of strong family ties to Cali-fornia was compelling also. Southern California, a dynamic and expanding area was most popular among Japanese from Cleveland."[87] The government estimated that, by 1947, "slightly more than 60 per cent of the evacuees have returned to their former homes, or other parts of the evacuated area, and slightly less than 40 per cent have remained east of the evacuation boundary."[88] In comparison, in 1940, 88.5 percent of all people of Japanese ancestry lived in Washington, Oregon, and California, and, by 1947, approximately 55 percent of the population lived in those three states.[89]

Yasu Momii, who lived and worked at the Cleveland Hostel during the war, eventually returned to California. But she always remembered Cleveland fondly. Momii and her husband married in 1945 and stayed in Cleveland until 1948. In recalling her time in Cleveland, after the upheaval of camp and relocation, she said, "Cleveland it was really, it was a nice place to be." This sentiment rings true for many of those interviewed about their time in Cleveland.[90] Even as Cleveland proved to be a reprieve from the confinement of camps, most people eventually returned to the West Coast. For Yasu, even though Cleveland was a "nice place," ultimately she and her husband returned to California, because "my home was Los Angeles."[91] Yasu was among many Cleveland resettlers who both married in Cleveland and returned to the West Coast. And, as Figure 2.5 shows, the "farewell party/wedding shower" combination event happened on at least one occasion, but likely with some frequency.

According to the 1950 census, the Katayamas were still in Cleveland, both working full time and living at 1720 East 70th Street in the Hough neighborhood. Taro, by then thirty-six, was employed as a "line type operator" at a printing company and Yuki, thirty-three, was working in some type of "claim" position at the Social Security office.[92] It is unclear if their dwelling was two-units or if the couple was sharing a single property with another household. The other household listed at 1720 East 70th Street was composed of Kengo and Tori Tajima, a married couple, both born in Japan, age sixty-five and sixty-three respectively, and their lodger, Kai Matsuoka a thirty-year-old never married bachelor, born in California.

This page of the 1950 census, City of Cleveland E.D. Number 92–835, Sheet 13, started on April 5, 1950, by Anna M. Wilson, reveals the history of migration to the Hough neighborhood as well as the multiracial character of the street that the Katayamas lived on in 1950. On their street, of the neighbors that were home, in addition to the Tajima-Matsuoka household, there was one other household of color, a "Negro" couple and their lodger residing at 1736 East 70th Street. McKinlay Shay, age twenty-nine, was a Virginia-born "special delivery manager" employed at the post office married to Gladys Shay, age twenty, an Ohio-born "dietary aid" working at a private hospital. They shared their home with their lodger, Hammond Peak, a married forty-three-year-old South Carolina born "mail trucker" working for the railroad. The rest of the seven households surveyed were white. Many of the Katayamas' neighbors

Figure 2.5 "At Stouffer's in Cleveland—Another Farewell/At shower for Sachi Kashiwagi now Mrs. Geo. Sugimura." *(Courtesy of the Mabel Sugiyama Eto Family Collection, Densho Digital Repository, circa 1940s. Available at https://ddr.densho.org/ddr-densho -298-240-mezzanine-17697bbca3/. Licensed under a CC-BY 4.0 License, available at http:// creativecommons.org/licenses/by-nc-sa/4.0.)*

were migrants to Ohio who were born in places like California, Washington, DC, Pennsylvania, South Carolina, West Virginia, Virginia, and Japan.

By looking at 1940s Cleveland, we can see that the "Japanese problem" of the West Coast was a "solution" of sorts in the Midwest. First, Japanese Americans were shifted to places where there was a labor shortage, to fill the demand for jobs in regions that were most in need of workers. Second, at the regional and local level, we can begin to see how Japanese Americans disrupted the presumed Black-white racial binary of the 1940s arsenal of democracy. The construction of Japanese Americans as "alien" and then, ultimately, "citizen" was not only a discursive but a spatial process. By focusing on 1940s Cleveland, we can see how Japanese American "inclusion" into the city is divorced from their prior exclusion on the West Coast as well as rendered in relationship to Cleveland's rapidly growing population of Black Southern migrants.[93] While scholars have written about comparative racial formations on the West Coast,[94] this chapter contributes to an analysis of the formation of Japanese American racial identity in the larger context of the Black-white framework of Northern urban cities. By focusing in on the East Side Hough neighborhood, the place with the highest concentration of resettlers, we can map the transition of the neighborhood itself from one composed of middle class white Clevelanders through Japanese resettlers and multiracial migrants from the South to a primarily Black neighborhood by the 1960s (see Chapter 4).

This transmutation of Japanese Americans into "model citizens" during World War II is both an important context for the regional understanding of Asian Americans in Cleveland at large and is the regional racial framework for the community and commercial development that is discussed in Chapters 3, 4, and 5. In the next chapter, I turn to the specific history of Chinese American settlement in Cleveland and redevelopment efforts during the city's period of population, economic, and reputational decline in the late twentieth century. By examining specific local histories of different Asian ethnic groups (Japanese American in this chapter, Chinese American in Chapter 3), we can see the complications of panethnic "Asian"–themed development (see Chapters 4 and 5) within the larger context of Cleveland's rise, decline, and rise again narrative arc.

3

The Provisions of Life

Restaurants, Grocery Stores, and the Anchors of Community Development

When Asia Plaza opened, it was the first time I saw AAPI representation. While there were other Chinese restaurants in the suburbs, this was the first time I saw mostly Asian patrons—I felt welcomed, heard other people speaking other languages like Mandarin. I had seen this in cities like Chicago, and NY, where my family would stock up on various foods, but this was the first time in Cleveland that I saw so many people who looked like me. I was excited—it was loud, with carts filled with familiar foods. I loved that it was a regular weekend destination, it felt easy and like I belonged.

—Participant, "We're Growing Home"[1]

A weekend visit to the "Park to Shop" grocery store in Asia Plaza requires no small amount of patience as you, indeed, need to try to "park" in order to shop. The back parking lot of Asia Plaza closest to the grocery store is usually full, and, although the angled spaces serve as some indication that there is one way to enter and exit the lot, waiting cars are circling for available spots in all directions. The jockeying for a parking spot is in many ways a prelude to the brisk and bustling interior of this pan-Asian grocery store. The cars mostly sport Ohio license plates, but often cars with Pennsylvania and sometimes Michigan plates are parked while their owners shop or dine inside. Park to Shop, and Asia Plaza more generally, is a regional hub for Northeast Ohio, some customers even crossing state lines to make this grocery run—filling carts with spices, sauces, and vegetables more commonly found in Shanghai and Seoul than the Rust Belt. From prepackaged snack foods to noodles made from rice, buckwheat, and potato flours and cuts and types of meat and seafood that lend themselves to the preparations that are popular in countries throughout Asia, Park to Shop is a large "modern" store with aisles full of "Asian" foodstuffs that in a Midwestern grocery store like

Kroger or Dave's may take up half an aisle at best. Given its location as some-what of a "destination," many of the shoppers have carts piled high with fresh, frozen, and packaged foods. The fresh foods to be prepared soon, and the frozen and packaged foods to fill a pantry for when particular tastes and flavors are a drive to AsiaTown or a plane ride away.

Park to Shop, and its presence as an anchor store in Asia Plaza mall, rep-resents a shifting form of consumption that began in the 1980s, where "Asian Americans could shop at supermarket chains targeted to them. . . . H-Mart on the East Coast and 99 Ranch on the West Coast were among the most suc-cessful."[2] These large supermarkets, typically found in suburban retail cor-ridors, are often anchor businesses in "Asian malls" and shopping plazas that were colocated with other ethnic businesses and targeted services.[3] Asian malls were built as a response to an overall growth of the Asian population, alongside a pattern of increasing suburbanization of Asian American com-munities.[4] These two factors combined to create market demand beyond the small grocery stores that had long existed as part of central city ethnic econ-omies for decades. Like the role of their central city predecessors, these newer form shopping plazas and grocery stores met the basic needs of supplying foodstuffs that are familiar and necessary. And these spaces also serve as sites of community development and community connection. The aisles of Park to Shop for example are transformed annually by the Dragon Dance as the dragon frolics its way around and through the aisles as part of the Asia Plaza Lunar New Year Celebration (See Figures 3.1 and 3.2). Much more than a "grocery store" or a "shopping mall," this chapter considers food, and the places it is produced, prepared, purchased, and consumed, as essential sites of development of Cleveland's AsiaTown. Beyond simply calories or culture, food is a key part of economic and community development.

AsiaTown is neither a "downtown Chinatown" nor a strip mall plaza in a suburb or an Asian Mall in an ethnoburb.[5] The AsiaTown neighborhood is located in a light industrial area of the city, just east of the downtown core—offset by one- and two-story mid-twentieth-century worker's cottages inter-spersed between hulking early twentieth-century factory footprints that have been repurposed into apartments,[6] mixed-use retail, industry, and some that are still in use as industrial concerns.[7] While this is, indeed, part of Cleve-land proper, it is a location that was, and remains, a primary place for light industry due to its proximity to both freeways and waterways. In many ways it both confirms and defies the typologies that are in place for ethnic malls, ethnoburbs, or urban Chinatowns. As discussed in Chapter 1, even though Cleveland's population as a whole began to steadily decline in each consecu-tive decade since 1950, in that same time period, the Asian American com-munity has steadily increased in population. This decline in white popula-tion that Cleveland experienced in the latter half of the twentieth century

Figures 3.1 and 3.2 Park to Shop interior, Lunar New Year Celebration, Asia Plaza, February 2018. *(Photos by author.)*

was similar to cities across the country as federal, state, and city governments subsidized the suburbanization of white residents. In the 1950 U.S. census, 765,264 white people were counted in Cleveland, and, by 1980, that number was 307,264, a decrease of 58.85 percent. In the 1950 U.S. census, 1,499 Asian people lived in Cleveland, and, by 1980, the number rose to 3,384, an increase of 125.75 percent. In comparison, in the 1950 U.S. census, 147,847 Black people lived in Cleveland, and, by 1980, the number rose to 251,347, an increase of 70.00 percent.[8] While the population of Asian people is a proportionally small racial group, the rate of population increase is significant.[9]

From the late twentieth century to the present, there was an increase in the Asian American population in Cleveland, and the United States as a whole. This time period also overlaps with rapid suburbanization across the United States and the marked decline of the center city across the United States, and in industrial and manufacturing centers like Cleveland in particular. Cleveland, like its Rust Belt counterparts began its continual contraction of the white population starting in the years immediately following the end of World War II. It is important to note here that the movement of white people out of Cleveland was fueled by several factors including, most definitively, the subsidization of whiteness by local, state, and federal governments and financial institutions through the processes of building suburban infrastructure, the federal highway system, and mortgage lending. In addition, cities and municipalities often enticed corporations to build sprawling new automated suburban industrial parks near communities where their white workers were building and buying homes.[10] Still other jobs were shipped overseas or lost to ever-increasing automation. These movements resulted in the loss of city tax dollars and population, as public monies underwrote suburbanization.

Just before the postwar suburbanization boom, Chinese exclusion came to an end, with the repeal of the Chinese Exclusion Act in 1943. As Xiaojian Zhao suggests, the time between 1940 and 1965 "profoundly altered the lives of Chinese Americans."[11] In direct contrast to the deleterious impacts World War II had on Japanese Americans (see Chapter 2), World War II profoundly shifted Chinese American legal status and opened a door to immigration, most directly for Chinese women.[12] Although family unification is most typically associated with provisions of the Immigration and Nationality Act of 1965, legislative shifts in the 1940s enabled family unification as Chinese American male veterans were able to bring their wives and fiancées to the United States free from the existing quota limits set forth in the 1924 Immigration Act. In this legislative opening, Chinese American families were reunited and made, well before the post 1965 demographic changes in the Asian American community at large. In what had heretofore been a majority male society, these shifts were measurable and clear, "in 1940 there were 2.9 Chinese men for every Chinese woman in the United States (57,389 men versus 20,115 women). By 1960 this ratio was reduced to 1.35 to 1 (135,430 men versus 100,654 women)."[13] By the time the 1965 Immigration Act passed, for Chinese Americans, a pattern of family formation was already in place.

As a result, in Cleveland, there was a modest but steady increase in the Chinese population from 308 people in 1940 to 740 in 1970, which amounts to a 41.6 percent increase.

The current iteration of what is now called AsiaTown really began to take distinct root in the 1980s and early 1990s as the developers of Asia Plaza aimed to recenter a "New Chinatown" in the area just east of the I-90 freeway in MidTown. Asia Plaza's development as an ethnic mall in the 1980s, in the city proper not in the suburbs, like we see in places like California's Monterey Park or Fremont, or a strip mall or stand-alone restaurant and small businesses, like we see in places like metro Detroit, is particularly unique. As this chapter shows, Asia Plaza aimed to serve as an ethnic mall and an anchor development that knit together the existing Chinese community church and longtime ethnic markets and restaurants dotting the neighborhood. The neighborhood is currently home to a diverse ethnic and racial population of about two thousand people with the majority of the residential life taking place between Payne and Superior Avenues on the numbered streets running north–south between E. 30th and E. 40th Streets. The commercial life of the neighborhood occurs along the light industrial avenues that run east–west, meaning that the residential life of the neighborhood is often just out of view of those visiting AsiaTown. The neighborhood has grown slowly and steadily into a commercial hub of panethnic Asian restaurants and grocery stores, with two malls, Asia Plaza and Asian Town Center, serving as anchor points.[14]

This chapter takes as its central through line that "food" operates as a way to make connections, community, and a living. More than simply flavors, or production, or restaurants, or small businesses, as Mark Padoongpatt suggests, food and foodways "must be understood as more than just a confluence of private practices centered on personal consumption but as a broader set of activities that involves multiple levels of interactions, public sociability, and community engagement."[15] In this particular Rust Belt city, with a small Asian population throughout the past two centuries, placemaking through food has operated as both a means of survival and a way to build community. While much has been written about the history of Chinese food in the United States,[16] this chapter considers food beyond production or flavors and as a way of understanding the historic and contemporary formation of the Asian American community in Cleveland. By considering food—grocery stores, restaurants, sites of consumption—we can begin to understand the ways that those who develop, run, and consume at these establishments are what Natalia Molina calls, "placemakers."[17] More than simply providing calories or the flavors of home, these placemakers serve as spatial and community anchors of development historically and today.

Community Placemakers: Ethnic Entrepreneurs, Small Business Owners from the Nineteenth Century to Present

Since the late 1800s, laundries, restaurants, and other small businesses have been a central location for Chinese Americans to carve out a place in the United States.[18] The earliest Chinese American restaurateurs and laundrymen were usually not plying a trade that they had come to America to pursue; rather, in the face of discrimination at the mining and railroad camps, many Chinese men, and other men more generally, began to operate businesses that catered to the needs of other workers: food, lodging, and laundry.[19] Beginning in the late nineteenth century, as Chinese people and businesses moved from workers' camps on the West Coast to bustling urban centers throughout the country, many cities could count a small Chinese population where many of its community were working in restaurants or laundries and creating "enclave economies" that rely on the "co-ethnicity of entrepreneurs and workers" existing in a "spatial concentration of ethnic firms with a wide variety of economic activities."[20] By the late nineteenth century, in cities like New York and Chicago, most of the "so-called slums and red-light districts" were "inhabited by recent southern and eastern European immigrants, blacks, and Chinese."[21] Although a distinction between "ghetto" and "ethnic enclave" would be employed by the late twentieth century to mark a distinction between a "Black" neighborhood and an "immigrant" neighborhood, in cities in the Midwest and on the East Coast, Chinatowns were often multiracial and multiethnic neighborhoods housing people of color and immigrants, more generally.

As Chinese migrants built commercial enterprises within residential neighborhoods, an "enclave economy" emerged.[22] A version of enclave economy has persisted from the early development of "traditional" Chinatowns (1880s–World War II) through the revitalization of historic Chinatowns (1940s–present) through the creation of "commercial" and "satellite" Chinatowns (post-1965–present).[23] Enclave economies rely on the continual participation of entrepreneurs to open and operate businesses. Entrepreneurship relies on a variety of factors including: "human capital, financial capital, social capital, and access to family and coethnic labor,"[24] some of which is secured prior to migration and some of which is built in the United States. As Lisa Sun-Hee Park argues, "The everyday reality of immigrant entrepreneurialism is a difficult one. The romantic notion of small family businesses ignores the existence of social structures that limit one's self-employment options, including the ability to mobilize resources such as capital and labor. In addition, quality of education, racial and gender discrimination, intense competition within a small market, and difficult working conditions pose significant barriers to successful self-employment."[25] It is within this tension of basic survival on the part of both small business owners and customers that community businesses persist as locations of community placemaking.

These locations of immigrant entrepreneurship have served as places for coethnics to find niche services and products, work, and carve out a place in the United States.[26] And, they have also served the larger narratives and persistent beliefs of Asian immigrant entrepreneurs as "good" immigrants serving to reify the model minority myth[27] through an embodiment of neoliberal ideology.[28] Indeed, it is the role of the "entrepreneur" and the neighborhood as the possible site of consumption that helps create the distinction between ghetto and enclave within Asian American Cleveland. For example, during the war years discussed in Chapter 2, Japanese Americans were concentrated in and alongside Black and immigrant Clevelanders in "ghetto" neighborhoods. But, by the early twenty-first century, as part of Cleveland's diversity marketing and branding, there is support by city and private developers to brand "AsiaTown" as an ethnic neighborhood (see Chapter 4). It is in the space between these two narratives that the development of Asia Plaza and the focus of this chapter emerge.

Steve Hom, the property manager of Asia Plaza, is a key member of the family that developed Asia Plaza and a member of the AsiaTown Advisory Committee (ATAC) (see Chapter 4). Steve is also a fourth-generation Chinese American on his paternal side and first-generation Chinese American on his maternal side. His family history of migration in and through the Ohio River Valley provides rich texture not only of secondary migration from the West Coast but of the continuing migrations of his family in search of work and home. Steve's family's movements and migrations are traced in the family oral history to a late nineteenth-century entanglement with railroad history. "Supposedly [my great-grandfather], would have come over with the railroads in the 1880s. Supposedly, after the railroads were finished they had this abundant pool of labor, and there was a lot of demand here in the Midwest for laborers in the steel mills. So they settled in Pittsburgh originally."[29]

Although Steve is not certain if his grandfather, like his great-grandfather worked in the steel industry, Steve's family history maps directly onto the history of American industrialization: first railroads and then steel. He does know that by the time his father was born in 1923, "in either Canton, Ohio or Youngstown, Ohio, somewhere around there . . . sometime they transitioned from the railroad to steel mills" and eventually to the laundry business. Steve's grandparents had a laundry in Canton, Ohio.[30] They operated the laundry "for quite some time, but I think, once the Depression hit in '29, '29 and '30, my dad would have been 6 or 7, they went back to China. They stayed there for about 10 years before coming back, that would be '39." After they returned, Steve's father and his uncles were all drafted and served in World War II. After the war, "in the '50s they transitioned from laundry to restaurants. Chinese restaurants really became really popular."[31] Steve's family story of movement in and around Ohio and Pennsylvania and moving to and returning from China in the 1920s and 1930s was not unique to his family. As historian Charlotte Brooks shows, "Census and immigration statistics for this period suggest that up to half of all native-born Chinese American citizens may have relocated to China between 1901 and World War II."[32] In Cleveland, the population of "Asian" was 330 in 1920, 649 in 1930, and 377 in 1940, reflecting the pattern that Brooks draws, nationally, and Steve Hom's family experienced, regionally.

This is a particular movement that is often not accounted for in the shifting landscape of the growth of cities in the 1940s. Brooks shows this missing element in stories of migration to the urban North. She writes, "The peak years of the Chinese American exodus also paralleled those of the Great Migration of African Americans from the Jim Crow South to the urban North. . . . About fifteen percent of the entire black population of the South migrated to the North between 1915 and 1930 alone. An even larger percentage of Chinese American citizens emigrated to China in the same years."[33] Brooks notes that both African Americans moving out of the South and Chinese Americans return migrating to China, during these years, "left their native homes for the same reasons: to escape racism, gain access to educational opportunities, and enjoy better job opportunities."[34] Throughout this period of Chinese return migration, the threat of war and invasion loomed as Japan's imperial ambitions rumbled throughout Asia in the late nineteenth and early twentieth centuries. The war between China and Japan triggered a return migration of many Chinese Americans back to the United States.[35] Steve's family story, while seemingly unusual, in fact, parallels a lesser-known history of Chinese American circular migration between China and the United States.

Steve Hom's family history illustrates a Chinese American family arc that begins prior to Chinese Exclusion and persists in Cleveland, Ohio. Although Steve is unclear when exactly his family made their way from Pittsburgh to Ohio, there were Chinese people living in cities throughout the Midwest in places like Chicago, St. Louis, and Columbus by the 1880 census.[36] In many ways, Cleveland is no different in that, "for the most part, the Chinese who settled in Cleveland came from other urban areas, particularly along the West Coast," and "nearly all came seeking relief from the intense anti-Chinese hostility on the West Coast and new economic opportunities."[37] Opportunities for service work abounded in the growing industrial city. Of these earliest settlers, "most had some education and work experience, and they typically opened small service businesses when they arrived, such as laundries, restaurants, groceries and clothing stores."[38] Like in most cities in the industrial Midwest, the Chinese were the first Asian ethnic group recorded in Cleveland newspapers and census documents. They began to emerge in the newspapers and documents of white settlers as early as the late 1840s when there was a community of about ten people, with the population dropping to only one Chinese person by 1870.[39] By the 1890 census, there were thirty-six Chinese people and the population in Cleveland grew slowly and steadily.[40] The Midwest was not an outright destination for most Chinese immigrants, and the people who arrived in the late nineteenth century often rode the railroads that Chinese workers had built to places with a train station and a growing economy.

Cleveland's Chinatown, like most around the country, began in the "traditional"[41] form in the 1900s, settled primarily by Chinese men as residentially segregated communities as a result of anti-Chinese white supremacy. In Cleveland, the first Chinatown was on Ontario Street near Public Square. Like many Chinatowns across the United States that began in the urban core, this Chinatown was uprooted by the 1930s, as, first, rents rose and, ultimately, the neighborhood was razed to make room for downtown development. By the time two Chinatown buildings were targeted for demolition in 1929 to erect the new parcel post building, the On Leong Merchants Association had already moved, in 1927, to Rockwell Avenue.[42] While some relocated to the Rockwell Avenue location as it was reestablished as the Chinatown, some of the community left Cleveland altogether for other cities and to return to China.

Cleveland Connections: A Grocery Distribution Hub

The importance of food as a location of business and employment is part of Chinese American community history and present. In the early twentieth century, Chinese food became all the rage for "urban slummers"[43] who ventured into Chinatowns from San Francisco to New York for late night chop suey. By 1920, La Choy Foods, one of the most well-known mass consumer brands of Chinese food was started by Ilhan New, a Korean immigrant, in Detroit,[44] so that people could make American Chinese food at home. As American Chinese food increased in popularity, restaurants popped up all across the country, including in the Midwest. Just as today, Cleveland's AsiaTown is a "destination" that meets the needs for Asian restaurants and groceries, with people driving in from the near suburbs and across state lines, Cleveland historically is also an important hub. Well connected to both New York and Chicago, with easy routes to Detroit and the entire state of Ohio, Cleveland emerged as a node in a regional system of Chinese food distribution.

Tony Louie was born in 1949 in Cleveland and grew up in the Rockwell Avenue Chinatown. As a teenager, Tony worked at the Sam Wah Yick Kee Company (see Figure 3.3), a Chinese food distributor. While Tony's father

CMP ClevelandMemory.org

Figure 3.3 Sam Wah Yick Kee Company, 2146 Rockwell Avenue, 1966, Cleveland Press. *(Special Collections, Cleveland State University Library. Available at https:// clevelandmemory.contentdm.oclc.org/digital/collection/press/id/15340/.)*

had a full-time job at Sam Wah, in Tony's teen years he worked after school shucking bean sprouts at Sam Wah. Tony recalled, "I would ride with George Hwang, he's a driver for the Sam Wah Yick Kee Company, I go with him to Chinese restaurants, distribute Chinese food and everything. Bean sprouts, noodles, everything. Then we have a Chinese noodle factory run by Sam Wah and a guy that makes all the noodles and we fry at Sam Wah, in the kitchen at the back, and then we ship them out to all these restaurants."[45] Tony Louie, and all of the other employees at Sam Wah Yick Kee worked to keep Chinese restaurants that were catering to the American love affair with Chop Suey, Egg Foo Young, and, in Ohio and Detroit, the regional specialty of Almond Boneless Chicken (Wor Sue Gai)[46] in provisions and supplies.

Lisa Wong, president of the Greater Cleveland chapter of OCA-Asian Pacific American Advocates[47] and a cofounder of the Cleveland Asian Festival (CAF) (see Chapter 5), shared that her dad grew up in the Rockwell Avenue Chinatown. She recalled that "the old Chinatown is a long building, storefronts on the bottom, apartments on top. When my dad grew up there, all the merchant restaurants, all the merchant stores there, catered to the Chinese American restaurants. They would have a lot of shipments from New York, Chicago, Canada, then they would come to Cleveland, and from there take it to all the Chinese American restaurants that catered to the American community."[48] Indeed, North Americans have had over a century-long love affair with Chinese food, which became popular in the early twentieth century and has yet to cease.

However, because the businesses were targeting restaurant distribution, this made it difficult for a customer who might want to buy enough just for a family. Lisa Wong reflected that, even though the Rockwell Chinatown existed and Tony Louie had a job at Sam Wah Yick Kee devoted to shucking bean sprouts, "my mom couldn't buy bean sprouts, she had to grow her own. She had to grow all her own vegetables in her own garden because there wasn't a grocery store for the community, they only catered to restaurants. So unless you wanted to buy a crate of bean sprouts, you didn't buy from those stores."[49]

Alongside the long history of Sam Wah Yick Kee on Rockwell, there are long-standing legacies of panethnic grocers in the greater Cleveland metro area. The 1977 book, *Asian Americans and Their Communities of Cleveland*, featured the three-decades-long history of a Korean American grocer in the Akron-Cleveland area.[50] In 1948, Ilsun Khim[51] "settled in Akron, taking over a food business."[52] When Khim was sixteen years old Japan annexed Korea, and he fled to Manchuria and then traveled to Shanghai. Khim hoped to emigrate to the United States but was initially denied before eventually gaining entry and settling in New York City.[53] In 1977, at the age of eighty, he was still active as a merchant, although semiretired. "When asked about the circumstances which made him decide to get into that line of business, Mr. Khim mentioned that occupational alternatives for Koreans, and Asians generally, were limited because of discrimination. Commonly, immigrants chose activities that were primarily a service to, or could be supported by, their own community. The food business, for example, working in Chinese restaurants, or, as he was engaged, distributing particular commodities to Asian food stores and restaurants was typical."[54]

Fugita et al.'s *Asian Americans and Their Communities of Cleveland* also outlined the history of Japanese grocers in Cleveland, along Payne Avenue. "After the inauspicious effort to provide some Japanese food staples by the Matsuya Company, a more complete store was founded at 3811 Payne [Avenue] called Toguchi's Grocery." Weaving together not only the history of Japanese settlement in Cleveland, Toguchi's, "cater[ed] principally to Japanese, its clientele also included some Caucasians who developed a taste for Japanese food during their military occupation duty in postwar Japan. Pickled radishes, fermented bean cakes, and soy sauce in wooden tubs, Japanese candies, bean cakes, napa (Asian cabbage), raw tuna, dried squid, bean sprouts, and the ever popular 100-pound bags of short grain rice, were but a few of its many treasures."[55] Although Toguchi's was a stand-alone ethnic market, "it served as a social meeting place, in the way shopping malls do for teenagers today, where old friends met and gossiped on Saturdays. The store changed ownership in the late 1960's and has expanded its range of merchandise both in types of food and art objects. [By 1977 it was] called Omura's."[56] The legacies of these stores as places of both community and provisioning lasted well beyond the 1960s and 1970s, as their locations served as the footprint for the late twentieth-century AsiaTown.

When John Louie opened Hall One on St. Clair Avenue at E. 31st, Lisa Wong recalled, "So when we had Hall One, they start catering to the restaurants as well as the community. They broke open the case and you can buy a size for a family."[57] The 1981 guide titled, *East Asian Resources in Ohio*, lists the Sam Wah Yick Kee Company store and John Louie's Hall One, in addition to three other food markets.[58] Sam Wah was located in the Rockwell Chinatown, and the other four stores scattered around a ten-block radius, representing Chinese, Korean, and Japanese grocers, served as a footprint for what would become "AsiaTown" by the mid-2000s. Today, AsiaTown has five grocery stores.[59]

Cooking for Clevelanders: American Chinese Restaurants and Community Development

In 1970, when Steve Hom was five, his parents moved their family from Youngstown, Ohio, another Rust Belt city with its own history of industrial rise[60] and subsequent decline,[61] to the West Side Cleveland suburbs, "thinking that there was more opportunity here."[62] With a little chuckle, he added, "We think they should have moved further west to San Francisco."[63] The Hom's had seen that "Youngstown started its decline in the '60s, once they started importing steel from Japan, Canada. It started its decline in the '60s and my parents knew that it was going down the hill, Sheet and Tool closed, a bunch of steel plants closed in Youngstown, all along the Mahoney River."[64]

By 1970, Steve's father had transitioned from working in steel mills and completed a civil engineering degree at Youngstown State, and they moved to Cleveland for his father to pursue a job as a civil engineer for the county. But Cleveland's industries, much like Youngstown, were also on the decline. Steve's mother, Donna, "opened a restaurant after a couple of years in Cleveland. She found an old bar, on the West Side, and she converted the bar into a Chinese restaurant."[65] Her restaurant, like most in the Midwest at that time, catered to white customers. "I mean back then Chinese food was very exotic . . . now it's kind of passé."[66] Steve remembers that, in the early 1970s when they opened King Wah, "because we were in the restaurant business my father would always drag us down to Rockwell. And back then, that was the Chinatown, here in Cleveland. There were still a couple shops where you could buy specialty products, noodles or vegetables. I think they would get deliveries from New York every once in awhile. I mean, no real grocery stores, but if you needed a product, that's where they would be."[67] The restaurant Donna Hom opened, King Wah in Rocky River, Ohio, did so well that Donna opened two more,[68] Ho Wah in Beachwood, in 1979,[69] and Li Wah in Cleveland, in 1991.[70] All three restaurants are still in operation and being run by Steve's brothers.

Joe Fong, an AsiaTown resident in his late twenties at the time of our interview, was born in Cleveland and grew up in the metro region in the 1990s and 2000s. Initially, his parents emigrated from China to San Francisco, in the 1980s, but left California after a few years because of the high cost of living. When Joe's family left California seeking economic relief, they followed a well-worn path, arriving in Cleveland as a location of secondary migration in the 1980s. Joe mentioned that they moved to Cleveland because they had some relatives in the area.[71] However, likely because of the city of Cleveland's state of decline, they did not settle in the city proper. Although Joe currently lives in Cleveland's AsiaTown, he grew up in a small community about thirty-five minutes west of Cleveland, where his parents owned and operated an American Chinese restaurant. He described the place where he grew up: "It was rural, but it was split between Caucasians and Africans.[72] There really wasn't much Asians or other ethnicities out there." The racial isolation that Joe felt in the late 1990s and 2000s echoes what Steve Hom said about his family moving to the West Side suburbs, two decades earlier, "there were almost no Asians at all in the '70s, here in Cleveland,"[73] and that did not change much for Steve as he was growing up in the 1970s and 1980s. Lisa Wong similarly described the racial isolation growing up on the West Side in the 1980s and 1990s. Although all of their families found their way to Cleveland in pursuit of economic opportunities when they were young or before they were born, the move to a place with a very small Asian population came at a cost.

For Joe and Lisa, the racial isolation resulted in harassment and discrimination. And the social isolation was deeply felt by Joe, as he reflected, "We dealt with a lot of racism out there, a lot of discrimination, especially growing up in school. 'Cause my graduation class was only like, besides me, there was two other Asians, so it wasn't really diverse." This is a reflection similar to Lisa Wong's experience of growing up in the 1980s and 1990s "on the West Side of Cleveland, and it wasn't a very progressive community at all."[74] She draws a comparison: in the Heights, "because they're next to the university, a lot of professors in the community, they're less racist. Not on the West Side, life is very hard. There's two auto factories nearby. What happened? Daily calls. Daily calls. Ching, chong daily."[75] This harassment continued for years, but as she grew older, "I would not let them get away with it. And over the phone you're not as shy as in school, so you can say whatever you want. So that's where my advocacy began. I found that I have a voice."[76]

Joe, Lisa, and Steve's experiences in Cleveland and the Cleveland Metro Area span from the 1970s–present. Steve and Lisa reflected on their relationship to the Rockwell Chinatown, and they all discussed AsiaTown, which developed from the 1990s onward. Like Steve and Lisa, Joe recalls that his family would go to AsiaTown for groceries. Joe said that his family spent weekends in AsiaTown. "Every weekend, yeah. We had to, my family had to get restaurant supplies from the Asian supermarkets, because the Asian supermarkets would sell restaurant supplies so we had to go back and forth. We also got restaurant supplies from Sysco, the restaurant suppliers, but other things we got from the Asian supermarkets."[77] Joe's family was working to carve out a business and make a living. But those weekend trips to AsiaTown proved essential to the family's restaurant to round out their specialty supplies as well as it being a respite from the battle of the racial isolation of growing up as the only Asian family in town. Monica Mong Trieu's study shows that Joe's experience is common among Asian Americans in the Midwest.[78] The majority of people in Trieu's study are "isolated ethnics," meaning that they "experience spatially defined isolation, live at a distance from Asian co-ethnics (at least outside their families), and experience ethnic community and culture only on weekends or occasionally through the year."[79] AsiaTown, and the Rockwell Chinatown before it, have functioned for generations as an important places for the Chinese American community, serving as a touchpoint of racial mirroring and ethnic community.

Sites of Meaning Making and Engagement: Asia Plaza

Since its development in 1991, many consider Asia Plaza the geographic and cultural heart of the AsiaTown community. The footprint for the plaza began, in 1988, when John Louie, a lifelong Clevelander, moved his grocery store, Hall One, to a seven-acre lot at the corner of Payne Avenue and E. 30th Street in the St. Clair Superior/Midtown Corridor.[80] This was the impetus for the Asia Plaza development that still stands today.

Steve Hom, current property manager of Asia Plaza, is part of the team that initially developed Asia Plaza. He reflects that in his experience, "I mean growing up here, there were no Chinese people, there was no real Chinese community, so it was interesting trying to come back [from the East Coast] to help establish the Chinese community, and so, that's how I got involved in Asia Plaza. It was actually the brainchild of a grocer named John Louie, he envisioned the idea. He was actually a very successful grocer, the first modern Chinese grocer here in Cleveland. He had been working for a food distributor. And then he opened his first grocery store, Hall One."[81] This original grocery store, the same that Lisa Wong recalled in the prior section, was grown and built with Louie's vision of creating a "modern" Asian grocery store akin to a Dave's or a Kroger. A participant in the AsiaTown visioning process shared:

> I remember [the neighborhood] from the 1970s when it was one grocery store owned by John Louie. The smell of the dried food section is still an indelible memory along with John handing to me a square box with a tiny straw filled with sweet soy milk. It was a tiny store compared to the stores we have today. In 1986, I worked for John Louie as a delivery person and in the warehouse for his grocery store Hall One which is today Asia Plaza. For a teenager, it was easy to get lost in this enormous warehouse filled with Asian groceries and freezers the size of 40-foot containers.[82]

Steve Hom recalls that Hall One "was the first modern grocery store. They had all the departments: canned foods, dried goods, vegetables, some meats, it was very innovative at the time. I mean they had them elsewhere, but for Cleveland, it was very innovative."[83] Louie was growing his store, and, in addition to retail operations, he "expanded into the distribution business, providing Asian food to Ohio restaurants and grocery chains." All the while,

Louie was growing his business by sometimes serving literally as the direct shipper from New York to Cleveland, "stock[ing] his store with fresh food he purchased on almost weekly driving excursions to New York."[84] As Louie's business grew, he developed an ambitious plan for a restaurant, food market, and retail space, "Asian Village," anchored by his grocery store at the current location of Asia Plaza.[85] However, efforts to finance the large-scale development project fell through, he sold the business, and the building remained undeveloped. Hom remembers about Louie, "by the late '80s he had enough confidence that he thought he could build a really large grocery store over by where Asia Plaza is now, but he bit off more than he could chew.... I mean he had a successful grocery store, he was making money, and he thought he could take over this other building, and have a big grocery store, and it just didn't work. So there was this need for someone to come in and find a use for the building."[86] Louie, unsuccessful in his attempt to finance, had to let the business go.

The reality of taking an ambitious dream from conception to completion is one that John Louie struggled with for his plan for Asian Village. The Homs, inspired by Louie's efforts, spearheaded a team that conceptualized the building and land at E. 30th and Payne as Asia Plaza, Cleveland's first Asian mall. The Homs as well really struggled to secure the funding and build Asia Plaza into a full-capacity mall. As Steve remembers, "It was a struggle, it was a big struggle. We had a restaurant anchor, we had a grocery store anchor, and we had to infill everything else. And everybody thought that we were crazy, and we were crazy, 'cause it was a tremendous amount of risk involved. We couldn't get financing from anybody."[87]

Part of the difficulty with securing funding was likely due to the stigma against opening a retail development in the urban core during a period when the city's tax base, white population, and overall financial security was in steep decline. While at this time there was a national trend of developing "Asian malls," most of these were in suburban locations with growing Asian ethnic populations.[88] And, although Cleveland's Asian population had grown by 125.75 percent from 1950 to 1980 and was showing continual growth,[89] financing for the Asia Plaza project was difficult to secure. But the Homs were committed to investing in Cleveland, and they believed that the existing footprint of Asian ethnic markets and restaurants in the area could be knit together into a commercial neighborhood. Steve Hom underscored the difficulty of raising capital to develop Asia Plaza, remembering that "it was very, very hard. Finally, we were able to get some assistance from the state, their Minority Business Assistance Program, as well as the City of Cleveland. So once the state and the city kicked in, finally chipped in, it was just enough, just enough to get started. Not nearly enough to keep us, to really build out everything we wanted. So we've been, we've been making it up as we go along.

We started with just the grocery store, the restaurant. We would add a shop or two every few years. So finally, after like five years we filled up the first floor, after six years we were able to fill most of the second floor. And, finally after maybe, maybe after eight years we were about to find a small tenant for the third floor, Cleveland Housing Network."[90]

When Asia Plaza opened in 1991, it was part of a national cohort of Asian malls that were developing at a similar time frame in both northern and southern California Asian suburbs as well as in growing East Coast communities in the New York, Boston, and DC metros, which were taking root replete with malls and shopping plazas.[91] Most of these new structures were taking place in suburbs and in places with rapidly growing Asian populations. Steve Hom and his parents drew from his knowledge in financing and, also, the trend nationally for economic development for Asian malls and plazas.

While Asia Plaza was groundbreaking for Cleveland, the development itself was part of a larger trend of what Willow Lung-Amam calls, "Asian malls." Lung-Amam notes that these shopping centers, "neither in form nor function are particularly, 'Asian,'"[92] rather, they are called "Asian malls" to signify their role as "vibrant hubs of Asian American social and community life."[93] The growth of Asian malls beginning in the 1970s represented an important part of Asian American community making. These commercial spaces serve not only as places to buy products, services, and foods that may be difficult or impossible to access in other malls or grocery stores but also as locations that reinforce Asian Americans' everyday practices. As one person explains, at the Asian grocery store, "I don't feel I am a minority at all," and, for many people, Asian malls and the "products and practices that bridge their multiple cultural identities help many Asian Americans see themselves not as 'hyphenated' Americans but instead as constitutive in the very definition of American."[94]

Most Asian Malls have some prototypical features: typically, they are anchored by a grocery store and feature robust dining options and a food court alongside ethnic specific stores and businesses. However, even when studying malls within one region, it is evident that "Asian malls reflected and shaped the diverse character of the places around which ethnic Asians from many different walks of life congregated."[95] Even as malls are sites of placemaking, it is the people that make that place.[96]

Asia Plaza in Cleveland in both size and features is a prototypical Asian Mall. The mall itself is about 70,000 sq. ft.[97] with office space tenants on the upper floors and retail space on the ground level, and anchored by a restaurant (Li Wah) and a grocery store (Park to Shop) (see Figures 3.4 and 3.5 for exterior views of Asia Plaza). In 2023, the retail tenants include a pharmacist, an herbalist, gift shops, a pho restaurant,[98] a jewelry store, a Hong Kong–style

Figure 3.4 Payne Avenue entrance to Asia Plaza during the Cleveland Asian Festival, May 2023. *(Photo by Thomas Guibert.)*

Figure 3.5 Asia Plaza west parking lot with Asia Plaza in the background, transformed for the Cleveland Asian Festival, May 2023. *(Photo by Thomas Guibert.)*

bubble waffle and tea café, and more. However, its location in Cleveland renders it distinct in geography, both its location in the city proper and its midwestern location.[99] And, for the Cleveland Asian American community, Asia Plaza was a central node of placemaking and a key piece of the contemporary recentering of AsiaTown itself, east of the Innerbelt Freeway.

Steve's parents, Donna and Willie Hom, were successful restaurateurs and active members of the Cleveland Chinese American community. In the late 1970s the family had opened two restaurants bordering the city of Cleveland on the West and East Sides.[100] When the opportunity to develop Asia Plaza emerged in the late 1980s, the Hom's saw an opportunity to pursue a dream of Donna's. "My mother had always been interested in opening a real Chinese restaurant, as opposed to these American style Chinese restaurants. By the late '80s, Bo Loong had already been established. It was the first real dim sum restaurant here in Cleveland, I mean there was one that was attempted back in the early '80s on the East Side, but it failed. But Bo Loong by the late '80s was very successful, was started probably in '85 or '86 so my mother saw Bo Loong being successful, and she had these two other successful Chinese American restaurants so she wanted to open an authentic Chinese restaurant, and a lot of people thought that she was crazy, 'cause this area [AsiaTown] was still really rough and tumble back then."[101] But they went for it. And, when Asia Plaza opened in 1991, their third restaurant, Li Wah was almost exactly the geographic midpoint between their other two restaurants.

Li Wah opened in 1991, as the anchor restaurant in Asia Plaza (see Figure 3.6). In terms of menu, Li Wah was created to serve *not* American Chinese food but "authentic" Chinese food catering primarily to Chinese and Chinese American people. This was in marked contrast to the places throughout the region that served American Chinese cuisine.[102] More than simply targeting an "ethnic market niche,"[103] wherein a business seeks to meet ethnic specific demands of a community, the restaurant itself served as a place for Chinese Americans from around the region to come for dim sum or dinner or weddings or celebrations. It was a place with a bilingual menu that served up dishes beyond the American Chinese food fare commonly found in most restaurants in the region. Lisa Wong remembers that after Li Wah opened in Asia Plaza, her family began going there. During our second interview, which actually took place on the Lunar New Year weekend at the small bar at Li Wah, she shared that "this is not like the Chinese-American restaurants, this one catered for the Chinese community . . . Like my parents are not going to eat out. Why would they go to a Chinese-American restaurant? My dad used to work at those. He won't eat at those. They'll come here for celebrations, birthdays, weddings, because it's authentic."[104] Li Wah emerged as a place

Figure 3.6 The wait for Li Wah in Asia Plaza during Lunar New Year Celebration, February 2018. *(Photo by author.)*

that centered dishes catering to the Chinese American community. This was a marked departure from decades of restaurants opening and catering to customers seeking American Chinese food.

Conclusion: Growing AsiaTown in the Twenty-First Century

In 2008, Asian Town Center, a second mall, opened eight blocks away in a former lighting factory with a footprint of 115,000 sq. ft.[105] Like Asia Plaza, a large supermarket, a number of restaurants, and retail and event spaces anchor Asian Town Center.[106] However, despite the efforts of business owners and community members, both malls often feel empty of the bustling foot traffic outside of special events and weekends. AsiaTown continues to serve as a nodal point of the Cleveland Asian American community, but the residential presence is growing older. Lisa Wong underscored this point by stating:

> A lot of Asian communities, new immigrants, people who have limited language, usually start out living here. Once they make enough money to buy a house in the suburbs so that their kids can have a better education they'll move out. Sometimes the parents, the grandparents will still stay here because they can travel, they can get gro-

ceries. They don't have to speak the language, they don't have to drive. They can just walk to the market, you know that's why it's an older community.[107]

The lingering impacts of both continued suburbanization and the light industrial footprint of the neighborhood are barriers to residential growth and development.[108] Therefore, one of AsiaTown's challenges is generating the neighborhood buzz to sustain the restaurant and retail culture of a neighborhood that relies on a steady stream of local and regional visitors to augment the small residential population. Where an ethnic business might be seen in a densely populated urban Chinatown, what the post-1965 development shows are examples of immigrant communities that bypass the urban core and settle directly into a suburban or exurban community. The next two chapters look at the challenges of growing the visibility of AsiaTown to both serve the Asian American community and attract local and regional visitors. There is a delicate and challenging balance of prioritizing and serving the needs of longtime and existing residents and business owners alongside new investors and visitors to the neighborhood which is further explored in Chapters 4 and 5.

Asia Plaza serves a small neighborhood population that comes to the plaza on foot or by bus, but, given the overwhelming reliance on car transportation within the city of Cleveland itself, the majority of its patrons arrive via automobile. Even the malls built in the late twentieth century in more densely urban spaces like San Francisco's Japantown and in Flushing, Queens, were constructed with the expectation that many people would arrive at the shopping mall via car. These malls and plazas, part of the postwar architecture, first of "retail strips" and then of regional shopping centers, "aimed at attracting patrons living within half an hour's drive who would come by car, park in the abundant lots provided, and then proceed on foot."[109] One of the big challenges for the AsiaTown neighborhood is creating a footprint that feels cohesive and linked together spatially at a walkable scale in a neighborhood built around light industry. As discussed later, a focus on growing the visibility of AsiaTown restaurants and businesses is one of the main priorities of the AsiaTown Advisory Committee (Chapter 4) and the Cleveland Asian Festival (Chapter 5).

4

The Politics of Visibility

AsiaTown Advisory Committee as Organizing Hub

No CDC has ever hired Asian American staff to oversee
AsiaTown.

—JOYCE PAN HUANG, DIRECTOR OF PLANNING AND
PLACEMAKING, MIDTOWN CLEVELAND INC.[1]

Joyce Huang, an Asian American woman in her early thirties warmly greets
people by name as they arrive one by one into a large room just adjacent
to a conference room at Ariel International Center in April 2018. The late
afternoon early spring sun is streaming in through the large windows fram-
ing views both north to Lake Erie and west to downtown. Even though some
of the attendees have been to this meeting space before, and the agenda was
sent with a map and directions, this suite of rooms is a bit of a challenge to
locate within the cavernous building itself. Ariel International Center is a
68,000 sq. ft. one-hundred-year-old brick building that has been converted
from its former use as an industrial building to office space and a conference
and event venue on the northern edge of AsiaTown. As people enter the room,
some are visibly relieved to find the meeting location. And as Joyce encour-
ages people to help themselves to food from the Li Wah take-out boxes lining a counter, the energy shifts. Some of the attendees are clearly happy to
be there, glad to "be done with work," and in warm conversation with others.
Still others are arriving, tired, and still "on the clock" for what is hopefully
their last work commitment of the day, a Monday night meeting from 5:00
to 7:00 P.M. This particular meeting is the third time this group of folks is
coming together, and some, like me, are in attendance for the first time.[2] Each
person makes their way to a seat around the large conference table, which
will eventually hold about twenty people, convening for the quarterly meeting of the AsiaTown Advisory Committee (ATAC). Joyce Huang, director of
planning and placemaking at MidTown Cleveland, Inc. (MTC), one of Cleve-

land's approximately thirty Community Development Corporations (CDC),[3] is the convener of the meeting, and Radhika Reddy, CEO and founder of Ariel Ventures, LLC, is our location's host and a highly active member of the development community in Ohio.

ATAC is a committee composed of a core group of stakeholders in the neighborhood: business owners, nonprofit leaders, community volunteers, residents, CDC representatives, city planners, and real estate developers. Many of the people who are actively part of the AsiaTown community play more than one of the above roles. The group was first formally convened in October 2017 as an advisory body to MTC, weighing in on and leading the agenda for AsiaTown-related development and planning priorities. However, the first item on their first meeting agenda was the following:

> Unless we can know ourselves and our history, and other people and their history, there is really no way we can really have positive kinds of interaction where there is real understanding.—Yuri Kochiyama, Civil Rights Activist[4]

By beginning the conversation on planning for the future of AsiaTown by firmly rooting the committee in the importance of history, Joyce, emphasized the commitment to preserving and amplifying the history of Cleveland's Asian American community as a core principle of ATAC. Joyce brought together ATAC as a place, where she, as a newly hired MTC staff member, relying on her own personal network and engagement with AsiaTown community leaders, sought to begin to formalize relationships between AsiaTown stakeholders and MTC with two primary objectives for ATAC: Advisory group, "to communicate needs and issues to MTC CDC," and Working group, to "deliver projects that will enhance AsiaTown."[5] At their first meeting, in 2017, there were sixteen attendees and the meeting minutes reveal a highly engaged conversation, where ATAC members outlined the structural concerns of having no formal CDC representation and a desire to increase the visibility of the placemaking efforts of the group. In the end, "Overall—group wants to work on nuts and bolts. There are lots of ideas and plans—we need to pick some and do them."[6] ATAC collectively decided: which projects to prioritize, how often to meet, and other people who should be invited to participate in meetings. The engagement of community members, the ability to point to structural issues, and the desire to work on nuts and bolts projects to grow the community are the earmarks of the ATAC. And the ATAC model is a key framework for considering *how* community representation happens in community planning.

This chapter shows how ATAC and its inception became a central point to growing the organizing capacity of AsiaTown. Although its role is as an advisory board to MTC, it is an organizing hub of action. ATAC began formally in 2017, composed of a diverse group of stakeholders—community organizations, local residents, large-scale investors, small business owners, CDCs, and city agencies. Led by Joyce Huang, an Asian American staff member from MTC at the time, this was but one portion of her workload. Joyce was first hired as a planner at MTC, a neighborhood CDC in the spring of 2017. Later in 2017, based on her existing relationships and ongoing conversations with community members in AsiaTown, and the critical feedback MTC received from AsiaTown community members, Joyce, with the support of MTC, decided to formally convene a group of stakeholders as ATAC. While this group of people had gathered in various formations over the years as the community leaders and initiators for events and development, this was the first time that a CDC had specifically invited AsiaTown community members on an ongoing basis to be part of the planning process. While community members had been invited in the past to take part in creating neighborhood plans,[7] this committee represented a unique opportunity to have a continued and sustained conversation with a CDC. This chapter shows how the targeted hiring of the first Asian American staff person at MTC was central to creating a climate for change and began to bridge the gap between the community, CDCs, and city planning during an era of neoliberal multiculturalism within city planning more generally.[8]

Even as the formalization of AsiaTown within MTC was cemented and, overall, has had a positive impact for the community and its representation, there remain complications of varying goals of development. The mix of funding, desire, and what is possible can be seen as both limitations and boundaries for development. Additionally, the formalization of AsiaTown's relationship through inclusion in MTC can exacerbate frustration over the sometimes contradictory goals of MidTown's desire for overall large-scale industrial development and smaller-scale types of residential priorities. In this chapter, evergreen questions of community participation in planning are raised and examined in the context of Asian American neighborhood branding for an Asian population that represents only 2.5 percent of the City of Cleveland as a whole and 23.5 percent of the neighborhood as a whole.[9] In an overall context where Asian Americans are often invisible within the city but represent a significant population and the namesakes of the AsiaTown neighborhood, how do Asian Americans mobilize for representation within the planning process?

From 2017 to 2020, Joyce Huang was the primary point of contact between MTC and ATAC. Joyce explained how ATAC began, "Michael Yap, Michael Byun (two ATAC members), and somebody else, went to the MidTown Strategic Plan unveil and asked, 'Why isn't AsiaTown a part of this?' Jeff (the MTC

Executive Director at the time) was like 'well we haven't historically done any-thing with AsiaTown.' So at that point, I was like why don't we just gather a bunch of key stakeholders. And a bunch of people had gone to Jeff and I think they were all kind of like we're not really being serviced."[10] This history of not being serviced is one that long predates the MidTown Strategic Planning reveal, where Michael Yap and Michael Byun asked why AsiaTown was not part of the planning process, and is the result of a number of overlapping and interlocking forces: the structure of Cleveland's CDC model, the shift-ing geography of the Asian American community, and the perception that there are no Asian Americans in Cleveland. In this chapter, I illuminate how a community that was never planned for and often rendered invisible cre-ated a space to directly engage in the planning process through both com-munity activism and structural change at the level of CDC structure.

We Are Here: From Invisibility to Action

Michael Byun, a Korean American man in his early forties, with a huge smile and warm demeanor, in the spring of 2018, was the outgoing CEO of Asian Services in Action Inc. (ASIA). ASIA "is the largest health and human ser-vices agency serving the AAPI community of Northeast Ohio."[11] They have offices in Cleveland and in Akron and serve the regional community with a whole host of services ranging from health services, legal services, translation services, and more. Byun led ASIA and was an integral part of its develop-ment for seventeen years.[12] He remembers a recent meeting he attended:

> Not too long ago, there was this project, this initiative. . . . There was some metric that they were looking at, that the community—Cuyahoga County and Cleveland, organized and did some planning. And they created this beautiful map of where all these neighborhood connec-tions centers were going to be. And it was all beautiful.
>
> But right there in 44114[13] there was a big black spot, it was notice-able. . . . Everything else was addressed and all these different com-munities, all these places were addressed. And on this map, there's a black spot. And I'm all going, "people look at this."
>
> And my comments and complaints were just falling on deaf ears. People were like, "there's no residents there, there's not a lot of resi-dents, it's all industrial." I'm like you've got to be kidding me, there are all these houses here. And in many of these houses, although they're single family housing units, there's probably multigenerational fam-ilies in there. And so that was one of the biggest things I had to argue against. Why is this going on? This is so unfair. This is like another

kind of way of redlining of sorts. I mean, yes there's a sizeable Black community that's been very vocal at uplifting and raising those concerns. And I totally agree with them and support them but there's also this other population that needs attention.[14]

The invisibility of AsiaTown and its residents that Michael experienced at this meeting is a common theme that appeared throughout numerous conversations with community stakeholders and others in the Cleveland community.[15] What is evident is that the current invisibility is partially an outcome of a planning model that did not respond to the changing needs of the neighborhood. As the neighborhood that would eventually be branded as "AsiaTown" grew commercially throughout the late 1970s to the present, the CDC model and its neighborhood-based geographies did not account for a place that was not on the map when the CDC boundaries emerged in the 1960s, and the three CDCs whose areas overlapped with AsiaTown (see Figure 4.1 Cleveland CDC Service Areas Map, numbers 4, 19, 28) were inconsistent in regard to their engagement with the community.

The CDCs are not the only places where the City of Cleveland is unsure of how to engage and meaningfully incorporate its Asian American community. For decades, the representation that the Asian American community has had in the city is through a "liaison role," which has been ill-defined at best and largely symbolic at worst. Cleveland's current "Asian liaison," Chia-Min Chen, is only the third person to occupy the position since its founding in the 1960s. When she introduces herself, she says, "Everybody calls me Chia, pronounced like Chai tea, a lot of people don't even know my last name."[16] Chia-Min Chen, is an outgoing and gregarious Chinese American woman in her fifties who can be found all across AsiaTown working in various capacities as a translator, an advocate, and a volunteer. At an ATAC meeting, she is in attendance partially due to her long-standing experience as a community volunteer and partially in her more formal role as, "City of Cleveland, Asian Liaison."

Chia-Min explained that the history of this role of Asian liaison, as part of the Cleveland Community Relations Board, whose mission is to "promote amicable relations among the racial and cultural groups within the community,"[17] is linked to the Hough Rebellion in the 1960s as part of the formation of the community liaisons, more generally. She recounted:

How the city came to have an Asian Liaison goes back to the '60s. Cleveland being one of the first cities to have a black mayor, with the civil rights, also with the racial riot, that's how the community relations board came into existence. So Cleveland was the first city to have such a department.[18]

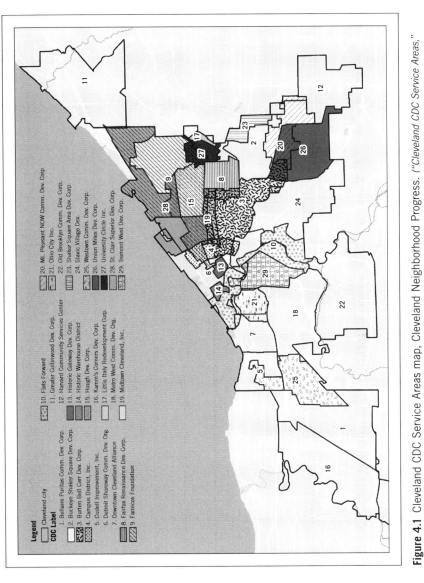

Figure 4.1 Cleveland CDC Service Areas map, Cleveland Neighborhood Progress. ("Cleveland CDC Service Areas," June 20, 2019, available at http://www.clevelandnp.org/cleveland-cdcs/cle-cdcs-map/, accessed May 9, 2023.)

The Cleveland Community Relations Board has a model of five district representatives across the five police commanding stations, plus a Hispanic liaison and an Asian liaison. When I followed up and asked if there were other ethnic liaisons, like an African American liaison, Chia-Min reiterated that, "nope, it's been like this since the '60s," the five police district reps and the Hispanic and Asian liaisons. Chia-Min explained during the course of the interview that she and the Hispanic liaison often were stretched thin because there is not a geographic location for the Asian and Hispanic liaison, and both liaisons cover the entire city of Cleveland "because Asians and Hispanics are everywhere,"[19] and presumably white people and African Americans are segregated into particular districts. Chia-Min did say that she typically attends the third district meeting, because this is where AsiaTown is located. In the course of the conversation, she noted that, despite the fact that the Community Relations Board emerged as a desire of the city to be responsive to the community, its structure relies on the existing patterns of neighborhood segregation and a model of community relations centered around improving police/community relations.

For Chia-Min, and the other Asian liaisons over the years, the formal role has been more representative than agenda setting and appears to be one that is largely symbolic more than anything. For example, Chia-Min recounted, although she knew and was friendly with the second Asian liaison, that when he retired, "I didn't know he retired, he forgot to tell me. And the position was open for over two years before the community realized, 'What happened to our Asian Liaison?' So the community raised a ruckus."[20] However, this story, more than simply the idea that the previous liaison was not that visible to community members like Chia-Min, also supports the idea that, within city governance, the role of the Asian liaison was more about an idea of ethnic representation than about the notion that the liaison would have direct and clear impacts.[21]

The official duties of the Asian liaison were described by Chia-Min as: "Official duties, just like the district rep, just like the Hispanic rep, we are here to help the area Cleveland residents in city or any entity, especially in racial relations issues. With that said, truly, most of the time, like the district reps work with residents having neighbor disputes. That's a big chunk of their job duties." For Chia-Min, however, she has taken the role and goes far beyond intervening in neighbor disputes and instead serves as an advocate, a translator, and a connector in various capacities. At the time of our conversation, she had been in the role about six years and reflected that

> I'm kind of everywhere simply because I'm doing the, I've been helping the community for nearly 30 years. So, in a nutshell I kind of expanded my job description myself, because I really, truly, know a lot of the issues and a lot of the needs of the Asian community.[22]

And, it is true, much of her work and the role she is in speaks more to her personal mission as an engaged community member. These days Chia-Min, being who she is, makes the role of Asian liaison more visible because of the work she does, some of which is part of her job and some of which is part of her continuing commitment as a thirty-year volunteer in the community.

The role of the Asian liaison is a good place to highlight both the sometimes performative nature of "race relations" in city government and also the ways in which a highly motivated and well-connected staff member can leverage a largely symbolic role to expand the prominence and needs of a community. The silver lining to an ill-defined and largely symbolic role is that there is a lot of room to grow it into a position capable of instituting systemic change. An example of a real change that Chia-Min as the Asian liaison was able to implement is a new protocol for calling 9-1-1 dispatch for Mandarin-speaking Clevelanders. Based on her professional skills and training as an audiologist, she was able to create a script based on communicating basic information in emergency situations for those who are not fluent in English.[23] She reflected that, while general fluency in English is helpful, knowing how to access emergency services can be lifesaving. She worked to develop a script for Mandarin speakers to contact 9-1-1. She said:

> Especially with 9-1-1. That's life threatening. It doesn't matter. They understand. And I taught the community and the dispatchers, I emphasized specifically the way to respond. First of all, most English speakers they think they know how to tell their needs. But how am I going to clue in the 9-1-1 dispatch? So, the script is, the first word out of the caller is Help! So that clues the dispatch. Anybody, their first word is help, is different from any other English speaking caller, that makes sense. Chances are good, it's a foreign speaker. Now, if they need a doctor, you say doctor. If you need police, you say police. If your house on fire, you say fire. Why I pick those words because P sound for police is very different from D sound for doctor, nowhere close to F for fire. So it doesn't matter how badly they butcher the sound, the initial sound clues in the dispatch so they know. Oh, I'm to dispatch the police, fire, or ambulance.... So you eliminate possible error. You pick distinct sounds. So you're not talking about how fluent you speak or how perfect.

And, after the dispatcher knows who to send, one of the next things that the dispatcher needs is a telephone number to help find the location. She goes on to explain how she directs Mandarin-speaking Clevelanders to communicate their telephone number:

Okay, so number 1 in Mandarin. So 1 sounds just like 10,000, okay? Number 2 sounds just like the word rabbit. 3 sounds like the word, You're sleeping. Okay, so you use these. So any users can spell out your phone number. So dispatch can help you. So the beautiful part is that it really works. And this commander is just thrilled, it really works. She said, "Chia, we can dispatch in under 10 seconds." And for dispatch, that's really fast.[24]

This is but one example of how the ill-defined role has room in it to create imaginative and proactive solutions to improve community access to city emergency services. However, the downfall to this approach is that it relies on the hiring and engagement of a particularly motivated individual to do this work.

Additionally, by linking a person's position solely to their racial and ethnic identity can serve to equate an official's identity as the primary and sole motivation for advocating for a position. As Wendy Cheng illustrated in the case of a proposed retail development in the San Gabriel Valley, the sole Asian American council member advocated on behalf of the development and was met with critiques that the development was "meant to serve the Chinese," which he found undermined his perspective that "it's to serve the whole community."[25] While many of the businesses' primary clientele were indeed Chinese and Chinese American residents, many non-Chinese would also patronize the businesses. In addition, the council person did not understand how detractors could not see that the overall economic development, tax dollars, employment, and revenue generation of the mall would benefit the whole community in myriad ways.

The role of Asian liaison is a good way to understand the City of Cleveland's historic orientation toward the Asian American community at large, which sets the stage for the context of Asian American community development. While Cleveland's CDCs were considered a "model" of community-based development throughout the United States for its neighborhood-centered approach, the model left AsiaTown as a district without a planning mechanism despite its very active community engagement. In the next section, I discuss the history of Cleveland's CDC model and how, although founded as a key tool for community representation and participation in neighborhood planning, because of the historical legacy of its neighborhood structure, it left the Asian American community without representation for decades.

Asian in the Middle: AsiaTown at the Intersection of Three CDCs

Lisa Wong (see Chapter 3) is the president of OCA, one of the cofounders of the CAF (see Chapter 5), and a member of ATAC. She is a Chinese American woman in her mid-forties, one of the key members of the region's Asian American community, and one of the biggest advocates for and of the Asian American community in Cleveland. Although less vocal in larger meetings, she is a person who knows the precise temperature of community constituents and can be found organizing an event, tabling for voter registration, making connections among people, and representing AsiaTown in various capacities. Here, she laid out the difficulties of AsiaTown's location within the context of the CDC model of representation and development:

> There cannot be a Chinatown CDC. There's not going to be one. There never will be. They won't allow anymore additions to CDCs, because there's only so much funds to distribute to CDCs there cannot be another one, cause then you're taking away from others. Whoever drew the lines in the beginning, AsiaTown is in the middle of two districts, maybe even 3 districts.[26]

As she explained AsiaTown's existence at the intersection of three CDC districts, we were sitting inside Li Wah Restaurant in Asia Plaza, which is at the northwest corner of East 30th Street and Payne Avenue. She gestured directionally as she pointed out the borders of the CDC districts that intersected with the area just outside of Asia Plaza: St. Clair Superior Development Corporation (SCSDC), MTC, and Campus, pointing out the areas of overlap and the fact that the borders mean that the north side of Payne Avenue, one of the major east–west thoroughfares in AsiaTown is in SCSDC to the north and MTC to the south, and historic Rockwell Chinatown (see Chapter 3) is located in Campus (see Figure 4.2). Lisa then raised an evergreen question, "So, who represents AsiaTown? There's 3 districts."[27]

This failure to appropriately represent AsiaTown is less of a willful act of dismissal than an inherited legacy of the nationally recognized CDC model of community development practiced in Cleveland, initially developed to combat anti-Black racism in neighborhood planning and development by centering neighborhood-led community development initiatives. In the wake of Cleveland's 1966 Hough Rebellion (see Chapter 2), the City of Cleveland implemented a CDC planning model that located neighborhood development within neighborhood CDCs. At its outset, this CDC model was nationally recognized for its emphasis on decentralization from central city planning departments to neighborhood-level initiatives.

The CDC model was born out of the activism of African American communities and neighborhood groups. The CDCs challenged anti-Black racism that shut out African Americans from suburbanization and created conditions that maintained inner-city slums (see Chapter 2). By 1965, a U.S. civil rights commissioner reported that "the conditions in Hough were the 'worst

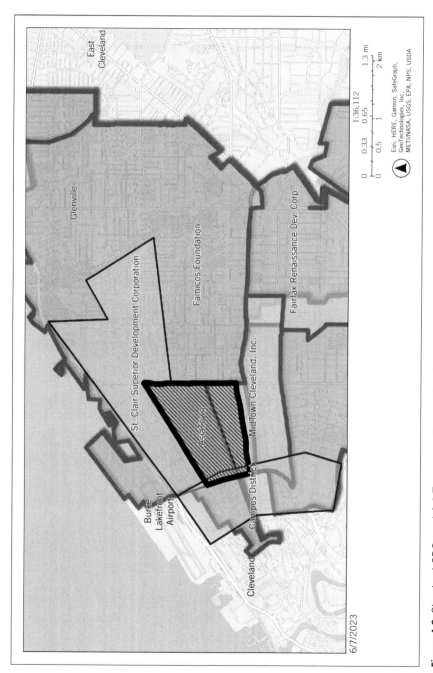

6/7/2023

Figure 4.2 Cleveland CDCs and AsiaTown map. *(Prepared by MidTown Cleveland Inc.)*

I have seen'" and that same year "Hough was considered too great an insurance risk by Lloyds of London."[28] As discussed in Chapter 2, the conditions of Hough, its transition from a nineteenth-century streetcar suburb to an intentional multiethnic racial ghetto in a state of inadequate housing and disrepair, led to the conditions of urban rebellion. In the wake of the long hot summers of the 1960s, and even though most of the recommendations of the Kerner Commission Report remained lodged in the document and never enacted, there was some financial movement as local, state, and federal[29] organizations began to allocate monies directly for community development. In the 1960s, when federal and state funding began to fund organizations directly for the planning of community development, CDCs emerged as one response to address some of the issues of inadequate housing and overcrowded conditions, "from the beginning CDCs were to accomplish bottom-up, comprehensive redevelopment."[30] As such the many grassroots organizations that were working on these issues before government funding became available were some of the first to take on the work. Ironically, as more government funding became available, this shifting funding landscape had an effect of consolidation of many of these types of grassroots organizations.

The entities we understand today as CDCs, while rooted in the structures of grassroots development and meant to combat inequity through neighborhood-centered and -facilitated planning, have shifted significantly over the past fifty years since their inception, in many cases to more market-driven and real estate–driven entities, begging the question of "who" the community is. Additionally, a legacy of the idea of community-centered planning exists in the contemporary moment, when no planning in any city in the United States would occur without "community" comment or participation. However, even though "disadvantaged neighborhoods appear more 'participatory' than ever," this participation has not necessarily translated into substantive influence or change in the process, partially, perhaps, because community participation is often engaged on a case-by-case basis rather than through a sustained and ongoing relationship.[31] Cleveland's CDC model was one of the first in the United States, and it still exists today. The City of Cleveland relies on neighborhood-level CDCs to initiate local planning projects and bring the projects to the planning department. As a result, Cleveland's neighborhood planning most typically originates in the CDC.

Part of the difficulty in the representational aspect of CDCs lies in the history of their development and funding structure, from grassroots neighborhood organizations to public-private partnerships that rely on a mix of city funding, private foundation grants, corporate philanthropy, national community development organizations, and revenue generation.[32] The Cleveland CDC model has "developed into an industry with a complex web of supportive relationships."[33] The shifting of the funding structure from grassroots-supported efforts to more formalized partnerships had the impact of growing and stabilizing the CDCs, while simultaneously creating "numerous tensions for CDCs as they became incorporated into initiatives led by corporate philanthropy and local government."[34] The funding structure itself speaks to what some consider inherent contradictions of the CDC model, since "understanding the problems with the CDC model requires understanding the relationship between capital and community. . . . Community's tendency is to preserve neighborhood space as a use value for the service of community members, while capital's tendency is to convert neighborhood exchange values that can be speculated on for a profit."[35] While overly simplistic in the case of AsiaTown, with developers as part of its community, it does speak to the oftentimes contradictory role of community investment and development—wherein "successful" development can result in the displacement of longtime residents through raising rents and hostile security measures[36] or even through policies that favor "greening."[37] As Joshua Akers argues, this practice of "orientation of urban governance toward managing territory as a collection of real estate markets is an internalization of neoliberal reason," which serves to reconfigure city governance toward "management for markets rather than population."[38] And, in Rust Belt cities like Cleveland, there is an outsize perception that the amount of "available" or "abandoned" land renders longtime community concerns over land use a nonissue.[39]

Cleveland's CDC growth is "an archetypal model CDC." It began in the internal neighborhood model of planning rooted in social movements to combat urban renewal practices that later shifted toward a more centralized "CDC industry" model of development wherein development relies on and is sustained through external support and collaboration across city, regional, and state organizations and funders.[40] In the Cleveland case, we can see, for example, how two neighborhood organizations that emerged in the 1960s and 1970s with the different priorities of low-income housing development and community-controlled enterprise, and housing rehabilitation, respectively, by the 1980s, had merged into one entity that took as its joint project housing as a fundamental part of neighborhood revitalization.[41] This merger illustrates the shifts from a rigorously neighborhood-led model to a model where the CDCs and the CDC industry "emerges together."[42] And the industry model, while it definitely has its benefits in terms of streamlining funding, technical support, financing, etc., moves away from a grassroots-grounded community-centered model.[43]

This movement from community-based organizations that run with a specific mission and aim to the incorporation of organizations that must compete for and rely on public and private foundation sources of fiscal support has created a complicated existence for many CDCs in that their primary role is to create economic revitalization, which can have varying impacts on current residents. In the late 1990s, urban planners began to note the ways in which the funding structure and streams of funding shifted the priorities of CDCs from neighborhood services to neighborhood real estate development.[44] Indeed, these are different "logics" of development, and social assets and market assets can often represent different priorities and values.[45] Many CDCs in the 1990s, due to funding support at the government and foundation levels, moved more toward real estate development—creating capital as a form of community development—which in turn created a whole host of problems and issues for neighborhoods themselves, such as skyrocketing rents, gentrification, and displacement, highlighting the challenges faced by CDCs as they diversified sources of financial support.[46] This has been an issue for at least a generation as the increase in public-private partnerships emanated throughout community development. For example, as early as the 1990s, scholars like Randy Stoecker noted the CDC model often puts at odds the contradictory relationships between exchange value of the market and use value of the residents.[47] Additionally, beyond the tensions of affordability, the ability of neighborhood residents and stakeholders to take charge and move agilely is diminished as CDCs become more like corporations, bogged down by bureaucracy and funders, and less like grassroots organizations.

Although AsiaTown is a neighborhood with an active community base, it was in between CDCs, which means that its planning priorities and agendas were often unclear. As previously discussed, AsiaTown lies at the intersection of two distinct planning districts, MidTown and St. Clair Superior, and the Rockwell Avenue Chinatown lies within the Campus CDC (see Figure 4.2). This "in betweenness" of the planning districts means that for much of its history AsiaTown was not well represented in terms of planning and only since 2017 have members of the Asian American community been on the board or staffs of any of the CDCs. Prior to 2017, AsiaTown was primarily overseen by SCSDC. It is in this context that Joyce Huang was hired at MTC, the neighborhood CDC that borders the southern edge of AsiaTown. Notably, Joyce was not hired to specifically connect AsiaTown to MTC. She was initially hired to work on economic development for MTC, which was not the urban planning job she originally applied for. However, Jeff Epstein, then executive director of MTC, said, "You seem like someone that would be good to add to this organization so why don't we place you in this other position that we're trying to fill which is an economic development job, with industrial, light manufacturing. But, we'll give you urban planning responsibilities on top of that."[48] So, initially, she was doing a variety of work in and on the economic development side. During this early period, she was working only a small portion of her week specifically on AsiaTown. Joyce began by strengthening the relationships she had started building, during her time as a Master's of urban planning student at Cleveland State University when she volunteered with the AsiaTown Night Market, the only Asian American on their team, to work with small business owners helping them become vendors for the event. She knew all along that "no CDC has ever hired Asian American staff to oversee AsiaTown."[49] Once she was hired, she took her role as a community advocate and planner very seriously. She was intent on mobilizing the very active Asian American community into direct conversations and planning. While, in the past, SCSDC had elicited community participation in the master planning process,[50] there was not a lot of sustained engagement with the AsiaTown community, as is discussed in the next section.

As mentioned earlier, when Joyce came on board at MTC, her role at the organization quickly morphed into a position that she crafted in relationship to the work that she was doing. Eventually, her work with ATAC, among other projects, resulted in the creation of and her new role as director of planning and placemaking. Throughout her time at MTC, from 2017 to 2022, she remained actively involved in AsiaTown planning. During this time, MTC took on a larger role of AsiaTown planning, part of which was due to the work that Joyce initiated during 2017–2018. However, the formalization of MTC's more active role was due to SCSDC's misfires. When SCSDC's continued missteps caused funders to withdraw support, MTC was ready to increase their already active role in AsiaTown, which I discuss in the next two sections.

What's in a Name? "AsiaTown" as an SCSDC Brand Strategy

As Lisa Wong relayed earlier, for about twenty years, until 2018, SCSDC was the primary CDC for AsiaTown's planning district.[51] During the time of my engagement with AsiaTown, SCSDC and MTC both claimed stakes in AsiaTown given their geographic boundaries. In 2018, MTC became more specifically responsible for planning AsiaTown, due to a number of factors that I discuss in the next two sections. However, the legacies of planning AsiaTown without sustained community engagement are apparent in some of the earlier efforts that SCSDC made on behalf of the AsiaTown community. Although none of the efforts made on behalf of the Asian American community were ill-intended, there were misfires that left the community frustrated.

As discussed in Chapter 3, the building of Asia Plaza was led by community-based developers in an attempt to knit together the existing stores and restaurants around a larger shopping center. While the Asia Plaza developers, in the late 1980s, struggled to secure financial funding for an ethnic mall, by the 2000s, there was a shifting discourse of diversity as celebration across broad sectors. In urban planning this discourse permeated in a shift to "thematic planning,"[52] wherein CDCs and city governments finally heeded the long calls of community activists to carve out planning districts bent on preserving and promoting the ethnic diversity and history of cities, as these ethnic districts also proved to be strong points of placemaking. This time-line and trajectory of development parallels what Jan Lin lays out, for example, in Los Angeles's Chinatown in the late twentieth and early twenty-first centuries.[53] Obviously, Cleveland and Los Angeles are two very different cities with unique local, regional, national, and global contexts. Yet, the dynamics of both multicultural planning and shifting attitudes toward urban life by suburbanites fueled an environment for growth in Chinatown neighborhoods in both cities.

In this general context of "ethnic thematic planning" SCSDC birthed the name "AsiaTown." This type of thematic branding was common across the country for decades. For example, in the 1980s, Philadelphia's Chinatown Development Corporation (PCDC) "worked to theme and brand Chinatown's landscape to improve neighborhood infrastructure and appearance," by "dr[awing] on a repertoire of spatial practices, including streetscaping and architectural theming, which allowed it to enhance the 'Chinatown-ness' of Chinatown."[54] What was more common in earlier efforts of thematic planning, like in Philadelphia and in Los Angeles, is that the impetus for the move was driven by community participation. In the case of Cleveland's "AsiaTown," this branding effort originated from a CDC rather than from the efforts of residents, or business owners, as we see later.

By christening the neighborhood "AsiaTown," SCSDC capitalized on the decades-long efforts of small business owners and developers in the neighborhood. As discussed in Chapter 3, while "AsiaTown" as a branded neighborhood did not exist until the mid-2000s, the commercial and residential presence of Asian residents and businesses extends back to at least the 1970s. Steve Hom reflected on the imposition of the name AsiaTown and stated:

> I know that they like to call it AsiaTown, but most of the population here is primarily Chinese. . . . It came from St. Clair Superior CDC . . . like '05, sometime around then. They wanted to help promote the area, and they felt that Chinatown was too restrictive, so they came up with AsiaTown. They came up with it, they had a logo, they had a website.[55]

As Steve Hom (see Chapter 3) outlines, the name "AsiaTown" was a creation intended to present a more inclusive neighborhood name, a nod to the pan-ethnic commercial and residential presence. The *Plain Dealer* records very briefly that the neighborhood unveiled its new name in 2007.[56] But, the context of the naming escapes actual meaning in the newspaper article, as the writer simply informs the readership that the new name was unveiled but does not discuss the process or who, in fact, was part of the naming effort and conversation.

The legacy of the racialized differentiation of neighborhoods and branding is apparent in neighborhoods not just in Cleveland. The idea that a neighborhood can be remade through a renaming of place plays out again and again in cities across the country.[57] In Cleveland, specifically, Joyce Huang reflected on this, stating:

> I mean MidTown at the end of the day is still a made-up neighborhood. It's a business district. And then Hough and Fairfax have been around forever, so parts of MidTown actually kind of cover Hough and Fairfax. And especially for the old-timers, they're like, "what is this MidTown?" Newer people are like whatever, "MidTown is MidTown." So I think it's about managing the relationship.[58]

The naming of the AsiaTown neighborhood reveals an effort both to brand the neighborhood and to showcase the ethnically diverse businesses in the neighborhood. However, the name AsiaTown still stumbles from the lips of many residents and community members who hold the community as Chinatown.

Part of the issue with the panethnic rebranding of Chinatown to AsiaTown is a flattening of differences and varied histories not only of different ethnic groups but of the history of Cleveland's Chinese American and Japanese American communities and the historical presence of these groups in the neighborhood (see Chapters 2 and 3). And, as Wendy Cheng argues as "municipal celebrations of diversity or multiculturalism" play out spatially, "multiculturalist narratives allow us to gloss over structured inequalities, conflicts, and heterogeneity among different racial, ethnic, and immigrant groups."[59] Lisa Wong reflects on the role of SCSDC's branding and community development, stating:

> St. Clair Superior Development Corporation they're the first ones to *brand* this as AsiaTown. It was always known as Chinatown. . . . They started branding this as AsiaTown, probably 12 years ago. . . . So their goal is to develop this community, and AsiaTown represents the fact that there are other communities here. . . . Although, the residents are all Chinese, many Chinese businesses are here.

Indeed, the commercial presence of AsiaTown is most clearly Chinese, with a smattering of Korean and Vietnamese businesses. However, based on the U.S. census American Community Survey (ACS) 2016, the five-year estimate for the zip code containing AsiaTown estimated 1,459 people identifying as "Asian alone," approximately 22.6 percent of the neighborhood. Of these, 740 Chinese, 514 Asian Indian, 89 Filipino, 31 Korean, 83 other Asian, and 0 Japanese and Vietnamese.[60] Yet, for Lisa, Steve, and others (discussed later in the chapter), the neighborhood is and "feels" majority Chinese, despite a number of Asian Indians and a handful of people of other ethnicities.

Even as some members of the AsiaTown community may continue to call the neighborhood "Chinatown," many are also well aware of SCSDC's broader strategy to highlight the neighborhood to enhance economic development and visibility. Increased economic development and neighborhood visibility are also shared goals of many of AsiaTown's most vocal supporters and promoters (see Chapter 5). Therefore, while Steve and Lisa represent community members that may be dissatisfied with the decision to brand the neighborhood AsiaTown and highlight the limitations of the name, there is also the recognition that there are benefits of neighborhood branding.

Although AsiaTown is not the most melodious of names, and no one seems entirely taken with it, it is the name that the placemaking efforts are literally putting on the map and appears on the multilingual blade signs that dot the neighborhood since they were designed through a joint effort by MTC and ATAC and mounted in the spring of 2019 as part of an effort to raise the visibility of AsiaTown (see Figure 4.3). The name AsiaTown does reflect the panethnic commercial presence in the neighborhood of Vietnamese, Korean, Thai, Taiwanese, Shanghainese, and pan-Asian businesses, and each blade sign is written in English on one side and another Asian language on the other side.

Lisa Wong highlighted many of the different ethnic businesses in the neighborhood during both of our interviews, celebrating the diversity of the neighborhood. However, in one of our conversations, she noted that there was a block that had three or four Vietnamese pho restaurants and that SCSDC named it, "Pho Row" (she intentionally mispronounces *pho* so that it rhymes with row).

> Pho Row. They know it is mispronounced, but it rhymes for them. . . . But now it is only 2 or 3 . . . one of them closed. A nail salon opened in one of them, Saigon Grill? I think they closed early, I think that they're going to reopen later on. But, because of that, where Koko Bakery is, the person who started that is Taiwanese. So some people call that a Taiwanese Bakery. It was a Taiwanese Café there, but they closed. Now the Map of Thailand moved in. . . . Now there's a Korean Association that was at Asia Town Center, they moved already. But there were Korean restaurants. So there was more Asianness going

Figure 4.3 AsiaTown blade signs, May 2023. *(Photo by Thomas Guibert.)*

on and St. Clair Superior recognized that, so they started branding it as AsiaTown, so now we all call it AsiaTown, but the Chinese still call it Chinatown.[61]

So, while SCSDC saw a potential branding move around the coethnic branding of a concentration of pho restaurants, it misfired in its execution as it perpetuated the mispronunciation of "pho" to rhyme with "row." But the naming of AsiaTown, more generally, did serve to create panethnic ties across groups and identities in an attempt to further enhance the panethnic identity of the neighborhood. Just like the historic work of Asian American activists to join together disparate Asian ethnic groups into a pan-Asian umbrella, SCSDC also attempted to join together various ethnic groups under the umbrella of Asian. The difficulty in doing this without the input of the community, however, is that it tends to flatten the distinct ethnic histories and cultures into a broad concept of "Asian."

The examples of the naming of AsiaTown and the "Pho Row" misfire speak to a larger history of SCSDC soliciting the engagement of community members but then having difficulty executing their ideas. For example, in 2010 and again in 2013, AsiaTown was the subject first of a neighborhood plan and then a master plan commissioned by SCSDC. In both of these plans, there was robust community participation, but, in the end, very little came of the process. Kim Scott, at the time of our interview, was the City of Cleveland planner charged with the AsiaTown neighborhood. Kim is a middle-aged Black woman and East Side resident, a deep and thoughtful listener, and a concise and frank speaker. In reflecting on the past AsiaTown processes she states:

> The AsiaTown Master was I will say somewhat completed, around sometime in 2012 or 13 or so. But I think that there were some gaps in the outcome. And I say that because I don't necessarily know whether we received a final document. So there was a group that worked to put that Master Plan together. I know that they had a very robust process that they went through. And they had a lot of good ideas, and it was very well participated in. So I do know from the perspective of the community, like the stakeholders that you mentioned, the residential and the business stakeholders, they're very much interested and they're very much engaged.[62]

The inconsistent engagement from SCSDC was a challenge for the community. When invited into the process, the community participated fully, however, these processes often did not result in action beyond the production and presentation of a report. On top of this, SCSDC's missteps and inability to extend and sustain relationships with the community members were points of contention. Both the naming of the neighborhood and the ill-fated Night Market, as I discuss later, served to somewhat undermine the relationship between SCSDC and community leaders.

The "AsiaTown Night Market" that SCSDC began in 2015 proved to be a spectacular and final misstep for SCSDC, drawing ire from the majority of the AsiaTown community, creating financial troubles for SCSDC, and, ultimately, serving to end the organization's stewardship of AsiaTown. The event drew its impetus from the experiences that the SCSDC executive director at the time, Michael Fleming, had as a tourist in Asia. Fleming's training as a chef inspired him to think about projects at the intersection of food and place-making. He reflected, "We wanted to do a Night Market because I knew these were starting to emerge in other communities and I took a trip to China and we stopped in Hong Kong and I got to see the Night Markets there. So I really wanted to bring some of the energy back here."[63] While the Night Market, basically an evening street fair, was a welcome and popular concept for Cleveland's summer scene, it was a flashpoint of tension for many Asian American community leaders.[64] The critique leveled at Night Market ranged from the event poaching vendors and exhibitors in its attempt to piggyback off of the success of the Cleveland Asian Festival (CAF) (see Chapter 5) without inviting in any of the CAF's organizing committee as consultants, to the Night Market organizer's seeking to profit off of "Asian" culture and community without actually bringing stakeholders from the community on board to plan and execute the event.[65] The Night Market ran sporadically in the summer months from 2015 to 2019 and ultimately created an enormous amount of ill will both from its marketing and promotion and from the string of unpaid vendors that the SCSDC-hired event management company failed to pay. When I met Michael Fleming for an interview in October 2016, he responded to the vocal community critique of the event by saying, "We don't run it [Night Market] internally, we actually hire out to run it. And now they have Asian people on staff,[66] but for the first year plus they didn't." When I asked him if the Night Market or the people they have hired out to run it are affiliated with the CAF, he said:

> No it's not. That's where that issue came up. We have these two highly successful events and one is largely run by the Asian community, one is not. And the one that is not, Night Market, is really not designed to be an authentic Asian experience. It is supposed to be an authentic Cleveland experience in AsiaTown. That's why we focus on artists and the Asian community and others and put them all together. But that was kind of lost and we have some tensions between these two events and we're [SCSDC] involved in both. 'Cause one says, "we're authentic because we're run by the Asian community, and you can't be authentic because you're not."[67]

This reflection on the Night Market (and its tagline) as "an authentic Cleveland experience in AsiaTown" rather than an "authentic Asian experience" is more than simply semantics. Rather, it forms the core of what many of the community members critiqued about the event; if you have an event in AsiaTown that is *not* run by the Asian community but calls itself an authentic Cleveland experience in AsiaTown, what authenticity is being marketed and sold? The frustration by the CAF organizers was primarily because the Night Market was riding the success of the CAF in its promotion without ever differentiating itself from the CAF until pressured to do so. The vocal critique of the Night Market did result in some marked changes, wherein, by early 2018, the SCSDC expanded its board to include Johnny Wu and Lisa Wong, two longtime and prominent AsiaTown community members and cofounders of the CAF (see Chapter 5). But the Night Market fiasco, while creating a big name for Michael Fleming and SCSDC, proved to be a bit of an albatross as the company that was hired did not process payments to many of its vendors. By 2017, SCSDC, itself in a financially perilous state, and in the midst of a reorganization, parted ways from the Night Market production team.

The Night Market example might be seen as a metaphor for the "good" intentions of the neighborhood development corporations to incorporate AsiaTown into its planning. The legacy of the Night Market for SCSDC was emblematic of a number of growth initiatives centered around food and placemaking that SCSDC pursued under Michael Fleming's tenure as the executive director. There was criticism leveled throughout the Cleveland planning community and the St. Clair Superior neighborhood that SCSDC was turning its back on its Black residents in favor of events to celebrate the more palatable and marketable histories of the much smaller Asian American and Slavic community connections to the neighborhood. A number of these initiatives, including Night Market, generated a lot of press but did little in terms of community development and revenue generation.

Ultimately, Cleveland Neighborhood Progress (CNP), the local "community development intermediary" and a primary funding partner of Cleveland's CDCs, withdrew its financial support for SCSDC and, instead, sought out MTC to take the leadership on AsiaTown community development, which I discuss in the next section.[68] As a result of the shifting funding partnership of CNP, MTC approached ATAC at the December 8, 2018, meeting to discuss the incorporation of AsiaTown into the MTC service area. This conversation at the meeting came on the heels of the highly public concerns over SCSDC's ability to exist as the organization had been in a state of public disarray, announcing a moving sale that included office furniture and file cabinets, as well as the public announcement on November 27, 2018, that Michael Fleming would be stepping down, effective November 30, 2018, with no accompanying announcement of new or interim leadership.[69] The five-year period between November 2018 and March 2024 was marked by continual instability for SCSDC. The organization was first run by the board for eighteen months before they launched a search for an executive director in July 2020. The new executive director was announced on October 30, 2020, and was in the position for less than six months. In May 2021, SCSDC announced another executive director search and a new executive director began in October 2021. In their short tenure that person helmed the CDC through a strategic plan and a new branding and marketing campaign that shifted its priorities back toward its primarily Black neighborhood residents. However, they quit abruptly in December 2023.[70] The interim director announced in December 2023 took over officially as the executive director in March 2024.[71]

Locating AsiaTown in a Changing CDC Landscape

The impending changes to the overall CDC landscape outlined earlier appeared to be in the ether during 2018, the time I conducted the majority of my interviews.[72] In May 2018, Kim Scott presciently predicted the shift that would occur between SCSDC and MTC coverage area, stating, "So here's what's going to happen. Within 3–5 years MidTown is going to absorb St. Clair Superior."[73] While MTC did not absorb all of SCSDC, it did absorb its AsiaTown service area. Kim elaborated on the context of both SCSDC and MTC's shifting roles in the Cleveland CDC landscape:

> St. Clair Superior for example has engaged in this area, but they've gone through changes over time so I think that their staff capacity is not what it has been over time. And I know, I see MidTown changing and evolving over time. Now, it seems as though they have moved into a more, I wouldn't say social service realm, but they're definitely doing much more outreach in terms of getting into the residential fabric and interfacing much more, and addressing, not addressing but giving consideration to more soft issues as opposed to we're just here as an association representing the businesses' interests. So they're changing.[74]

At the December 2018 ATAC meeting, Joyce Huang and Jeff Epstein (then executive director of MTC) brought a proposal on behalf of MTC to ATAC with an update on CNP's plan for MTC to take a lead role in planning for AsiaTown, shifting from SCSDC to MTC in the wake of the scaling down of SCSDC. Joyce presented six "Areas of Focus" for MTC in regard to AsiaTown: "Planning, Real Estate, Arts and Placemaking, Community Organizing and Safety, Economic Development and Tourism, and Policy Issues."[75] These six areas present an approach that is intent on growing AsiaTown, with emphases both on planning for the existing community and on attracting outside engagement. After the presentation, ATAC members engaged in a robust discussion centered on what would shift in a move from SCSDC to MTC: the hiring of dedicated staff for AsiaTown and questions and concerns over the precise planning areas. In the end, ATAC moved with cautious optimism into formalizing and enhancing the relationship with MTC.

The cautious embrace of AsiaTown as part of the neighborhood service area for MTC reflected a shift not only for SCSDC's management but also for MTC's work to build its AsiaTown engagement. This is where the CDC context of neighborhood planning areas is important, as MTC was wary of taking on a geographic service area that they were unfamiliar with and that has a different footprint than what they are used to. Joyce explained in March 2019, after the changes in the service areas were already completed, that "AsiaTown wise, you know CNP basically came to us in September or October [2018] and said to us, 'We would really like you to consider taking over a geography.'"[76] CNP proposed that MTC expand to include a large swath of SCSDC's existing area, including AsiaTown as well as a heavily industrial area close to Lake Erie. But MTC responded, "We do not have the capacity to do that. And it's just way different, right? You're talking about lakefront planning. Total industrial stuff over here that we just do not have the capacity to handle. But, we'll take between Payne and St. Clair." With MTC agreeing to take on the areas between Payne and St. Clair, as that is the majority of the commercial district of AsiaTown, the northern boundary of MTC's geography would simply be extended to encompass the majority of the commercial district of AsiaTown, increasing from simply the southern edge. This adaptation made sense to MTC, as Joyce explained:

> We can take AsiaTown because we've already worked there with the stakeholders. We're not planning to expand our service area but to house a team of AsiaTown staff under MidTown so they're CDC supported.[77]

By July 2019, Karis Tzeng began work as the first full-time dedicated staff as the AsiaTown project manager.[78] And, in August 2019, a job announcement went out for a part-time (twenty hours) position for a bilingual AsiaTown community organizer.[79] At the November 6, 2019, meeting, the hiring of the organizer was almost complete and the meeting focused on an AsiaTown strategic vision process, in full light and recognition of the prior two processes that were undertaken in 2010 and 2013.[80] On January 6, 2020, Xinyuan Cui came on board the AsiaTown team as a bilingual community organizer.[81]

Creating a Panethnic Neighborhood: Asian American Development

A focus on ATAC simultaneously shows how a group can form to advocate shared priorities, and it also reveals the limits of community organizing. Even as ATAC attempts to represent the entire Cleveland Asian American community, the advisory committee members and the neighborhood business owners and developers primarily represent the Chinese American community. The gesture toward panethnicity is one that is embraced by some segments of the community, in addition to the nonprofit CDCs spearheading development, however, there are limitations to this umbrella of inclusivity. Partially, this could be attributed to the fact that for Cleveland, like in other places throughout the United States, the historic downtown districts were settled by primarily Chinese American communities and, therefore, historic panethnic connections must be created.[82] And, given the ethnic population demographics of the AsiaTown neighborhood (as discussed previously), the panethnic neighborhood is what ATAC and MTC have identified as the model for growth.

ATAC member Radhika Reddy is one of the biggest proponents for panethnic AsiaTown growth. Radhika is a founding partner of Ariel Ventures, an economic development finance firm, and was awarded distinction by *Crain's Business Cleveland* list of "Notable Women in Real Estate"[83] and is a "Notable Women in Entrepreneurship."[84] In addition to being a nationally recognized "expert in New Markets Tax Credits,"[85] she also actively serves with six nonprofits, including organizations like Global Cleveland, India-Ohio Chamber of Commerce, ASIA, and ATAC, among others.[86] Radhika's expertise as a development finance authority is apparent in any meeting discussing the financing of development. In addition to her expertise in development, as one of the few active South Asian members of the ATAC and the Asian American community, broadly, her professional and personal perspectives bring a unique and important voice for diversifying what and how "Asian" is imagined within the community.

Radhika's Ariel International Center is located at the northern edge of AsiaTown and served as the meeting location for nearly all of the ATAC meetings held from 2018 to 2020. Ariel International is an "incubator for multiple startup ventures in which [Reddy] has made seed investments, and several tenants who have business connections in technology or from other parts of the globe. The building's top floor serves as a banquet center she launched to provide a meeting place for many of the region's ethnic groups as part of her self-appointed quest to make the region more welcoming to immigrants."[87] Her focus is on real estate development that will continue investment and also grow the area of AsiaTown for the Asian American community at large.

While there are representations of a panethnic Cleveland Asian American community, much of the most visible representation in the community and most prominent advocates of and for the community are East Asian, generally, and Chinese, specifically. This mirrors a larger and long-standing omission of South Asians, more generally, in representation and conversations about Asian American panethnicity.[88] The AsiaTown community is not unique in that it, like many representations of "Asian American," frequently centers East Asians (Chinese, Korean, Japanese) and their experiences, food, and culture. Despite the inclusion of Vietnamese and Thai businesses in the AsiaTown neighborhood, the community notably centers around a Chinese American representation.

When reflecting on the ethnic makeup of Cleveland's AsiaTown, Radhika told me, "I'm very involved and in AsiaTown I find that it's more heavy China, Korean, Vietnam, but I don't see any Indian presence."[89] This parallels Lisa Wong's earlier comment of primarily Chinese representation, despite the residential demographics that tell a different story, 740 Chinese, 514 Asian Indian, 89 Filipino, 31 Korean, 83 other Asian, 0 Japanese and Vietnamese.[90] Radhika continued on, "It was interesting and it's amazing that some people don't even consider Indians to be Asian, which was news to me because I didn't know that."[91] This idea of panethnicity has been a complex one from the beginning of the Asian American panethnic movement in the 1960s as a group of diverse ethnic groups came together to politically form an alliance. And, to this day, the ways in which East Asians still tend to dominate conversations of Asian American identity continue both within the field and outside of it.

Radhika speaks to this notion of how the East Asian experience is seen as the definitive Asian experience by many, even though she takes a view of broad solidarity with other groups, she reflects:

> So I always when I think Asian I think all of us, so it's interesting. And in fact I was working with some of the Middle Eastern guys from Syria, Lebanon. He's like, "we're also Asian, why don't you consider us Asian?" So it's interesting how many people are Asian but, somehow Asian has got attached to the Pacific Rim or something.[92]

These ongoing conversations within the community about how they define themselves and how to balance a diverse history and experience within Cleveland, specifically, and the United States, more broadly, continues as an undercurrent of conversation throughout AsiaTown organizing and planning (see also Chapter 5). In particular, this conversation became more apparent when the announcement came in 2017 that one of the neighborhood anchors, Dave's Supermarket, a huge 1.25 acre property, would be closing their original AsiaTown location. Long before the neighborhood's current iteration as AsiaTown, Dave's opened at E. 33rd and Payne, in 1930, and had been in continual operation since then. Dave's is a Cleveland-grown local grocery chain that has served generations of customers. To keep up with trends in prepared foods and Whole Foods–type models of grocery stores as community hubs of education, classes, and experiences, Dave's built and opened a brand new flagship location 1.5 miles east of AsiaTown in February 2019. Shortly after the opening of the new store, the AsiaTown location closed its doors leaving a hulking vacancy in the middle of AsiaTown.[93] The site of the former Dave's on Payne Avenue in AsiaTown is a huge 1.25 acre property including the 45,000 sq. ft. store and four surrounding parking lots. The space has remained vacant since 2019. The Dave's closure is a loss for residents and also for the neighborhood fabric. Since it occupied an entire city block with the footprint of the store on the north side of Payne and its primary parking lot on the south side of Payne, the closure creates a gaping hole in a neighborhood that already had challenges in cohesion.

In the intervening years since the closure, the Dave's site is a continual topic of conversation about potential land use. While still without a buyer or clear sense of what and how this now-abandoned store will develop, ATAC and the AsiaTown project manager have worked hard both to imagine a future for the space and also actively attempt to populate the spaces surrounding the empty store. The adjacent parking lots have been seasonally reconfigured as pop-up parks with some tables, trees, and defined spaces and hosted events including a pop-up library and exercise classes throughout the summer and fall months of 2019, 2020, 2021, and 2022.[94] The efforts have proven modestly successful, but during the winter months the area lies empty, as a bare block-long abandoned parking lot.

Throughout the period of 2018 and 2019, ATAC discussed options for the Dave's Supermarket site and the committee as a whole and individual members worked actively to propose plans for the space. The pie in the sky dream was for a community center for AsiaTown. In the end, the plans faltered, primarily because of the lack of financing. And the site remains vacant with the hopes that a mixed-use developer will purchase the location for retail and housing. As a real estate developer positioned in AsiaTown, Radhika was one of the core ATAC members who researched the potential of a community center. The subcommittee identified quickly that

> the biggest problem, you cannot cash flow a building. The rents are very low. And the costs to build it and maintain ADA accessibility and those sprinklers all to the building department standards, and the cost of construction is more than the rent you'll get. So you don't even break even unless you get a lot of subsidy, it's hard.[95]

However, Radhika believed that, although it would be a lot of work,

> AsiaTown should be able to raise a lot of grants and be able to do it. It's just a matter of having people committed to going around and doing, having a campaign. So, yeah, someone's got to have the time

and dedication to go raise a capital campaign, do a $6 million dollar raise. Go to individuals, you know. 6–10 million you'll need to do it. The rents you get won't pay for it, so I mean if someone rents it. But who's going to rent it? The community center has to earn money to keep up its operations.[96]

The complications here to undertake and finance a project like a community center are reminiscent of the difficulties in initially fully leasing Asia Plaza. The market calculation is very precise: the building manager needs to secure enough rent to maintain operating costs, and the market is not such that the amount of money needed is sufficient to maintain the building. Radhika was hopeful that "it's a matter of time before the whole area develops. So downtown has happened after 20 years so you know, you've got to wait out years. But I think it's coming, the market rate after the RNC[97] it's gone up a little, where you may start seeing some market rate."[98] Radhika's expertise was central as the subcommittee tried to secure funding for an AsiaTown community center; she spoke with fluency about the possible tax credits that the group scaffolded together to attempt to get to a workable funding plan. At one point, there was a plan where, "If we could raise the other $6 million, maybe we could do $3 million through tax credits." And "if that foundation had given us that 50% we could have done it. That was the plan so, that's why, it was pretty close, but they backed out." For now, Radhika was an advocate of place-making efforts to raise visibility of the neighborhood with hopes that a building might come later with continued effort, stating,

I still think we can do simple things like signs. Like what we are doing. So we've got the momentum going. So if we put that little signage there it creates a little sense of place. I was suggesting some arches into the entryways, by Li Wah here or we have these beautiful Indian architectural poles, that you can do one part there and do a China thing there, so we can create that sense of place. So simple things we can do for a low cost. But building a building, that will take a few years.

It is possible, it's just a matter of dedication and someone having the wherewithal to hire the staff to do that. You need a development director who knows how to raise money, going to foundations, writing grant applications, so reaching out to individuals. So you need someone dedicated like that and you need some real estate experience. And then you need to know committed tenants who are going to do the programming and know how you'll raise revenue, who'll pay the mortgage, who'll pay the operating costs. 'Cause there's a lot of operating costs, real estate taxes. Utilities, insurance, all that you have to cover. So for that you need operations, profitable operations to do that, or the ability to raise continuous annual funds. So you need to have all that.[99]

ATAC has spearheaded placemaking efforts such as the creation of neighborhood blade signs on the streets (see Figure 4.3), numerous online maps, walking tours, and "date night" itineraries as well as "Where to Eat" brochures. These efforts, while small in the grand scheme of things, have worked to maintain and modestly increase the visibility of the neighborhood. Yet, as I turn to in the final section, a continued tension for development is the long-lasting legacy of anti-Black racism in Cleveland and the role of AsiaTown as a "diverse" nonwhite and non-Black neighborhood.

The Continuing Legacy of White Supremacist Land Use: Neighborhood "Buzz" as Code

AsiaTown is not, obviously, an island in Cleveland. Like neighborhoods across the country, it is dealing with the continuing systems of racism and racist lending policies. AsiaTown, as discussed previously, also must contend with multiple tensions in terms of economic development. On the one hand, as scholars have long shown, "uneven development does not occur, as some would have it, 'naturally,' or simply as a result of the actions of the 'invisible hand' of the market."[100] Yet, in the contemporary model of urban economic development, one of the primary ways that neighborhood revitalization occurs is through economic development in the form of residential and commercial investment. This focus on real estate as a prime location of neighborhood growth is often structured around the assumed but seldomly verbalized question: Will middle-class consumers (who are rendered in Cleveland's landscape as white) come to the neighborhood?

Rob Curry, then executive director of the Cleveland Housing Network (CHN),[101] met me in his office, located on the third floor of Asia Plaza in May 2018. CHN is one of the longtime tenants of Asia Plaza and rents one public-facing ground floor office as well as suites of offices on the building's second through fourth floors. Rob, a white man in his late fifties, had been the executive director of CHN for twenty years.[102] While meeting with Rob, we discussed the long-standing east-west racial divide of Cleveland.[103] The Cuyahoga River serves as a natural boundary that divides the city into an East Side and a West Side, and the river serves as a boundary for an unnatural racial formation; a primarily white West Side and a primarily Black East Side.[104] While, this unnatural racial division takes places against the geological divide formed by the river, the racial segregation is sedimented in generations of willful discrimination, as discussed in Chapter 2. The present patterns of racial segregation are most recently rooted in late twentieth-century history, as Rob discusses here:

> So you have just these, you know, 50 years ago, the Kerner Report. You've got two Americas, one Black, one white, separate and unequal. You have two Clevelands, very separate and unequal. The neighborhoods that are working, that have a buzz in the neighborhoods and the neighborhoods that have almost no investment ... picture in your mind a map that showed all the low and moderate census tracts that are principally minority.[105]

As Rob outlined, the differing fortunes for housing stability and the disproportionately negative impact of the 2008 housing crisis, where "what happened on the East Side, and the East Side is the historic Black side of town, is [that the] median sale prices were $80,000[, and] when the financial crisis hit they plummeted to around $15,000." And, even still, a decade later, "in these neighborhoods, kind of the same neighborhoods, property values have only worked their ways back up to around $20,000. So what you have cooking here is, you've got two realities."[106] As our conversation continued, we discussed the ideas of development and buzz, Rob was very clear to elucidate that "buzz" has a racially situated component. The differences in development in a place like Detroit Shoreway versus MidTown or St. Clair Superior are discussed here by Rob:

> Detroit Shoreway developed the big tent approach: we are firmly committed to our low income residents, low income housing, firmly committed to middle class housing, firmly committed to the gay community, we're firmly committed to our churches, we're firmly committed to theater. And so Detroit Shoreway created a theater district. But that works because racism is not playing out. Even though they have a very significant number of Hispanic and African American residents, it's kind of viewed as an economically and racially integrated community. When you have a nearly 100% low-income African American community, it's just almost impossible to create that buzz.[107]

The sentiment that Rob presented about the West Side neighborhood of Detroit Shoreway appeared again and again in conversations about neighborhoods experiencing large amounts of growth and investment. People often mention Detroit Shoreway as a model Cleveland neighborhood that has "successfully" developed as evidenced by stabilized and raised residential and commercial values and high levels of buzz. Kim Scott recounted, "in Detroit

Shoreway, . . . the development, the residential development is booming right now and the market is able to absorb $300,000, $500,000 housing units."[108] The East Side and West Side are two different housing market realities, even in 2018.

AsiaTown is unique in that it is an East Side neighborhood rendered as non-Black. Rob pointed out:

> So let's take AsiaTown, which is kind of the western edge of Goodrich-Kirkland Park. You can create a buzz here. You've got great restaurants all around this neighborhood. So it's not that surprising that Mueller Lofts was developed. There's a perception that it's not a low-income African American community, the people who rented on E. 31st are worried about break-ins because the parking lot is not fenced in and secured, but break ins are kind of, you've got this whole network of homeless shelters here and just a group of people who have no qualms about breaking glass in a car, breaking a window if they see a quarter on the dashboard. But it's got that stable home ownership and commitment to remaining in the community. You have lots of people, lots of Chinese have moved to the suburbs, yes. But you've got a great core of committed folks in AsiaTown.[109]

The legacy of Cleveland's anti-Black segregation is palpable in the real estate market and the common racial narrative about the East and West Sides. Despite the work of housing industry players to acknowledge the legacy of racism, the entrenchment of its legacy as a market driver continues to play out in all aspects of development. Contemporary AsiaTown then has the potential for buzz, despite the fact that it is adjacent to housing shelters and primarily Black communities, because, as Curry stated earlier, the *perception* is "that it's not a low-income African American community." The history of residential racial segregation is founded both on systemic inequities and on how this intersects with neighborhood "perception."[110] Although very few respondents besides Rob Curry and Kim Scott have mentioned the overall racial dynamics of the city and the specific location of AsiaTown as being not a majority-Black neighborhood within the majority Black East Side, this context matters, both because of the historical legacy wherein Chinese and Japanese were also segregated to the East Side during the late nineteenth and much of the twentieth centuries and also because it speaks to the spatialization of Asian American space as "ethnic enclave" rather than "ghetto." In a primarily Black East Side, AsiaTown is a neighborhood that is garnering development "buzz" on the East Side. In the next and final chapter, I turn to the ways in which the tensions of panethnic economic development play out through the CAF.

5

The Cleveland Asian Festival as Scenario

Performing and Unsettling Racial Scripts

I live in Cleveland, so I know how times have changed where it wasn't popular to be Asian or looked upon well. Or there's lots of negative stereotypes and a lot of things that come along with it. So I'm hoping to make life here better for my kids and their kids and for future generations because I know what I grew up with, and I know, and people shouldn't have to live through that crap. I'm American. My father's American. Why do we have to deal with this? You know. Right now there's a big thing on the news, a TV reporter, who said, "Go back to China," excuse me I grew up with that. So the Cleveland Asian Festival was born out of that question of how do we showcase this culture.[1]

—Lisa Wong, cofounder Cleveland Asian Festival

For two days every May, the streets, parking lots, and sidewalks of Payne Avenue between E. 27th and E. 30th become transformed into a center of Asian American cultural performances, cuisine, activity, and festival. During this weekend, the Cleveland Asian Festival (CAF) typically draws about thirty thousand to forty thousand multiracial and multigenerational Clevelanders packing the sidewalks and parking lots adjacent to Asia Plaza with the sounds of music and laughter, the smoky smells of grilling foods, and bright pops of color reflecting from performers' costumes, vendors selling jewelry and clothing, and clear plastic cups full of vibrantly hued boba teas.

The visitors to the festival arrive in every possible configuration: families with young children in strollers, groups of elderly folks, young people in their teens and twenties out for an afternoon of fun, middle-aged people solo and in groups, and on and on. Visitors arrive, some for their first time and others who participate or attend the festival every year. There is no entry fee for the festival, and attendees can watch a full program of performances ranging from classical instruments, pop dance competitions, traditional forms of dance, martial arts demonstrations, and more under two separate performance tents. The food court and the food truck lane are full the duration of the festival, with lines of people snaking out from the vendor tents waiting to buy a green onion pancake or okonomiyaki from the popular restaurants and food trucks that converge at the CAF food court. In these two days, you can sample Asian cuisine and culture right from the streets of Cleveland.

The CAF is held annually in May in celebration of Asian American and Pacific Islander Heritage Month,[2] and it is the focus of this chapter. On one level, the CAF can be interpreted as an ethnic cultural heritage festival, a version of which happens in cities and communities across America. The CAF, however, is unique in that it occurs, annually, in Cleveland, Ohio, a city with a census-identified Asian population of 10,517, or 2.5 percent of the city.[3] The CAF exhibits some of the phenomena that are common across ethnic heritage festivals, in that the cultural festival, more generally, was born in many communities with the initial goals of strengthening economic development, celebrating cultural identity, and showcasing culture for the community at large.[4] The ethnic festival form also often has other outcomes, as Chiou-Ling Yeh shows, public celebrations can be both a disciplining force, "a place where governments and group leaders exercise their control over their citizens and group members,"[5] and, simultaneously, a space for festivalgoers "to bond among themselves, to connect with their family members and relatives."[6] As Yeh shows, San Francisco's Chinatown festival has grappled with the tension that exists within the Chinese New Year Festival as both "a platform to display patriotism and to Orientalize Chinese American identity" and "a space in which many Chinese Americans have been able to empower themselves and identify with their ethnicity."[7]

The common goals and tensions that others have shown in the production of ethnic festivals[8] also exist in the production of the CAF. However, because of Cleveland's smaller Asian American populations, the CAF was intentionally created as a panethnic heritage celebration, which, given the wide range of histories and cultures that span "Asian," creates a continual tension for any panethnic Asian cultural festival. While showcasing culture was and is one of the main goals of the CAF, as established by its organizers, the CAF has multiple goals of economic growth, education, celebration, and community engagement. By revisiting the quote from Lisa Wong that opens this chapter, we can see that the role and goal of the festival is doing the work of much more than simply cultural performance and celebration. In this chapter, I analyze the CAF as it presents, represents, reinforces, and unsettles Asian American racial scripts. By examining the festival as both location and performance of Asian American place, we can understand how the pervasive racial scripts—Asians as model citizens and cultural other—continue to circulate, even as the festival works to unsettle anti-Asian discrimination in its mission for education. The CAF reveals the complexity of putting on a festival that does the work of both celebrating community and Asian American placemaking. Ultimately, the CAF raises the perpetual positioning of Asian Americans as included, so long as that inclusion is a palatable multiculturalism: simultaneously nonthreatening, easily digestible, and enhances diversity.

The perniciousness of long-standing racial narratives of Asian Americans as the "forever foreigner"[9] racial other fuels the CAF's mission of education, but it often does so through an articulation of Asian Americans as "good" community members. To understand the interconnectedness of these tropes, we might consider what Natalia Molina calls, the *racial script*: a relational and repetitive process[10] that "expands our focus from *representations* to include the structural conditions that produced them."[11] The racial script of Asians as "other,"[12] undergirded the segregated spatialization of Asian communities.[13] Yet, as is evidenced in the case of Asian American place, as discussed throughout this book, the racial script of Asian American place shifts in the years after Japanese incarceration as Asian Americans transition from what Charlotte Brooks shorthands as, "Alien Neighbors, Foreign Friends."[14] The shifting narrative of Asian American place from "ghetto" to "enclave" from "alien" to "neighbor" occurs alongside a shifting racial script of Asians as model citizens.[15] Yet, as others have shown, even as Asian Americans have moved to suburbs and satellite cities, Asian American businesses and residential pockets continue to be met with suspicion and derision by some "longtime" neighbors.[16] By analyzing the CAF as a site of Asian American placemaking and meaning making, we can see how racial scripts are simultaneously produced, disrupted, and reinforced. The CAF, and its inherent tensions, are a microcosm of the contradictions and complexities of cultural representation as it performs within the racial scripts that have been generated and are in circulation about Asians, and Asian place, while also exceeding the spatial script of Asian Americans as the festival literally takes place and commands space in the Cleveland streetscape.

One of the regional racial scripts discussed throughout this book, the idea that Asian Americans are an "invisible" group within the Midwest, in particular, is a key point of departure for this chapter. This idea of the "invisible minority" is both a spatial and an ideological rendering. Lisa reflected on this notion of "invisibility" and the ways in which the CAF counters this narrative of invisibility, stating:

> Chinatown *has always been here*. AsiaTown *has been here*, but we're never like on the map. There's Little Italy, everyone knows, you know Cleveland promotes ethnic neighborhoods they always promote Little Italy, but they don't always include AsiaTown. So one of the goals of the Cleveland Asian Festival was to bring people to AsiaTown, let

them know what is here. . . . *It's always been here*, it's just more people finding out about it.[17]

Lisa's articulation not once but three times that Asian American place "has always been here" elucidates the common racial script of Asians as invisible. This is a trope that plays out not just in Cleveland or Ohio, but throughout the Midwest.[18] Yet, Lisa's naming and repetition of the idea that Asian American place "has always been here" is in itself an act that defies the racial script of invisibility. The CAF places the Asian American community center stage for a weekend every year as it takes over the streets of AsiaTown, a physical performance of presence.

Indeed, as Josephine Lee notes, "Public performance has been of particular value for Asian Americans, who have been called the 'invisible minority.'"[19] Angela Ahlgren's study on taiko drumming in Minnesota reveals the tensions of Asian American public performance by noting that, even as the idea of showing up is crucial and operates "as a supplement or correction to pervasive whiteness, either that of the audience or of Minnesota more generally,"[20] the group is mostly hired to fulfill their clients' "two seemingly contradictory goals—cultural enrichment for white audiences and providing role models for Asian American students—both deploy taiko as a corrective to a lack of racial diversity."[21] Yet, the highly performative aspect of festivals themselves can unwittingly reinforce existing racial scripts, as "festivals are also a highly visible public means of reinforcing, reviving, and even inventing ethnic identity by drawing cultural boundaries between 'Us' and the 'Other'"[22] through the presentation of a palatable multiculturalism. bell hooks was prescient to the rising tide of multiculturalism, noting in 1992 that a desire for "contact" in the form of consumption is often read as a representation of a progressive change in white attitudes toward nonwhite people.[23] hooks's notion of consumption, of "eating the other," is a useful lens for considering how food, performance, and history are presented in a festival form. As others have noted, "Multicultural festivals are often premised on the logic that they provide minority ethnic groups with opportunities to demonstrate the value of their culture to the white 'host' culture. As such, they work to reinforce the position of dominant groups as 'hosts,' who may 'enrich themselves' through their participation in the festival experience."[24]

In this chapter, I show that the work of counteracting racial scripts of invisibility can result in an overcorrection, in which visibility is claimed through a hyperperformance of the racial script of Asians as assimilable "good immigrant." This double bind reveals the limitations of Asian American representation in the Midwest, as either visible as "good" or simply invisible. While visibility as "good immigrant" has a different tenor than visibility as "enemy alien," as showcased in Chapter 2, the point here is that to exist as only one-half of a binary means that the script can always flip. The CAF can be understood, therefore, as a large-scale multiday public performance of presence; the event and its attendant ephemera producing what Molina might call a "counterscript," the production of the event itself a refutation of a narrative of visibility. Yet, the work of producing the event takes place within a larger narrative of "Asian as racial other," making the event one that, on one hand, disrupts the racial script but, on the other hand, does so in a way that at times reproduces the racial script of Asians as "model minority."

In the pages that follow, I analyze the CAF and its ephemera to reveal the simultaneity of unsettling and representing racial scripts. I begin by discussing the history and founding of the CAF and the way it claims space and literally makes the community visible. I then discuss how the festival program booklets' are a way of scripting presence through "goodness" as the text firmly situates anti-Asian racism in the past and highlights educational and economic data that reaffirm Asians as "model minorities," an important group that showcases the promise of America's multicultural present and future. I then turn toward the idea of "performing Asian" by discussing my simultaneous performance of unsettling the script of racism as confined to the past while relying on my embodiment as an Asian American woman in my role as a festival volunteer. Finally, I conclude the chapter by examining the interrelated tensions between community economic development and "consuming the other" through the role of the CAF as an incubator for restaurants and other food-oriented businesses.

Setting the Stage: Cleveland Asian Festival

Lisa Wong is one of the most dedicated and well-known volunteers in the Cleveland AsiaTown community. It does not even seem appropriate to call her a volunteer. Although she labors unpaid in her various capacities—advocate, board member, chair, cofounder, president—her work on behalf of the community amounts to more than a full-time job. As discussed in Chapters 3 and 4, Lisa is a leader in the community-led development of AsiaTown and is one of the community's most active and visible members. If there is an event involving Cleveland's Asian American community, there is a good chance that Lisa is organizing it or involved with it. Lisa sat for two interviews, both occurring simultaneously with her work on behalf of the community, evidence of her seemingly boundless energy to support and promote Asian American cultural and political participation. We first met as she was tabling for Asian American "Get Out the Vote" and "Know Your Rights" election information in Asia Plaza. The second time we met was for a scheduled interview, during Lunar New Year weekend 2018. She asked me to meet her at Li Wah Restaurant, on one of their busiest days of the year. The restaurant was full of Chinese and Chinese Americans, panethnic Asians, and Clevelanders of all races and ethnicities coming to AsiaTown to take part in the annual Lunar New Year celebration. When I arrived, she was seated at the bar helping organize the day's rapidly increasing pile of receipts and kept her hands busy filing receipts as we talked. From filing receipts to being a cofounder and principal organizer for the CAF, Lisa is a key figure in putting and keeping the AsiaTown community on the map.

The CAF, held annually in May in celebration of Asian American and Pacific Islander Heritage Month, began in 2010 as a one-day event where even the organizers were not sure how many would attend. Ten years later, the 2019 all-volunteer produced and run festival hosted over forty thousand people over two days.[25] The festival began as a way for the larger panethnic Asian American community to both come together in celebration and invite outsiders to join them. While the larger event is successful in increasing community visibility, engagement, and economic development, the diverse audience can also produce some tensions as many attendees are unfamiliar with particular ethnic groups and/or Asian America more generally.

The CAF is a product of community organizing that shifted over time from smaller and more targeted ethnic-specific celebrations to a larger panethnic event. Lisa recounted the history of the festival as part of a longer legacy of individual groups holding events to highlight group-specific ethnic heritages and other Asian Americans supporting these events.[26] Eventually, the organizations decided to come together and create a panethnic celebration. Before the first iteration of the festival occurred in 2010, Lisa recounted that it was typical practice during Asian American and Pacific Islander Heritage Month that "many of the different ethnic group organizations would come together and each ethnic group would showcase performance, [and] have a sample of Asian food to share with the public. We got up to 500 people for that event."[27] These earlier events were more grassroots, produced by and for the community. Lisa discussed various precursors to the festival, recalling that, "over the years, when we moved to City Hall to get the officials involved, we started losing attendance."[28] And, as attendance went down, the organizers of the events began to ask: "How can we make this better? All of these wonderful cultural performances and no one to see it. Because we were down to less than 100 people at that event."[29]

Lisa began to have conversations with other Asian ethnic community groups around Cleveland about how they could grow Asian cultural programming. A longtime presence in the community, going back to her days as an undergrad at Cleveland State in the late 1990s, Lisa recalled how each group would typically have its own cultural celebration and performance, "well each Asian ethnic group, when they have their own event, we used to have events at Cleveland State, we used to have dinner galas, fill up the restaurant. At the most we used to get 300–500 people, right? Whether it's for an audience or a dinner program, that's our max. In the Indian community, any community, that's our max."[30] Out of this realization and cross-ethnic support that was already happening on the ground between Asian American organizations, Lisa suggested:

> Why don't we just do what the other ethnic groups do in Cleveland, which is a very diverse community with lots of ethnic groups, there's a Little Italy, you know, and they do the Feast of Assumption, there's Greek Festivals, Italian Festivals, Irish Festivals. I'm like, why don't we do an Asian Festival? So, out of that conversation was born the Cleveland Asian Festival. And OCA even though the leadership group was from that, we decided not to give all the credit to any one or two organizations because then other organizations would not want to participate. So it was just individuals from different organizations and communities, Filipino community, Indian community, coming together to say hey, let's organize a festival that highlights Asian culture during Asian Pacific American Heritage month.[31]

So, that is what they did. In 2010, the first year of the festival, the organizers were not entirely sure how many people to expect. They promoted the festival widely among the different groups' existing networks and reached out and advertised in the Cleveland metropolitan community generally. Their efforts promoting in and outside the Asian American community paid off. Lisa recounted, "We thought, if we get 10 groups together and they brought their 300–500 people, we'd get up to 5000 people. We got 10,000 people!"[32] They were thrilled and somewhat shocked by the support, having doubled their anticipated attendance, and, as Lisa exclaimed in remembrance, "We were like oh my god there's an interest!"[33] From this first year, which overwhelmingly exceeded expectations, the CAF organizing team has run the event annually, each year growing in size and prominence.[34] As the festival grows, it has proven to be a success on many levels, as different groups figure out how to share leadership and vision for the event and as the event draws in more people new to the Asian American community in Cleveland.

The CAF's multiple goals and functions are spelled out in its mission, composed of four distinct goals:

- Strengthening the identity of AsiaTown and supporting its economic growth
- Educating and promoting Asian culture and traditions
- Celebrating Asian Pacific American Heritage Month and Cleveland's Diversity
- Uniting Cleveland's Asian Community[35]

The festival itself in its organization and structure acts on each of these goals in a variety of overlapping ways. With each of its goals, it seeks to highlight the physical and cultural presence of Cleveland's Asian American community. The CAF accomplishes its mission through a sophisticated organizing structure that relies on a central organizing committee that is then broken down into subcommittees that work with hundreds of volunteers to put on the festival. The fourth goal of the festival, *Uniting Cleveland's Asian Community*," is enacted first and foremost through the organization and running of the festival. The neighborhood's signature event relies on the support of multiple organizations and individuals, as Lisa shared, "We have over 200 volunteers. We have committee members, they're all volunteers who do this out of a passion to grow AsiaTown, to help the community."[36] Lisa spoke at length about the origins of the CAF as a way to bring the pan-Asian community together, stating, "I mean it's a great collaboration. It's supposed to be many different things. First, to bring the Asian community together."[37] This happens in the enactment and attendance of the festival as various groups come together to perform, volunteer, operate food stands, run vendor booths, and attend the festival.

For a weekend in May the otherwise quiet streets of AsiaTown are transformed. The Asia Plaza parking lot is filled not with cars but with tents sheltering restaurateurs preparing delicious bites of culture in makeshift kitchens. The east–west artery of Payne Avenue is transformed from a light industrial thoroughfare to a pedestrian pathway bustling with pedestrians and performers walking to and from the performance tents, stopping to learn about community organizations or spinning a game wheel for the chance to win a prize from one of many Cleveland businesses that have set up a booth to market to festivalgoers (see Figure 5.1). As the festival comes to life on the streets and parking lots adjacent to Asia Plaza, the taking of space itself is one way to address the goals of the festival. As the geographer Michael Hawkins argues, "Performances of ethnic identity delineate physical space, whether it be the temporary 'festival space' or a large urban park or the territorial boundaries of an ethnic neighborhood."[38] Indeed, the festival itself is a way to create a narrative and literal boundary of place. As Hawkins suggests, urban ethnic festivals are places where "ethnic boundaries are spatially and symbolically negotiated and ethnic identities have been invented and redefined"[39] as festival organizers "consciously creat[e] a multiethnic sense of place by displaying a diverse array of ethnic markers—dance, music, food, and crafts—which signify that this place is special or outside the mainstream of the dominant national culture."[40] Since AsiaTown's typical footprint on the other 363 days of the year is a car-centric light-industrial streetscape, the CAF is transformational in its use of space.

Figure 5.1 Cleveland Asian Festival crowd, May 2023. *(Photo by Thomas Guibert.)*

The CAF is held annually the weekend in May prior to Memorial Day weekend, "for Asian Pacific Heritage month to celebrate that month, to draw attention to that month,"[41] which meets the third goal of the CAF mission, "Celebrating *Asian Pacific American Heritage Month and Cleveland's Diversity.*" Ideally, because the event is near the end of the month, it leaves plenty of time for individual organizations and businesses to promote Asian American and Pacific Islander Heritage Month, as Lisa suggests, "there's lots of opportunity for other Asian ethnic organizations or businesses to have things throughout May that lead up to the finale, that's the Cleveland Asian Festival."[42]

These goals of the CAF mission and the order in which they are presented are clearly reflected in the ways in which the festival is organized and produced. It is the second goal, "Educating and promoting Asian culture and traditions," that is primarily highlighted within the visitor experience as performances and the food court are the primary draws of the festival. The CAF's performance committee books acts on two performance stages (see Figure 5.2) on both days of the festival—collectively showcasing approximately sixteen to thirty-two hours of total stage time.[43] Annually, there are usually two national or international acts that appear on the main stage for one headliner performance each day. In addition, the festival draws local dance groups, mar-

Figure 5.2 Cleveland Asian Festival main performance tent, May 2023. *(Photo by Thomas Guibert.)*

tial arts, drumming groups, and more. Beyond the performance stages other main draws are the food area that features over twenty-five local restaurants and food vendors, the World Marketplace of one hundred plus vendors and exhibitors, trolley tours of AsiaTown, health screenings, children's pavilion activities, and games.[44] All of the events and programming for the festival are free except for purchases from the food area and World Marketplace vendors.

Perhaps one of the reasons the second goal, "educating and promoting Asian culture and traditions," is so prominently on display in festival programming like performances, an egg roll eating contest, the "Colors of Asia" Fashion Show, and an Asian Pop Dance Competition, is due to the demographics of the attendees.[45] As Lisa stated, "The thing is, the majority of people who come to this is, they're not Asian."[46] The racial demographics of the CAF attendees are immediately apparent when arriving to the event. In contrast to the Night Market (see Chapter 4), which is primarily white, the CAF attracts a racially diverse group of festivalgoers and volunteers. The tension of producing this festival as both an in-community celebration and an entry point for a diverse group of outsiders is most clearly evidenced by the basic historical context that the CAF presents in the program booklet, which I discuss in the next section.

Program Book as Script: Racism in the Past and the Multicultural Promise of Today

Beyond simply combating invisibility through presence, the CAF takes seriously its mission of education. Part of the work that the CAF does is to introduce non-Asians to the Asian community in Cleveland. In this section, I focus on how the CAF program books do the work of educating the audience about who Asian Americans are through a selected portrait of Asian American history and contemporary demographics. I argue that the program book's purpose of education, is written in such a way that it performs the racial scripts of anti-Asian racism as in the past and the promise of Asians as good immigrants in the multicultural present. This represents the double bind of needing to perform visibility. It is hard to know how a group can highlight itself without redeploying the good immigrant scripts, yet the reinforcement of these narratives perpetuates the long-held narrative that Asian Americans in Cleveland belong because they are "good" rather than simply suggesting that they can just belong (see Chapter 2).

Since at least 2017, the CAF has produced a high-quality sixty-page full-color standardized program. The CAF organizers use the festival program booklet in multiple ways: to feature advertising from sponsors, show the political and cultural significance of the festival through official messages and proclamations, provide information about the performers and vendors, and as a wayfinding guide. The program book is another way that the organizers communicate to festivalgoers information about the Asian American community, generally, and the Cleveland Asian American community, specifically. An analysis of the program book shows how a pervasive racial script of Asians as good immigrants manifests within the festival scenario. This is not a critique of the work the CAF is doing but rather an acknowledgment of the limited ways that Asians in America have been scripted into the larger scenario of the United States, reoccurring as either "unassimilable other" or as "model minority." The perniciousness of these racial scripts suggests that as Yến Lê Espiritu argues, even if Asians are included, it is only in and through their difference.[47]

In the balance of this section, I discuss the elements of the program books from 2017, 2018, and 2019 that circulate the performance of good immigrant assimilation by discussing three overlapping and interlocking main elements: the performance of multiculturalism, the performance of history, and the performance of Asians as economic citizens. In terms of form, the book is standardized annually as evidenced by the unvaried format, many of the same ads, and much of the same content appearing from year to year.[48] The booklet begins with welcome letters and proclamations from local officials, includes festival wayfinding information like schedules and maps, and closes with educational information about the Asian American community.

The performance of multiculturalism and inclusion is rendered most clearly through the pages of welcomes and proclamations from local and regional officials and the wide range of advertisers and sponsors listed in the program book. Sponsors and officials put forward messages of support that both welcome visitors and commend the festival and festival organizers for their hard work. In 2019, messages from the mayor Frank G. Jackson[49] and the city council member Basheer Jones both include this same sentence, "One of our community's greatest assets is our diversity."[50] This sentence can be read as what Sara Ahmed might consider an "official diversity speech act,"[51] wherein the performative utterance stands in as an affirmation of an idea, without actual interrogation of what that idea means or if it is true. Ahmed argues, "The use of diversity as an official description *can be* a way of maintaining rather than transforming existing organizational values."[52] In this case, then, rather than telling us that diversity is important, the onus on the City of Cleveland's government is to prioritize diversity. Similarly, proclamations from a congressional representative, a U.S. senator, and other city and county officials speak to the celebration and showcasing of "official diversity." Officially, Asians are important, but what does that look like when juxtaposed against, for example, Lisa Wong's prior need to claim not once, but three times, that "we are here"? If a group is officially important, then shouldn't the visibility of the community be a given?

The CAF takes place within the larger national context of Asian American and Pacific Islander Heritage Month. The program book devotes three pages, including some photographs, to discuss the origins of Asian American and Pacific Islander Heritage Month, "a national celebration established in 1977 with the participation of civil rights organizations such as the Japanese American Citizens League and Organization of Chinese Americans."[53] After outlining the congressional legislation and then formal recognition of the heritage month some very basic historical information is presented.

Even as Lisa recalls incidents of ongoing racism facing Asian Americans in Cleveland, the CAF program booklet repeats the multicultural narrative that situates racism as in the past, as over and done with. The section "Asian-American History: From Chinese Laborers in the 1800s to Millions of U.S. Citizens Today" begins with an overview of the exclusion and discrimination of Chinese in the 1800s. The next sentence skips to, "Today, Asian immigrants have a high rate of assimilation and participation in the American mosaic."[54] The sections that follow then detail the history of exclusion and discrimination alluded to in the introduction, "Gold Rush Boom," "Violent Protests," "Japanese Arrive," "Contact with the Philippines," "Japanese Internment," "Increasing Numbers," and "A More Diverse Group." This three-page history is striking for what it emphasizes, and, in this emphasis, what is lost. And, notably, the data and history focus on the national rather than the Cleveland-specific communities and histories.

As anyone who teaches Asian American history knows, it is complicated to figure out how to weave together into a coherent and digestible form the history of Asian America. What is apparent in the choice to reproduce this history[55] among countless other possible histories is the way it hews closely to racial scripts that generations of Asian American Studies scholars have sought to disrupt: discrimination is in the past, Asian America is primarily East Asian (Chinese and Japanese), the United States is/was a benevolent receiver of immigrants seeking "a better life," the varied and complex histories are assimilated into the narrative of the United States as a nation of immigrants.

While this historical narrative is part of the CAF's mission of "educating and promoting Asian culture and traditions," it tells only part of the story. The choices of data and information that the organizers present in the program book do the work to reconfirm the most pernicious Asian racial script, the model minority myth: Asians as striving, good immigrants, working to assimilate into America. The idea that Asians are highly educated workers and laborers, always hardworking, never a problem, while maintaining just enough of culture to be exotic, is the scenario that plays again and again on a loop in cultural representations of Asian Americans.[56]

The reasons for migration to the United States are never fully clarified in the history outlined in the booklet. For example, although the essay mentions that Filipinos migrated to the United States as a result of "the U.S. control of the Philippines," the history of colonization is not mentioned; rather, the author suggests that "because most Filipinos are Roman Catholic, their integration into American life was somewhat easier than for other Asians," and "Filipinos arrived with English skills, making assimilation easier."[57] While both statements are grounded in truth, to present these as unmitigated facts facilitates a narrative of American dream desire rather than the economic, political, and social instability created by first Spanish colonization and then the continued U.S. occupation of the Philippines. This nation of immigrants narrative paints over the U.S. role in militaristic interventions in Asia, suggesting instead that "in 1975 following the Vietnam War, more than 130,000 refugees fleeing from the Communist governments of Vietnam, Cambodia, and Laos arrived on U.S. shores."[58] The United States is painted again and again in this short essay as a benevolent host.

The work of situating discrimination against Asian Americans as firmly in the past is evidenced by the authorial suggestion that these issues have been resolved. For example, the issue of Japanese "internment"[59] is rendered resolved when "in 1988 Congress passes a measure giving $20,000 to Japanese

Americans who had been interned during the war. President George H.W. Bush signed it the following year."[60] Likewise, in this telling, the history of Asian exclusion begins with Chinese in the late 1800s, and the note, "eventually other Asians [too] were excluded from citizenship," is rendered resolved when anti-immigration laws are repealed, and Asians are no longer barred from immigration and naturalization. The work here of making the festival and, by extension, Asian Americans palatable to outsiders is palpable.

In the program book, it appears that the only rhetorical recourse to mitigate a presumption of Asians as "other" is through the narrative of Asians as good citizens. The program features a two-page layout of "Asian American and Pacific Islander Heritage Month, Facts and Figures" with four sections of graphs that are meant to situate the Asian American and Pacific Islander community.[61] The first section, "Population," situates the 2015 national Asian American and Pacific Islander population, of 16.2 million people, as 5.2 percent of the total U.S. population. The section goes on to further break down the ethnic representation, highlighting the six largest Asian ethnic groups (Chinese, Asian Indian, Filipino, Vietnamese, Korean, Japanese) and a category of "other Asian."[62] As the history essay in the program booklet revealed, there is no easy way to describe the history, culture, and migration patterns of multiple ethnic groups that only becomes a singular "Asian" in the late twentieth-century United States. Often, the default becomes a focus on the largest groups which is a detriment to the heterogeneity both within individual ethnic groups and the far-encompassing category of "Asian."

Yet, the experiences are all combined and collapsed into one, for the purposes of the next series of graphs, in order to compare Asians to other racial groups. The next section of graphs delineating "Education," "Finances," and "Employment" compare "Asian/Pacific Islander" (the graph's labeling) in some cases or simply "Asian" in relationship to "Black, White, Latinos, American Indian/Alaskan Native." And, in these graphs, the data work to show that Asians have the highest level of education compared to all other racial groups,[63] have the highest median income compared to all other racial groups, and have nearly $1 trillion of buying power, even as they represent "only" 6.16 percent of the employment participation rate.[64] These data reveal Asians to be highly educated superworkers with a lot of money. More important to my argument than these "Facts and Figures" is what racial script these data points aim to represent.

The statistics[65] presented mimic an argument that Asians should be included in the fabric of the nation not necessarily because they are people and important but because they are good consumptive citizens.[66] In featuring information on education, employment, and buying power, the booklet, whether knowingly or not, puts forth a narrative that Asians should be included as either consuming or laboring bodies, a retelling of the narrative of economic inclusion rather than social inclusion. And the numbers then lean on and reaffirm the narrative of Asians as "good immigrant" and "model minority" because of their successes in education and employment.

As much as the program book itself is a festival wayfinding guide, including maps, as well as biographical information about the annual headliners, the work of educating the public who comes to the festival is part of the work of the program book itself. Granted, while most people are not going to read sixty pages during the festival, the idea that they will take the booklet home and read through the pages lingers as part of outreach. This is why the work of the AsiaTown Trolley Tour (which I discuss in-depth later) is a crucial part of the in-person festival. Since there is no way to know who or how many will read the booklet, the other primary way that history and information about the Asian American community is transmitted is through the trolley tour.

History and Performance: Body in Scenario

The AsiaTown Trolley Tour is one of the only places where the history of AsiaTown is communicated directly to the CAF visitors and provides the opportunity for CAF volunteers to go "off script." The tour runs every thirty minutes over the two days of the festival and is approximately fifteen to twenty minutes in duration.[67] At the 2017 festival, I went on the tour twice and, at the 2018 festival, I was a volunteer tour guide and led six tours. While the organizers set the tour route and provide a basic tour script that each guide follows, the "Tour Guide Instructions and Guide Booklet" reminds volunteer guides, "This is NOT a formal script. Read from this guide if you must, but it is also ok to become familiar with this guide and then ad lib as you feel comfortable. Feel free to add details that you may know about AsiaTown and some of the sites."[68] The personalization of the tour is evident from the tours I have both led and attended. In May 2017, at least two different guides offered tours that highlighted different facets of the neighborhood. While both guides covered the same broad contours, one of the guides seemed much more deeply engaged in the neighborhood, knew its current status, and also had a deep knowledge of the history of the neighborhood and the built environment. This second guide, an Asian American woman in her late twenties, discussed the history of redevelopment and the project of highway building that cut off the eastern edge of the historic Chinatown and also spoke of the differences in housing stock and the historic senior apartment buildings in the neighborhood and the importance of walkability for seniors.[69] I eventually learned that this second volunteer guide was Joyce Huang, an integral part of AsiaTown organizing (see Chapter 4). When I became a volunteer for the trolley tour in 2018, I quickly learned that the most compelling information that Joyce told her 2017 tours about the roles of discrimination, destruction, and development on and in the AsiaTown community was almost entirely information that she brought in with her own personal knowledge, not information included in the "official" script.

In my experience as both an attendee and a guide, I find the tour itself one of the most popular events, each tour running at full capacity, even as it also feels slightly ungrounded and disjointed from the festival itself. This could point to a number of factors: the geographic range and dispersal of the neighborhood (see Chapter 1) is reflected on the tour, the fact that we are on a moving trolley car and the trolley does not stop to pause in front of any specific location, and changes from tour to tour based on traffic patterns. While I have notes on my experiences as a festivalgoer in 2017, my role as an actor within the scenario as a trolley tour guide in 2018 enabled me to understand the inherent contradictions in performing Asian American racial scripts. By focusing on the ways in which I, as a social actor, both perform scripts and can maneuver inside and between the scripts presents a way to think through the contradictions in performing presence at the festival. The ability to maneuver the tour narrative "on" and "off" script required reproducing a relationship of host/visitor to create rapport alongside a willingness to introduce potential discomfort for both me and the attendees. As was clear from my experience, it was easiest to remain at the level of benign assimilation as this is the narrative that upholds the multicultural fantasy. Therefore, attempts to disrupt the narrative that places racism in the past are difficult to broach in the context of an ethnic festival.

Every year there is a mandatory training session for all festival volunteers offered on two or three separate occasions in the lead up to the festival. During these general training sessions, the organizing team highlights an overview of the festival and volunteer responsibilities. The tour guide position is one that must be sought out separately, general volunteers to the festival cannot simply sign up for a slot as a tour guide. The people who are tour guides typically already have a relationship to AsiaTown, and I specifically asked the organizing committee for the assignment after explaining my role as a researcher.[70] Because at the time of the 2018 CAF I lived almost three hours from AsiaTown, my tour guide training took place remotely via email exchanges. In May 2018, I volunteered on the first day of the festival in another role as a trolley ticket taker and took a tour. On the second day of the festival, I began a shift of three-straight hours of tour facilitation, six separate thirty-minute tours. I began my shift knowing that I wanted to add more about the history of the neighborhood, consciously intending to model my tours after the meaningful tour led by Joyce at the 2017 festival. However, this was much more difficult than I anticipated, and I reflected that "the first tour was terrible,"[71] both because of the physical setup of the tour and also trying to balance the content.

Although I have walked this neighborhood countless times and had even attended this tour multiple times in 2017 and 2018, the first go around "live" was disorienting and hard to manage. The fact that I was not the person driving the moving vehicle and had no control over the speed or the pacing of the trolley meant that my timing was often too late or too early. This difficulty in pacing was exacerbated by the fact that I was sitting in the front of the trolley, facing the tour group, and, therefore, the direction we were heading was always behind me. After the first difficult tour, I regrouped and started again, ultimately getting into the groove of things, reflecting that "tours 2–6 were much better" as "I added in information about my favorite restaurant, the history of the first and second Chinatowns, and also the history of Asian immigration to Cleveland/Midwest, as well as urban renewal."[72]

Part of the disorientation between the community history I wanted to share and the scripted experience of the tour is that first and foremost the tour is primarily a pro-business and economic development tour. The script itself points out the spaces of economic interest in the neighborhood both historically, like the Rockwell Avenue Chinatown, and currently, the numerous restaurants, event spaces, groceries, and small businesses in the neighborhood. AsiaTown itself, not "naturally beautiful" with parks or trees or full of architecturally significant structures, is of interest to those on the trolley primarily as a space of consumption. To come to AsiaTown is to eat, shop, and explore.

Regardless of how confident I was in the pacing and material, after the first tour went terribly, I realized I needed to perform mastery. I began to preempt the questions from the audience and drop "insider tidbits" about my favorite restaurant, where to find "the really spicy Szechuan food" and the "secret karaoke room." It was also during these tours that I began to add in and emphasize the history of urban renewal and displacement (see Chapter 1) and the regional racial violence that spurred movement initially from the West Coast to Cleveland. As I aimed to ground the "unpleasant" history, I amped up my own performance of the racial script: I divulged how and where to consume Asian culture and food, and I offered myself up for and as part of that performance, to make the "hard stuff" more palatable to the mostly non-Asian tour-goers. I was self-conscious of this dichotomy in the moments of the tour as I reflected in my field notes afterward:

> It's very strange because in the tour I felt torn over not wanting to self-Orientalize, but then in many ways I did. . . . After tour 1 I began to use claiming language like: we, us, etc to suggest that I'm part of

the community. I also began offering "secret" or "insider" tips (i.e. "secret karaoke room," "secret parking in the back of Bo Loong," etc.). It was so so weird. On one hand the script was written and oriented to make something that was less familiar more familiar and "known."[73]

Indeed, as I discuss my researcher subjectivity in Chapter 1, I am not a Clevelander. I do not even live in Ohio. Yet, my Asian American body, my embodied presence, lent me "credibility" with tour groups. They did not ask where I lived, how long I lived in Cleveland, how I came to the area. They did ask what my favorite restaurant was, where to get the best noodle soups, and is there a place to buy Asian souvenirs. And this is where the multiple levels of performance for me, and by extension the festival, are revealed. I am not of this community, yet, because of the limited racial script of "Asian" my *localness* did not matter, because my *Asianness* could be verified vis-à-vis my racialized and gendered body as an Asian American woman.

At the same time, I was providing history and context of structural racism I was also serving as "an insider" to Cleveland's AsiaTown. The irony of this dual position was not lost on me as, at the time, I was living in Detroit, not even in the same state as AsiaTown. I continued to reflect on this as I mentioned this experience during a later interview with Michael Byun, one of the original organizers of the festival, and, at the time of our interview, the executive director of ASIA Inc. (see Chapter 4). As I recounted to him my experience of being a CAF tour guide, I remarked:

> The whole job is to serve as a guide and make these spaces that are unknown accessible. And there's this tension because that's what you need for community development and economic investment from outside the community. When I was reading the script and thinking it through, I was like "oh my gosh, I'm totally performing self-Orientalization." "Asians, we're just like you," "come to this restaurant it's really good."[74]

In reply, he laughed and affably commiserated by saying, "no, I totally feel it."[75] What we were both gesturing toward is the discomfort of "performing" for the audience this narrative of "insider" and knowing that my role is to be and do just that. Michael empathized and reflected:

> I mean the inherent tension is there, because in an economic development space, part of it is, how do you draw more investment? Either through consumers coming in through their purchasing powers or developers coming in. And at the same time look at it from the community's perspective, what does it mean to be the long-term commu-

nity, where community who want homes have access to homes, where community who want opportunities have access to that. And, you know I think it's, in my mind it's not one or the other, it's this constant negotiation that occurs and the key to that is having the right set of values that helps to negotiate that.[76]

The tensions that Michael and I both identify between the CAF as space for community to come together and also as a site of economic development is germane to the ethnic cultural festival format in general. Studies on contemporary urban cultural festivals often point to their primary role as an engine of city-led branding and economic development.[77] Many contemporary festivals are primarily seen, for better or worse, as place-branding events that will lead to further tourism and development of a city, with international events like the Olympics being the largest scale.[78] Indeed, much like other forms of placemaking, cities utilize festivals and the "idea" of culture to achieve noncultural goals, including: "place promotion, image restructuring, urban regeneration, employment opportunities and economic development. In an increasingly competitive environment, cities seek to highlight that they are exciting places to visit and live, which often involves offering a myriad of cultural attractions and activities."[79] However, even as festivals are associated with overzealous attempts at development, scholars also note that "certain festivals can, and do, still have community-building and identity-forming elements, especially with regard to ethnic minority and marginalized communities."[80] Indeed, the literature generally situates "the Festival" from either an economic or a cultural standpoint. This bifurcation suggests that festivals are typically considered through a framework either of placemaking as a form of branding and economic development or of community-generated showcases of cultural identity, which also are sometimes linked to placemaking and economic development. The ethnic festival, in particular, has been considered as a place of diversity engagement, seen as a place to showcase multiculturalism and "where it is hoped that opportunities to engage with difference within the relatively 'safe' framework of a festive event may lessen potentially divisive responses to difference and demonstrate a commitment to creating a welcoming, inclusive, and accessible community."[81]

However, seminal work such as Lon Kurashige's *Japanese American Celebration and Conflict: A History of Ethnic Identity and Festival, 1934–1990* shows that cultural festivals can be equally engaged in both the cultural and the economic project of placemaking and celebration.[82] Kurashige's study of fifty years of the Nisei Week Festival in Los Angeles's Little Tokyo neighborhood reveals both the multiple roles an ethnic festival plays in an ethnic community and the challenges inherent in putting on the festival within larger social, economic, and historical contexts. For the Japanese American community in

Little Tokyo, the impetus for Nisei Week was both cultural and economic. The festival operated to bring both business and economic development to the Little Tokyo neighborhood and as a means of encouraging ethnic pride in the second-generation Japanese American community.[83] A festival can be both a street party and a carnival, and so much more. The tension of both performing Asian place for investment and economic development and celebrating cultural pride is what I turn toward in the final section, the role of economic development for Cleveland's Asian-owned small businesses and the CAF.

Eating the Other: Food and Festival as Economic Development

The CAF is a community-conceptualized and -led festival, one of the primary ways in which the AsiaTown community showcases and celebrates itself. In the case of the CAF, the economic development priorities are one of the festival's main goals. Lisa Wong views the festival as a way to introduce outsiders to the neighborhood, businesses, and restaurants in AsiaTown. The idea is that the CAF is an initial point of contact and that visitors will continue to support the businesses throughout the year. Lisa stated,

> And hopefully they'll come back, other than just the festival. That's our contribution in the economic realm of this area. 'Cause we're hoping that the businesses will grow, that more businesses will come because they see that they're a niche here. It's always been here, it's just more people finding out about it. So we're hoping that all that builds up this community.[84]

The CAF does the work of economic development vis-à-vis cultural engagement in the various ways I described earlier: introducing festivalgoers to the neighborhood, area restaurants, and small businesses in the form of the food court, performances, and the trolley tour. Additionally, festival organizers have intentionally built opportunities for business incubation. As Lisa Wong discussed:

> We have ice cream vendors, an ice creamery started out at the CAF. They had a business plan, but they kicked off, being the first, their first vending was here, at the CAF. Now they have a brick and mortar store, and they had like taro ice cream, black sesame, lychee. Because of this festival they had to have an Asian theme, one of the people of the creamery is Asian. But we have restaurants catered toward making Asian flavored ice cream and even had people doing Asian shaved

ice. We're educating people, yet we're giving people opportunity to open businesses, like Miega restaurant. The people who I first went looking for the first year for CAF, who did the Korean association food, the next year they opened a restaurant, Miega, in Asian Town Center. I mean they get their start. They get the feel of community. They get a following, people know, you know.[85]

As Lisa's anecdote illustrates, food vending is one of the primary modes of economic development at the festival. The food court both meets the CAF mission of "supporting AsiaTown's economic growth" and, for many of the festivalgoers, proves to be the most easily accessible forms of sampling Asian culture.

The food area is one of the most important aspects of the CAF. It is a place where festivalgoers refuel and eat something out of their everyday culinary experience. All day long lines snake from the food vendor booths crisscrossing around the dining tent in the middle of the food court area. The vendors prepare and sell foods just as quickly as they can make it and in 2017 several vendors ran out of food before the end of the festival. One vendor told a line of disappointed customers that they were sold out, but "we're going to prep more food tonight and be ready with more tomorrow, so come back and we will be here!"[86]

In a typical year there are over twenty exhibitors dishing up a variety of food. The range of food is wide and represents a large swath of panethnic Asian cuisines. For example, in 2019, there were twenty-two, in 2018, there were twenty-eight, and, in 2017, there were twenty-one vendors.[87] Vendors are listed in the program by name. Some of the business names indicate a specific ethnic cuisine like "Indian Delight,"[88] or the business is named after the specific foods it specializes in like "Banh Mi & Noodles,"[89] or there is a general name like "KoKo Bakery."[90] At the festival, a visitor does not need to know in advance that samosas are, indeed, an Indian delight, or that a Banh Mi is a Vietnamese sandwich, or that KoKo Bakery specializes in bubble tea and Taiwanese-style baked goods because, as they walk through the marketplace, they are able to see and smell and learn the names and sample the flavors of these items. Many vendors sell both larger meal-size items and smaller bite-size items that can be shared or sampled among many. The festival features a wide range of foods and ethnic cuisines in addition to the ones listed earlier: Korean, Thai, Japanese, Chinese, Nepalese, Pho, Shaved Ice, Biriyani, and Pinoy Street Foods, just to name a few.

For the organizers, the wide range of foods and the opportunity for festival visitors to try different foods is seen as a way for visitors to become familiar with Asian cultures. As Lisa states:

The more the general population knows about Asian culture, and Asian people, the more they will love it versus hate it or think negatively or stereotypes. If they've never met anyone of Asian descent they have preconceived notions in their head, they're stealing our jobs, or they're all criminals, or this or that. *But, if they can try the food, they might like it.*[91]

In this way, Lisa Wong expresses the idea that consuming Asian food will be one of the primary activities that attendees engage in and knows that the "general population," which can be read here as "non-Asian," will be interested in trying new foods. As the food historian Amy Bentley notes, "When examined through the lens of culinary tourism—understanding 'food as other' is a dynamic process running along three axes: from exotic to familiar, inedible to edible, and unpalatable to palatable."[92] Lisa and the organizers know and anticipate that the festival is a first point of contact with Asian food for many of the visitors and, as such, most of the foods that are offered at the festival lean toward Bentley's points of the familiar, edible, and palatable in order to be nonintimidating. And this pans out in Lisa's discussion of visitors consuming food at the festival:

It's great when you're walking around and they're trying boba tea and they're sipping a tapioca ball and they're like mmm. It's wonderful to see people trying new food. So maybe a group will come down, or a family will come down and one person will be like I'm not going to try anything, I'll have a hot dog. But you'll find a Chinese hot dog. We almost had Chinese pizza with shitake mushrooms and Chinese sausage. I mean you find unique things that cater to everyone and you're gonna find something you like.[93]

And, it is true, because of the accessibility of most of the food on offer at the festival, everyone will find something to like. In some ways, Lisa's statement here and the work of the festival generally echoes Anita Mannur's research on the ways that early Asian cooking show stars like Ming Tsai and Padma Lakshmi served an American audience not simply exotic flavors but "model minority fusion cuisine"—an easily accessible and consumable racial other, nonoffensive in terms of both a mainstream American palate and mainstream American multiculturalism.[94]

Lisa's initial statement in this section reflects a desire for food to serve as a gateway to the humanity of Asian ethnic groups and combat what she calls "negative stereotypes." And, if we read this combating of negative stereotypes in the ideas of mainstream palate and mainstream multiculturalism then in some ways the organizers have done just that, created a palatable and consumable bite of Asian American culture. Robert Ji-Song Ku argues that "Chinese food, as well as the people associated with it, appear perpetually foreign and conspicuously alien, even as eggrolls, wonton soup, pork fried rice, etc. are undeniably American."[95] For Ku, although Asian food is easily consumable and even understood as American, there is still a tension between how acceptance of a food culture does not translate into an acceptance of the cultural heritage and people that produce those flavors.

Indeed, as bell hooks might suggest, the point of an ethnic festival food court is not about breaking down barriers or battling negative stereotypes, but to have a chance to "sample" the racial other in an easily digestible form. If we situate the CAF as a scenario of encounter, it becomes a location where "members of the dominant group" can "eat the other" through the consumption of culture.[96] The idea is that "when race and ethnicity become commodified as resources for pleasure, the culture of specific groups, as well as the bodies of individuals, can be seen as constituting an alternative playground where members of dominating races, genders, sexual practices affirm their power-over in intimate relations with the Other."[97] This practice of "urban tourism" has roots that extend back for over a century. Chad Heap's work on the early twentieth-century trend of "slumming" shows how bohemian white people entered into zones of the city where people of color, immigrants, and the vice districts often cohabitated in search of "exotic" food, clubs, and adventures.[98]

This is precisely where the tensions inherent in producing an ethnic festival are most readily felt, in the economic desire to expand business and clientele, even at the potential cost of catering to outsider tastes. Throughout this chapter, I have shown how combating a racial script of invisibility can also require a performance of "good" citizens, hosts, and guides. The dual missions of economic development and placemaking are about creating an environment that is welcoming to prospective visitors and consumers and that sometimes requires the reproduction of racial scripts. In this way, we can understand the tensions and contradictions of creating Asian American place vis-à-vis the CAF within the context of existing racial scripts. However, the action of taking over the space of the streets to embody presence is a powerful counterscript to invisibility. And, in this act of claiming place the CAF organizers, volunteers, and attendees create a community beyond what typically exists the other fifty-one weekends of the year. In the Conclusion, I turn to the "Imagine AsiaTown" visioning process to see how AsiaTown residents and stakeholders are envisioning the community they are actively creating.

Conclusion

Imagine AsiaTown

"We're Growing Home"

Amid the COVID-19 pandemic, the AsiaTown planning team, led by Karis Tzeng, the AsiaTown project manager at MTC, laid the groundwork for a strategic visioning process. With feedback from ATAC and other community stakeholders, the AsiaTown Strategic vision process launched in September 2020. For about six weeks, the community at large was invited to "Imagine AsiaTown" in several forms and formats including: storytelling interviews, celebration through arts, and a collaborative mapping project[1] to highlight significant places, ideas for use, and areas of concern.[2] These various asynchronous activities all built to two online group conversations. The creative and multiple modes of engagement, partially to do with the limitations presented by COVID-19, also created a wider variety of formats for people to engage with individually, in small groups or pairs, and in a variety of sensory formats, in addition to a typical "community meeting" form. In doing so, the process yielded a variety of thoughtful and insightful responses presented in the *Imagine AsiaTown Visioning Report: "We're Growing Home."*[3]

This invitation into the strategic visioning process represents not a beginning but rather a moment that was years in the making, the outcome of years of hard work on the part of community members, and a nimble and forward-thinking CDC. The community-based "Imagine AsiaTown" visioning process is a form of centering placekeeping as the community imagines its future. In response to the prompt: *"AsiaTown is a place that . . ."* community members offered these aspirational answers:

Fosters pride for Asian Americans and helps show who Asians are
way beyond stereotypes!

. . . is welcoming and radically connected, a place for Asian people
to feel safe and to belong

. . . lets Asian people feel accepted and understood in a country and
city where we often aren't

. . . is bustling and full of energy

. . . is valuable and fundamental to Cleveland

. . . makes me proud

. . . blooms with flowers

. . . we can ALL call HOME.[4]

These responses reveal several factors that shape what place means to a community—connection, safety, visibility, in addition to the association of a place with beauty and energy.[5] Centrally, the themes of place are about keeping and growing AsiaTown as a location where the Asian American community feels belonging and home.

The subtitle for the "Imagine AsiaTown" visioning report, "We're Growing Home," emerged from the series of conversations that fueled the process and the multiple and common experiences that Asian American Clevelanders have had of being told, "Go home! Go back to where you came from!" AsiaTown community members reported that they are "all too familiar with being on the receiving end of this painful racist taunt."[6] Asian Americans in Cleveland share a common experience of many Asian Americans more generally of being rendered as "perpetual foreigners, not 'real' Americans, of not mattering and not belonging."[7] And, to add to this commonly experienced narrative of Asian American life is the local context of invisibility. *Mapping AsiaTown* has traced experiences of "growing home" in Cleveland as Japanese Americans resettled during World War II and Chinese Americans sought opportunity, both groups seeking refuge in the urban Midwest, with later generations creating community spaces and keeping community in the built forms of Asia Plaza, AsiaTown, and the CAF. These spatial locations map Asian American life in the city and center the contemporary community; and these places of presence embody the stories of many who came before.

During this research, I learned many more stories than I was able to relay in these pages that will live on in the memories and history of the community. There is one story, in particular, that I was unable to weave into the chapters, but it served as an inspiration throughout the writing. Early in my research, I spent time at the Cleveland Western Historical Archive searching for historical records of Asian Americans in Cleveland. Unsurprisingly, given that in general, "archives were designed through policies and practices of systemic racism,"[8] most collections, including this one, have sparse holdings regarding Asian Americans. There were, however, a handful of boxes and several files recording the activities of the Cleveland Resettlement Committee during World War II. These records, as government files so often do, center on the bureaucracy of operations: meeting minutes, budgets, reports. However, saved among the reports was a folder of correspondence from resettlers writing in advance from camp. And there is one particular letter that remains with me.

On June 11, 1945, George Inada wrote a letter from Topaz War Relocation Camp in Utah to Beatrice Burr, the executive secretary of the CRC. In beautifully flowing cursive penmanship, the first page of the letter reads as a formally penned missive discussing his father's recent departure to Cleveland, Ohio, in search of a job and housing, noting, "As soon as he finds a living quarter he will call us to relocate." It is not until midway through the first page that the reader begins to understand that George is a young person when he expresses that "I want to leave for Cleveland before the fall term starts." In this sentence, Inada reveals himself as school aged. The letter continues on the back of a half-page sheet of writing paper. And, it is in the last five sentences of the letter, tucked onto the back, that the writer's hesitations appear. His self-assuredness of the prior correspondence disappears, as he writes:

> If possible could you send me a map of Cleveland? I certainly appreciate your kindness. How What does the boys and girls do? Do they How do they dress? What do they do after school, on Saturdays?[9]

Both the tenor of George's questions as well as the two sentences begun and then crossed out to begin again reveal an apprehension that was not present previously. Whether these sentences reveal George's youth or are the result of three-plus years of being forcibly removed from his home in San Francisco, transferred to a racetrack in San Bruno, and, ultimately, to Topaz concentration camp in Utah,[10] or a combination of factors both inferred and unseen, the questions reveal concerns of: will I fit in? what is it like? After all, George Inada is a teenager about to move to a new school in a new city in a new state and has no idea what to expect. Of course, Inada's situation is much more fraught—he is likely worried about anti-Japanese racism given the social context of the moment; he also might simply be worried about what trends he might have missed in the time since he was forcibly evacuated from San Francisco in the early spring of 1942.

George Inada was thirteen years old when he penned the letter to Beatrice Burr in Cleveland in June 1945, and, in addition to wanting to know what the kids were wearing and doing, he also requested a map. Perhaps on his journey from Topaz he studied the map, making note of the location of the Cleveland Hostel, which, although it would close in July 1945, would likely yield a bit of information and community in their first month in the city. George wanted to be able to visualize the place he was moving to, to map the geography of this city. We know that George and his mother, Ishino, followed his father, Toraichi[11] to Cleveland in the summer of 1945, after Toraichi secured work, "perhaps a maintenance job."[12] After that, George and his family disappear from the Cleveland archive, and we do not know what their life in Cleveland was like. But I hope that they were able to "grow home," to find a bit of understanding and safety in the wake of multiple upheavals. And, that George found friends to spend Saturdays with.

While it might seem unusual to return to this letter since I cannot wrap this story up into a neat package, which, is often the goal of a conclusion. I do not know if the Inada's stayed in Cleveland and shopped at the grocery stores that would form the footprint of AsiaTown or moved to the suburbs or back to the West Coast. Instead, I take license here, armed with the inspiration of Saidiya Hartman to remember that a "historian(s) of the multitude, the dispossessed, the subaltern, and the enslaved is forced to grapple with the power and authority of the archive and the limits it sets on what can be known, whose perspective matters, and who is endowed with the gravity and authority of historical actor."[13] As both a scholar and a narrator, it is a delicate and significant act to both balance the "facts" and engage in "narrative restraint, the refusal to fill in the gaps and provide closure."[14] A conclusion requires one to sum up and also look toward the future. Yet, not all situations are ones that can be summed up. I like to think of George Inada and Yae Wada during World War II and Steve Hom's great-grandfather in the 1880s riding the trains eastward full of hope, trepidation, fatigue, and wonder as they gazed out over the ever-flattening landscape. We will never know with precision their experiences or thoughts, nor are we entitled to know what they held privately. Yet, with every upheaval, relocation, and step forward, there is the possibility, the moment to imagine what comes next.

The 2020 Imagine AsiaTown Visioning process invited community members to both tell and learn stories and to map places of significance and ideas for the neighborhood. In some ways, I bring George here in the Conclusion to do just this, think about the role of Cleveland in Asian American history and also Asian Americans in Cleveland history by centering the experience of individuals narrating and sharing their own stories, creating a map of their community. The future of AsiaTown is one that is being built each day by residents, neighbors, city planners, and community volunteers. And it is informed by histories, both those that are broadly and widely taught and those that still need to come to light. At the end of the day the core desire of belonging, of "making AsiaTown a thriving home for all" is the vision. In this way, the approach to planning for the future is not centered on creating something new but rather keeping and growing existing connections. And, as I aimed to show throughout this book, the complexity of the process is clear, as AsiaTown community stakeholders grapple with and within multiple and sometimes competing priorities of community development in a city that has at times rendered these stakeholders and their communities as invisible. Throughout these chapters, I suggest that part of the work of making AsiaTown visible, sometimes through acts typically associated with place-making—redevelopment, festivals, branding—are in themselves acts of place-keeping. As AsiaTown Cleveland placemakers continue the work of keeping place and growing home, this book is but one offering to situate histories of the imagination and labor that goes into crafting Asian American place in the Rust Belt by situating the past, present, and future of Cleveland's community.

Notes

CHAPTER 1

1. See, e.g., parts 2 and 3 of Rosie Tighe and Stephanie Ryberg-Webster's 2019 anthology, which focus specifically on Cleveland.

2. Here, Cheng makes the case for a departure from Michael Omi and Howard Winant's canonical formulation of "racial formation" (1994). Cheng highlights "regional racial formation" as connected to and engaged with the large-scale national social processes that Omi and Winant engage but situated particularly in the localness of place (W. Cheng 2013, 10–11).

3. W. Cheng 2013, 10–11.

4. See, e.g., Joshi and Desai 2013; Bow 2010.

5. See, e.g., Wilkinson and Jew 2015; Ahlgren 2018; Gupta-Carlson 2018.

6. Sumida 1998, 84.

7. E. Lee 2009, 248.

8. Scholars have made cases for why we should turn toward the Midwest and what that can and does do for the discipline. See, e.g., Sumida 1998; E. Lee 2009; Fajardo 2014; Trieu 2023; Ling 2022, 2012, 2004.

9. Fugita et al. 1977, 24.

10. Ling 2012, 2004.

11. Ling 2012, 2004.

12. Brooks (2009) also argues that the geographic inverse was true, noting that Black Americans residing in places like San Francisco found more residential mobility in the early twentieth century than their Northern and Midwestern counterparts at that same time. Brooks notes, "Lost among a much larger Asian American population in a region with unique racial traditions, African Americans enjoyed far more residential mobility in San Francisco than either Chinese Americans or Japanese Americans. Their relative mobility set San Francisco apart from other American cities of the early twentieth cen-

tury. Black San Franciscans owned homes in Sutro Heights, the Richmond, the Sunset, and other white middle-class neighborhoods where Asian Americans dared not venture, except as domestic servants" (31).

13. Brooks (2009) and Kusmer (1976) both make this argument. See also Freund 2007 and Sugrue 1996.

14. Brooks (2009) notes that, by the 1870s, "more than three decades before the residential segregation of African Americans became common in the urban North—the vast majority of Chinese in San Francisco lived in the compact Chinatown district north of downtown, not out of choice but because they lacked other options" (11–12).

15. As Kusmer (1976) points out, although Cleveland was a key point on the underground railroad and was a place that "the Fugitive Slave Act of 1850 became virtually a dead letter" throughout the region, he is quick to also point out that, throughout the North, "supporters of the anti-slavery cause did not necessarily also favor racial equality" (7). Kusmer's research reveals that Cleveland's "free persons of color" (11) mostly resided on the East Side, as early as 1860, noting, however, that prior to the 1880s, "there was no noticeable trend toward the ghettoization of the black population" (12). Kusmer notes that, prior to the 1880s, "no ward in the city was more than five percent black; and although blacks were concentrated essentially in three wards (the First, Fourth, and Sixth), they were thoroughly integrated in each. No segregated neighborhoods as such existed. Nor were blacks housed primarily in multiple-unit dwellings; in 1880 almost 70 percent of the city's Negroes lived in single-household units" (12).

16. Kusmer (1976) underscores that the economic and transportation systems resulted in poorer sections of the city. "To be sure, blacks—more so than immigrants or native whites—tended to be restricted quite often to the poorer sections of many cities, but this was primarily the result of economic factors (the lower income of many Negroes) and only indirectly to the result of racial prejudice. And in spite of this, it seems doubtful that anything even remotely resembling a real black ghetto existed in American cities, north or south, prior to the 1890s" (12). However, I wonder if Kusmer were writing today if there would be further discussion of the "racial prejudice" that created conditions of race-based income disparity.

17. Fugita et al. 1977, 24.

18. Brooks (2009) states, "A combination of factors enabled white northerners of all classes to segregate African American residents by the 1920s, however. These factors included turn of the century public transportation improvements; zoning and the creation of single-use districts in cities; the rise of eugenics and 'race science'; and the proliferation of the automobile. Chinatown emerged long before any of these developments" (12).

19. The affiliations listed here are drawn from Native Land Digital, an Indigenous-led Canadian nonprofit organization, available at https://native-land.ca/, accessed May 23, 2023. However, the National Parks Service lists different tribal affiliations for this area during the 1600 and 1700s, Lenape, Oneida, Ottawa, and Wyandot, on the National Park Services website, available at https://www.nps.gov/cuva/planyourvisit/the-land-of-refuge .htm. However, based on the standpoint of this chapter, I defer to Native Land Digital in text but would be remiss to not note and name the differing record of affiliations.

20. Dunbar-Ortiz 2021.

21. Elizabeth Sullivan, 2010, "Immigration," in *Cleveland History and Economics: A Discourse in Public Policy*, 2nd printing, 27–40, 29. Teaching Cleveland, editors. available at https://teachingcleveland.org/wp-content/uploads/2017/08/cleve-hist-and-econ-12 .2010-ful-book.pdf, accessed July 20, 2022.

22. Dunbar-Ortiz 2021.

23. Stradling and Stradling 2015, 5.

24. Stradling and Stradling 2015, 5.

25. In 1873, John D. Rockefeller bought a large tract of land about six miles east of his home on "Millionaire's Row." He ultimately developed the property into a large estate named, "Forest Hill," which served as a summer estate for his family until 1915. This area in East Cleveland was the first of many moves that other elites would make in the next few decades developing the farmlands in Forest Hills, Doan's Corner, and Wade Park into the stately neighborhoods of the rich. See Stapleton 2020, 30.

26. Stapleton 2020, 30.

27. U.S. Census Bureau, 1960, "Number of Inhabitants, Ohio," available at https://www2.census.gov/library/publications/decennial/1960/population-volume-1/37749282 v1p37_ch02.pdf, accessed December 16, 2021.

28. "Fire Strikes House Bought by a Negro in Cleveland Suburb," 1966, *New York Times*), September 25, available at https://www.proquest.com/historical-newspapers/fire -strikes-house-bought-negro-cleveland-suburb/docview/117388941/se-2?accountid =26417.

29. "Burning of Negro's House Deplored in Ohio Suburb," 1966, *New York Times*, September 26, available at https://www.proquest.com/historical-newspapers/burning-negros -house-deplored-ohio-suburb/docview/117395530/se-2?accountid=26417.

30. In this case, the purchaser, the Reverend John R. Compton, was a local minister and the associate secretary of the Ohio Society of Christian Churches as well as the executive director of its Cleveland Metropolitan Commission. Given his leadership positions and the timing of the home purchase less than two months after the July 1966 Hough Rebellion by Cleveland's Black community, in all likelihood this was a test case pushing the de facto segregation of suburban Cleveland. The following year, Reverend Compton was vice chairman of the Regional Church Planning Office when that body issued a report, "The Hough Riots," outlining the impacts of segregation on Cleveland's Black residents. For more information, see "The Hough Riots," Regional Church Planning Office, Report No. 43, July 1968, available at http://web.ulib.csuohio.edu/hough/HoughRiots.pdf, accessed December 16, 2021.

31. Boyle 2004.

32. Debra Kamin, 2022, "Discrimination Seeps into Every Aspect of Home Buying for Black Americans," *New York Times*, November 29, available at https://www.nytimes .com/2022/11/29/realestate/black-homeowner-mortgage-racism.html, accessed May 17, 2023.

33. U.S. Census Bureau, 2020, "Quick Facts Cleveland City, Ohio," available at https://www.census.gov/quickfacts/clevelandcityohio, accessed April 27, 2021.

34. Lipsitz 2011.

35. Gilmore 2002, 21.

36. Pulido 2016.

37. *Encyclopedia of Cleveland History*, available at https://case.edu/ech/articles/f/for eign-born-population-cleveland-and-cuyahoga-county.

38. Ling 2012, 30.

39. Ling 2012, 29–30.

40. Anderson 1987.

41. Shah 2001.

42. Lin 2011.

43. See Aronson and Kent 2008 and Campbell Gibson and Kay Jung, "Historical Census Statistics on Population Totals by Race, 1790 to 1990, and by Hispanic Origin, 1970

to 1990, for Large Cities and Other Urban Places in the United States, Table 36. Ohio—Race and Hispanic Origin for Selected Large Cities and Other Places: Earliest Census to 1990," Working Paper No. POP-WP076, February 2005, available at https://www.census.gov/library/working-papers/2005/demo/POP-twps0076.html, accessed November 20, 2021. Thank you to Linda Rich (and reference librarians everywhere) for help in wading through the census website. Thank you to Connor Glass and Lee Eitel for their initial census data analysis and interpretation of the 1940 census data for their Introduction to Asian American Studies Fall 2020 final presentations.

44. Gibson and Jung, "Historical Census Statistics . . . Table 36."

45. Aronson and Kent 2008, 314.

46. Aronson and Kent 2008, 315.

47. In Detroit, for example, the historic Chinatown was razed in the 1950s for slum clearance in the name of freeway building. The community associations opted to relocate in an area about a mile north and many moved to the suburbs. See Zuzindlak 2015, 50–69. And, in St. Louis, Hop Alley, the center of that city's Chinatown, was razed in 1966 to make a parking lot for Busch Stadium and the community moved to the suburbs. See Ling 2004, 1–2.

48. Brooks 2019.

49. Aronson and Kent, 317.

50. As I discuss further in Chapter 2, census race categories, racial projects in and of themselves, change over time.

51. Gibson and Jung, "Historical Census Statistics . . . Table 36."

52. See Thomas 1997; Sugrue 1996; Souther 2017.

53. See Wilson 2015; Ling 2012, 2004; Zuzindlak 2015.

54. C. Cheng 2006.

55. Most infamously the 1952 case of Sing Sheng who challenged the opposition to his and his family's purchase of a house in Southwood, a suburban neighborhood in South San Francisco. See C. Cheng 2006, 1082–1088; Brooks 2009, 194–236.

56. Frey 2018, 163.

57. Zachary Smith, 2022, "Where Are the Largest Asian Populations in Ohio? See State's Top 25 Cities in New Census Estimates," Cleveland.com, April 6, available at https://www.cleveland.com/data/2022/04/where-are-the-largest-asian-populations-in-ohio-see-states-top-25-cities-in-new-census-estimates.html, accessed May 21, 2024.

58. Cuyahoga County Planning Commission, "2020 Census: Population by Race," available at https://www.countyplanning.us/resources/census-data/decennial-census/2020-race/, accessed May 21, 2024.

59. Wu 2015, 141.

60. See, e.g., Wu 2014; R. Lee 2009.

61. Chang 2010, 26.

62. Chang 2010, 25–53.

63. Two infamous examples include both the *Time* magazine article published on December 22, 1941, explaining "How to Tell Your Friends from the Japs," which outlined the differences between Chinese and Japanese and the beating of Chinese American Vincent Chin in June 1982 in Detroit.

64. See Espiritu 1992; Omatsu 2009.

65. Cleveland State University Center for Public History, "Cleveland Population Change, 1800–2020," available at https://visual.clevelandhistory.org/census/, accessed April 24, 2024.

66. Cleveland State University, "Cleveland Population Change."

67. See U.S. Census Bureau, "U.S. Decennial Census Measurement of Race and Ethnicity across the Decades: 1790–2020," August 3, 2021, available at https://www.census.gov/library/visualizations/interactive/decennial-census-measurement-of-race-and-ethnicity-across-the-decades-1790-2020.html; Anna Brown, 2020, "The Changing Categories the U.S. Census Has Used to Measure Race," Pew Research Center, February 25, available at https://www.pewresearch.org/short-reads/2020/02/25/the-changing-categories-the-u-s-has-used-to-measure-race/#:~:text=Asian%20Indians%20were%20called%20%E2%80%9CHindus,write%20in%20a%20specific%20group.

68. Espiritu and Omi 2000.

69. U.S. Census Bureau, "Historical Census Statistics on Population Totals by Race, 1790 to 1990, and by Hispanic Origin, 1970 to 1990, for Large Cities and Other Urban Places in the United States," Working Paper No. POP-WP076, Campbell Gibson and Kay Jung, February 2005, available at https://www.census.gov/library/working-papers/2005/demo/POP-twps0076.html.

70. Cleveland City Planning Commission, "Population by Race Time Series," NHGIS, U.S. Census Bureau 1970–2010, 2020 Redistricting File 94–171, available at https://planning.clevelandohio.gov/, accessed April 24, 2024.

71. Ngai 2004; Espiritu 2003.

72. See, e.g., Aguilar San-Juan 2009; Võ 2004.

73. Gupta-Carlson 2018.

74. Bow 2010.

75. Tang 2015.

76. See, e.g., Saito 1998; Fong 1994; Lung-Amam 2017.

77. Hsu 2015.

78. Melamed 2011.

79. Molina 2022, 9.

80. This narrative of place cultivation, race, and gentrification can be seen in present day narratives of spatial notions of the return of whiteness to what were deemed "abandoned" downtown cores. See Montgomery 2020; Kinney 2018; Kinney 2017.

81. Zicter 2020, 279.

82. This citation is sometimes misattributed to Bedoya. Bedoya (2014) cites a direct quote from activist Jenny Lee.

83. Bedoya (2014) lyrically conceptualizes Jenny Lee's idea as: "*placekeeping*—not just preserving the facade of the building but also keeping the cultural memories associated with a locale alive, keeping the tree once planted in the memory of a loved one lost in a war and keeping the tenants who have raised their family in an apartment. It is a call to hold on to the stories told on the streets by the locals, and to keep the sounds ringing out in a neighborhood populated by musicians who perform at the corner bar or social hall."

84. Throughout my engagement with AsiaTown, Joyce Huang's role shifted. When we first met in May 2017, she was an urban planner for MidTown managing a few projects. Over the next five years, she was promoted within Midtown CDC to the director of placemaking for MidTown and, ultimately, vice president of community development at MidTown CDC. Her successful leadership on the AsiaTown development project rationalized the hiring of 1.5 more staff to fully run the AsiaTown project as her work shifted to more overall development for MidTown. In January 2022, she was tapped to join the team of Mayor Elect Justin Bibb as Cleveland director of city planning, available at https://

www.cleveland.com/news/2022/01/cleveland-mayor-justin-bibb-taps-joyce-huang-of
-midtown-cleveland-inc-to-become-new-city-planning-director-ricardo-leon-as-strategist
-for-equity.html, accessed February 2, 2022.

85. Respondent is referring here to Wilson 2015.

86. Joyce Huang, Interview 2, May 2018.

87. Souther 2017.

88. This event is one that was produced by the St. Clair Superior CDC in 2015–2016. I discuss this further in Chapter 4. This event is a prime example of the disconnect between CDC and community leadership. While the intentions of the CDC to produce the event were to promote the neighborhood, the management and organization of the event was much critiqued in the Asian American community. The event has a complicated history surrounding its fiscal management and vision. Nonetheless, it was my first entrée into the AsiaTown community.

89. This was evident to me during my period of active visitation, from August 2016 to March 2019, when, on two separate occasions, I randomly chose Airbnbs and during my stays I learned that each were hosted by people who either worked at a Cleveland CDC or worked as a partner with Cleveland CDCs. I stayed with one of these hosts multiple times, and the other host I eventually interviewed for this study. This speaks to the relatively small size of Cleveland and the active role many people engaged in community development play in the informal tourism of Cleveland neighborhoods.

90. United States Census Bureau. "Quick Facts: Cleveland City, Ohio," Available at https://www.census.gov/quickfacts/clevelandcityohio, accessed May 24, 2021. According to the 2019 U.S. Census estimate, Cleveland is: 33.8% white alone, not Hispanic or Latino, 48.8% black or African American alone, 0.5% American Indian and Alaska Native alone, 2.6% Asian alone, 0.1% Native Hawaiian and Other Pacific Islander alone, 4.4% 2 or more races, 11.9% Hispanic or Latino. Although this is not the most up-to-date demographic profile of the city, I am choosing to include this as the demographic profile during the period of study.

91. Due to the COVID-19 pandemic, this course was taught remotely. The upside to this move online was that we were able to work remotely with AsiaTown. This would have been much more difficult with a face-to-face course, as AsiaTown is approximately two hours' drive from the town where the university I teach at is located.

92. See Trieu 2023.

93. The examples of still surviving Chinatowns are unique in that they did not suffer the near complete demolition at the hands of politicians and planners who moved, removed, and demolished communities as part of city plans to stamp out blight and build freeways so that white suburban commuters could still easily make their way to their offices downtown. Asian American communities from San Diego to Boston and numerous places in between have been forever changed because of policies of urban renewal. See, e.g., S. Kurashige 2016 for a discussion of Asian American urban history.

CHAPTER 2

1. Yasu Koyamatsu Momii Interview, Densho Digital Repository, Densho Visual History Collection, October 25, 2011, denshovh-myasu-01, accessed December 5, 2022.

2. Throughout this chapter, I opt to use the terminology of concentration camps, incarceration, and forced evacuation except when quoting directly from historical documents. I do this under the guidance of Densho's terminology guide, available at https://densho.org/terminology/, accessed May 15, 2023.

3. Yasu Koyamatsu Momii was born October 23, 1921, in Seattle, and the family moved to Los Angeles in 1928. Her two eldest siblings were born prior to when her father came to Seattle in 1906. Her mother and two eldest siblings stayed in Japan, and they would be separated for twelve years. The family was reunited in Seattle in 1918, and, in 1919, her next eldest brother was born, and then she was born in 1921. She recalls, "Many of my friends, their parents were the generation of my brother and sister. My parents were rather old for, compared to my friends' parents." Yasu Koyamatsu Momii Interview, Densho Digital Repository.

4. One of the earliest groups of resettlers were Japanese American college students. See, e.g., Okihiro 1999.

5. On February 19, 1942, President Franklin Delano Roosevelt issued Executive Order No. 9066. This order was both vague and intentional, as it began by declaring that "the successful prosecution of the war requires every possible protection against espionage and against sabotage," and it gave the secretary of war and his designees the right to create military zones "from which any or all persons may be excluded." The intentionally vague language does not mention Japanese Americans or concentration camps, specifically, thereby imbuing the secretary of war, James L. Stinson, and his designee, General John L. DeWitt with extraordinary power. Although the Japanese community was not specifically named in Executive Order No. 9066, the order was the legal document that set into motion the massive removal of 120,313 Japanese Americans from the West Coast and into the custody of the WRA.

On February 25, 1942, the residents of Japanese ancestry of Terminal Island, California, became the first community under mandatory evacuation. They were given forty-eight-hours' notice to evacuate the island by the U.S. military. The expulsion of the Japanese American residents of Terminal Island became the first in hundreds of community upheavals. Bainbridge Island and Alameda were evacuated immediately following Terminal Island. And less than a week after the Terminal Island orders were issued, on March 2, 1942, General John L. DeWitt declared all of California, and the Western portions of Washington, Oregon, and Arizona, a military zone.

On March 18, 1942, the Office for Emergency Management officially established the WRA to carry out the program of relocation. The WRA "formulated and executed a program for removal, relocation, maintenance, and supervision in 10 interior relocation centers." These were established per Executive Order No. 9102. The WRA was the successor to the Wartime Civil Control Administration (WCCA), Western Defense Command, which was established as a result of Public Proclamation No. 1, which designated southern Arizona, western Washington, Oregon, and California as Military Area No. 1 on March 2, 1942. The WCCA was created, on March 11, 1942, "to implement army-issued civilian exclusion orders requiring the evacuation of persons of Japanese ancestry from the military area." The WCCA was in operation for one week until the WRA was established, on March 18, 1942. National Archives, "Records of the War Relocation Authority (WRA)" Finding Guide, last reviewed August 15, 2016, available at https://www.archives.gov/research/guide-fed-records/groups/210.html, accessed January 9, 2023.

6. Linehan 1993, 55.

7. The Cleveland hostel was funded by the American Baptist Home Mission Society in New York. This religious organization and others funded hostels in other cities as well (Linehan 1993, 65). There were hostels throughout the country in all of the major cities where Japanese relocated. Charlotte Brooks (2000) argues that "hostels provided Japanese Americans necessary shelter, but they also gave church groups the power to push assimilation as the primary goal of resettlement" (1661).

8. Linehan 1993, 65.

9. Yasu Koyamatsu Momii Interview, Densho Digital Repository.

10. "Very early on, when I first got there, I met him . . . he had been at the hostel and gone out already. He was not living there. He just happened to come and a mutual friend introduced me to him. . . . I saw him from time to at the hostel 'cause he'd be there with his friends, and then I think in '44 we started to go around together, so we were together about one year before we were married." Yasu Koyamatsu Momii Interview, Densho Digital Repository.

11. Isao East Oshima Interview, Densho Digital Repository, Twin Cities JACL Collection, denshovh-oisao-01, June 17, 2009, accessed December 5, 2022.

12. Linehan 1993, 67.

13. Linehan 1993, 67.

14. Linehan 1993, 54–55.

15. Executive Order No. 9066 authorizes the secretary of war to create military areas of which "any or all" people may be excluded on the pretext that "whereas the successful prosecution of the war requires every possible protection against espionage and against sabotage to national-defense material, national-defense premises, and national-defense utilities," available at https://www.archives.gov/milestone-documents/executive-order-9066.

16. Exceptions include: Okihiro's (1999) discussion of college students, Linehan's (1993) article on Cleveland, Brooks's (2000) discussion on Chicago, and Hayashi's (2004) discussion on the Midwest.

17. It is important to note that, while the census is a useful document for comparison, it is an imperfect data collection tool and most likely represents an undercount and also contains inaccuracies. However, even as an imperfect source, it can provide a sense of the overall population figures.

18. The language of the 1940 and 1950 censuses uses the terminology "Negro."

19. Iyko Day's (2016) formation of Asian racialization and the logics of settler colonial capitalism suggest that Japanese incarceration is a transformative moment in the mutation of Japanese labor. She argues that incarceration itself was "motivated by a perception of the excessive industry of Japanese labor" (118). In this logic, not only does the period of incarceration create conditions wherein, in camp, labor is rendered excessive, devalued, and surplus to the West Coast capital; in the camps and during the decades that follow, "Japanese labor transforms from a dehumanizing symbol of modernization into an ideal surplus labor force" (122).

20. Brooks 2000, 1661.

21. Brooks 2000, 1661.

22. In addition to the laborious and costly process of moving most people to first an assembly center and then mere months later to a permanent concentration camp, the assembly centers and camps themselves were shoddily built. The camps were often in isolated locations where even the logistics of moving food, supplies, and personnel required to sustain these hastily built cities of eight thousand to eighteen thousand people was difficult. In addition, incarcerees, a great majority of whom were arriving from more moderate coastal climates, faced extreme temperatures and weather and the conditions themselves were marred by poor nutrition and subpar living conditions.

23. U.S. War Relocation Authority 1946, 1.

24. U.S. War Relocation Authority 1946, 22–23.

25. Linehan 1993, 57.

26. Linehan 1993, 59.

27. U.S. War Relocation Authority 1946, 133.

28. U.S. War Relocation Authority 1946, 133.

29. U.S. War Relocation Authority 1946, 133.

30. Isao East Oshima Interview, Densho Digital Repository.

31. Isao East Oshima was one of eight children born to his parents, but one brother died shortly after birth. As a child, his family moved around the Bay Area to accommodate his father's frequent job changes. In 1942, they were living in West Oakland when Oshima was relocated first to Tanforan Assembly Center in the spring and then to Topaz in September with his parents and six younger siblings.

32. Isao East Oshima Interview, Densho Digital Repository.

33. Isao East Oshima Interview, Densho Digital Repository.

34. Isao East Oshima was only in Cleveland a few months, from late May to early September 1943. Over Labor Day in early September 1943, he went to the Twin Cities to visit his sisters, and, "well, I stayed and never went back." Not only did he not return to Cleveland; he stayed in the Twin Cities even after the West Coast exclusion zone was rescinded. In fact, no one in his entire family, parents or siblings, returned to California. After the war, his parents and many of his younger siblings came to Minnesota to join Isao and his sisters. At the time of the interview, in 2009, two siblings and one deceased sibling had remained in the Twin Cities, and the other three were spread among Washington, New Jersey, and Massachusetts.

35. Day 2016.

36. U.S. Department of the Interior 1947, 29.

37. U.S. Department of the Interior 1947, 30.

38. See, e.g., Babson (1984) 1986.

39. Fugita et al. 1977, 79.

40. The neighborhood's boundaries are defined as: bordered on the south by Euclid Avenue, north by Superior Avenue, on the west by East 55th Street, and the east by East 105th Street.

41. Souther 2017, 48.

42. Souther 2017, 46.

43. Souther 2017, 47.

44. Stradling and Stradling 2015, 49.

45. Sussman, White, and Caplan 1959, 5.

46. By 1950, about 5 percent of the population was nonwhite. By 1957, 59.3 percent of the population was nonwhite, Sussman, White, and Caplan 1959, 5.

47. And, by 1960, the population of Hough was 73.7 percent Black, according to Lackritz (1968) 2010, 39.

48. Only sixty-five units of housing were built in Hough in the 1940s, even though the neighborhood population grew by almost twenty-six thousand people in the same decade, according to Stradling and Stradling 2015, 49–50. In the period from 1950 to 1967, there were "about 150,000 units [of housing] constructed in the suburbs" throughout Cuyahoga County (Cleveland's city and suburbs), yet in the city of Cleveland itself "only 30,000 new units" were constructed. At the same time, only 5 percent of Cuyahoga County's Black residents lived in the suburbs, Lackritz (1968) 2010, 48.

49. Sussman, White, and Caplan 1959, 19.

50. Linehan 1993, 64.

51. Linehan 1993, 61–32.

52. Linehan 1993, 73.

53. Yae Wada Interview, Densho Digital Repository, Densho Visual History Collection, ddr-densho-1000-476, April 12, 2019, accessed December 5, 2022. Yae's father was a small business owner, running Ashby Laundry. Yae's mother was sick for as long as she can remember and passed away when Yae was fourteen. By 1940, Yae had a beauty shop, Alice Beauty Salon, in Oakland's Chinatown and was married to her first husband. In 1942, when mandatory evacuation happened, Yae, her husband, and her father were all relocated to one shared horse stall in Tanforan Assembly Center, and her sister was with her husband's family elsewhere in the camp. Yae's time at Tanforan was stressful and, notably, marked by a miscarriage of her first pregnancy. Yae, along with all of those at Tanforan, was moved to Topaz in September 1942. Yae became pregnant again and had a baby girl in 1943. She and her daughter were both in poor health. Yae was unable to breastfeed because she was so sick. Even still, each morning she had to wait in line for a daily ration of five bottles of formula. As she remembers, "the mothers in camp had a hard time." "I was so sick that I didn't have milk . . . the mothers that I know all wanted to breastfeed because then they would be assured that their babies would get milk. Those of us who had babies were expected to breastfeed, but because I wasn't able to . . . we kind of had to wait in line . . . that meant getting up early in the morning so you would get your five bottles of formula."

54. Yae Wada Interview, Densho Digital Repository.

55. Yae Wada Interview, Densho Digital Repository.

56. Yae Wada Interview, Densho Digital Repository.

57. Yae Wada Interview, Densho Digital Repository.

58. Brooks 2000, 1686.

59. *Cleveland Plain Dealer*, May 30, 1943. The digitized microfilm shows the printed page number as 6-A. However, the Newsbank automatic citation lists this as p. 13.

60. *Cleveland Plain Dealer*, May 30, 1943.

61. An article in the *Topaz Times* by Alex Yorichi includes the biographical information that "the bridegroom was working on a San Francisco paper before the evacuation. He was also the editor of the Tanforan Totalizer," 2. Additionally, Taro Katayama was also an editor and contributor for *Trek*, a literary and arts journal published at Topaz Incarceration Camp; digital versions are available at https://digitallibrary.californiahistorical society.org/object/ms-840-12.

62. Utah State University Digital Collections, Topaz Japanese American Relocation Center Digital Collection, "Central Utah Final Accountability Report," October 1945, 64; Katayama listing, under which Yuki appears beneath Taro, Yuki (see Shiozawa), available at https://digital.lib.usu.edu/digital/collection/p16944coll135/search/searchterm /Central%20Utah%20Final%20Accountability%20Report/field/title/mode/exact/conn /and/order/title/ad/asc, accessed October 6, 2022.

63. Yuki's father, Tetsushiro Shiozawa was born on May 11, 1885, and her mother, whose name is undecipherable in the digital version of the record was born on September 15, 1894. Both of their records are marked "A" for alien and were, therefore, presumably born in Japan. The Shiozawa listing shows Yuki's parents, her five unmarried siblings, and has a separate listing for her eldest sister, who was presumably married prior to incarceration and Yuki, with the notation that she married Taro Katayama. Utah State University Digital, "Central Utah Final Accountability Report," October 1945, p. 164. available at https://digital.lib.usu.edu/digital/collection/p16944coll135/search/searchterm /Central%20Utah%20Final%20Accountability%20Report/field/title/mode/exact/conn /and/order/title/ad/asc, accessed October 6, 2022.

64. Executive Order No. 9066, February 19, 1942, available at https://www.archives.gov/milestone-documents/executive-order-9066#transcript, accessed January 5, 2023.

65. Yorichi 1942, 2.

66. U.S. Department of the Interior 1947, 7.

67. U.S. War Relocation Authority 1946, 7.

68. U.S. War Relocation Authority 1946, 6–11.

69. U.S. War Relocation Authority 1946, 11.

70. U.S. War Relocation Authority 1946, 11.

71. U.S. War Relocation Authority 1946, 85–86.

72. On February 16, 1944, the WRA was transferred to the Department of the Interior and was abolished, effective June 30, 1946. After the end of the West Coast exclusion order, effective January 2, 1945, the WRA primarily shifted to a program of resettlement. The WRA was ended by Executive Order No. 9742, June 25, 1946, effective June 30, 1946. National Archives, "Records of the War Relocation Authority."

73. U.S. Department of the Interior 1947, 9.

74. U.S. Department of the Interior 1947, 9.

75. Linehan 1993, 72–73.

76. Tule Lake closed March 1946.

77. Fugita et al. 1977, 81.

78. Fugita et al. 1977, 91.

79. Fugita et al. 1977, 91.

80. Fugita et al. 1977, 100.

81. Fugita et al. 1977, 97.

82. Fugita et al. 1977, 84.

83. Fugita et al. 1977, 84–85.

84. Fugita et al. 1977, 99.

85. Fugita et al. 1977, 99–100.

86. Linehan 1993, 75.

87. Fugita et al. 1977, 91–92.

88. U.S. Department of the Interior 1947, 11–12.

89. U.S. Department of the Interior 1947, 12.

90. The Densho Digital Repository included a handful of interviews that discussed relocation to Cleveland. I read and listened to the following oral histories from the Densho Digital Repository when writing this chapter: Roy Ebihara, Harry Kawahara, Rokuro Kurihara, Yasu Koyamatsu Momii, Toshikazu "Tosh" Okamoto, Isao East Oshima, Henry Sakamoto, Cookie Takeshita, Betty Tanakatsubo, Ben Y. Tonooka, Yae Wada, and Yoneo Yamamoto.

91. Yasu Koyamatsu Momii Interview, Densho Digital Repository.

92. The cursive penmanship of the census taker is difficult to read and the second word after "claim" for Yuki's job position is visible but undecipherable.

93. Cleveland's Black population grew from 84,504 in 1940 to 147,847 in 1950.

94. See, e.g., Brooks 2009; Molina 2006; S. Kurashige 2007; Pulido 2006.

CHAPTER 3

1. MidTown Cleveland Inc. 2020.

2. Jayasanker 2020, 56.

3. Jayasanker 2020, 54–62; Lung-Amam 2017.

4. Jayasanker's work makes arguments about Asian as well as "Hispanic" population growth, but, for the purposes of this chapter, I am focusing on his Asian-specific argument for clarity.

5. Li 2009.

6. Mueller Lofts, "History," available at https://themuellerlofts.com/history/, accessed July 1, 2024.

7. See Cleveland Historical, "Tyler Village," available at https://clevelandhistorical .org/items/show/279/, for the history of the W. S. Tyler Co. Building, and Tyler Village, available at https://tylervillage.com/, for examples of the contemporary marketing and branding of the space, accessed September 11, 2024.

8. U.S. Census Bureau, "Historical Census Statistics."

9. As discussed in the Chapter 1, the role of race in the U.S. census is an imprecise category, yet it can be a useful demographic snapshot. See the papers U.S. Census Bureau, "U.S. Decennial Census Measurement" and Brown 2020.

10. See, e.g., Sugrue 1996; Freund 2007.

11. Zhao 2002, 1.

12. Zhao (2002) writes, "Not until the exclusion acts were repealed in 1943 and alien Chinese became admissible did the struggle for family unification begin to gain significant momentum. The 1945 War Brides Act allowed the admission of alien dependents of World War II veterans without quota limits. A June 1946 act extended this privilege to fiancées and fiancés of war veterans. The Chinese Alien Wives of American Citizens Act, enacted in August 1946, granted admission outside the quota to Chinese wives of American citizens" (1).

13. Zhao 2002, 1–2.

14. Anchored by the opening of Asia Plaza in 1991, the opening of the Asian Evergreen Senior Apartments in 1998, and the opening of Asian Town Center in 2008, and the development of the strip mall, Payne Commons.

15. Padoongpatt 2017, 2.

16. See, e.g., Banh and Liu 2020; Mendelson 2016; Liu 2015; Chen 2014; Cho 2010; Coe 2009; Jennifer Lee 2008.

17. Molina 2022, 9.

18. Kaplan and Li (2006) suggest that many immigrants are entrepreneurial out of necessity, and often are small-scale businesses that rely on family labor. Additionally, the ethnic "specialization" in a few economic sectors "stems from many factors: the skills that ethnics bring with them, the opportunities available in a particular context, the legacy of long-standing activity in a sector, and the structural barriers set by hosting societies that prevent ethnic minorities from penetrating certain sectors" (3).

19. See, e.g., Johnson 2009.

20. Zhou 2004, 41–42.

21. Heap 2009, 9.

22. Zhou 2004.

23. Aronson and Kent 2008, 308–312.

24. Zhou 2004, 49–51.

25. Park 2005, 15.

26. It is important to underscore that as Jan Lin (1998, 11) noted, "The ethnic enclave may be conceived as having a double-edged character that rewards bosses mainly at the expense of workers, who labor in jobs that mostly dead-end in terms of future occupational mobility" while also recognizing that "immigrant bosses also work hard, provide

opportunities for immigrants with limited English-speaking ability, give them on-the-job training, and may overlook undocumented immigration status."

27. Park 2005, 13–14.

28. Dhingra 2012, 5.

29. The "supposedly" here is not said with skepticism, rather it is yet to be "officially" verified. During this conversation, Steve mentioned that "it's kind of unclear, my dad never talked about it, and my grandfather on my father's side passed away a long time ago. . . . Although we haven't really proven it, we're [father's lineage] originally Toisonese, and supposedly go back to the railroad days." And, when I asked later if his father spoke much about his World War II military service, Steve replied, "No, he's um, he's your typical Chinese father, he doesn't say very much, you'd have to pry information out of him, and of course, being a traditional Chinese family, we never really pressed him."

30. The irony of this name was not lost on either of us.

31. Steve Hom, March 2019.

32. Brooks 2019, 3.

33. Brooks 2019, 8.

34. Brooks 2019, 8.

35. As Brooks (2019) notes, "Between 1937 and 1941, Chinese Americans who lived in Japanese-occupied areas had to decide whether or not to seek shelter in foreign concessions, flee to 'Free China,' live under Japanese rule, or leave for Hong Kong or the United States. Throughout the country, those who stayed in Japanese-occupied or neutral territory also gambled on whether relations between the United States and Japan would continue to worsen. The vast majority of Chinese Americans who made such choices found few of their options palatable. Professionals with successful careers in China pondered returning to an economically struggling country where racial discrimination usually confined Chinese Americans to menial work. Many Chinese Americans lacked the money to buy a ticket to the United States or the willingness to abandon noncitizen spouses and children inadmissible under American immigration law. Yet Chinese American citizens who did return to the United States before December 1941 ultimately fared far better than almost all of the those stranded in occupied China after Pearl Harbor. In contrast to the anxious uncertainty of the period between 1937 and 1941, the outbreak of the Pacific War meant almost certain deprivation and terror, and sometimes death, for those Chinese Americans who stayed in China" (53).

36. See Ling 2012, 2004; Yan 2013. Yan (2013) shows that the 1880 census, counted eighteen people of Chinese descent in Columbus where "laundry" was the most commonly recorded occupation. Yan's archival work shows that the first Chinese restaurant appeared in the city directory in 1901 and that, by the 1940s, restaurants had outpaced laundries as the dominant occupation (79–82).

37. Yee 1977, 24.

38. Yee 1977, 24.

39. Yee writes, "Reports from various sources indicate that perhaps 10 Chinese may have lived in Cleveland as early as 1848. By 1870, however, there was only one Chinese in Cleveland. Within the next three decades, the Chinese population in Cleveland increased to over 100, and their activities pointed to the development of a permanent Chinese settlement. The first Chinese restaurant was opened in 1895 by Wong Kee, an immigrant who came to Cleveland from Chicago" (1977, 24).

40. Yee 1977, 35.

41. The "traditional" form of urban Chinatowns generally developed from the 1880s to the 1940s, as residentially segregated communities in the face of rampant anti-Asian sentiment.

42. Aronson and Kent 2008, 315.

43. See Heap 2009.

44. Choi 2016.

45. Tony Louie, October 2016.

46. Yan 2013 attempts to pin down the origin story of this dish, and it tracks to either Detroit, Michigan, or Columbus, Ohio.

47. OCA, historically is the Organization of Chinese Americans, a national organization with regional chapters. In 2013, the organization rebranded its name at the national level to OCA-Asian Pacific American Advocates; more information is available at https://www.ocanational.org/about.

48. Lisa Wong, October 2016.

49. Lisa Wong, October 2016.

50. Fugita et al. 1977.

51. This is a very unusual spelling of the Korean surname that is typically Romanized as "Kim." This spelling of "Khim" appears throughout the original text so is likely not an error.

52. Fugita et al. 1977, 153.

53. Fugita et al. 1977, 153.

54. Fugita et al. 1977, 153–154.

55. Fugita 1977, 89.

56. Fugita 1977, 89.

57. Lisa Wong, October 2016.

58. The markets that are included in *East Asian Resources in Ohio* (1981) are Sam Wah Yick Kee 2146 Rockwell Avenue, Friendship Chinese Foodland 3415 Payne, Hall One Company 3126 St. Clair, Kim's Oriental Food Store 3411 Payne, and Omura's Japanese Food and Gift Shop 3811 Payne, 23–24. Additionally, there was one store listed on the East Side, Lee Road Oriental Trader in Cleveland Heights, 2295 Lee Road, 23.

59. Two of the five are large supermarkets: Park to Shop and Asia Food Company; three are smaller markets: Tink Holl Food Market, Kim's Oriental Food, and Good Harvest Food Market.

60. Teaford 1993, 53.

61. Teaford 1993, 220–221.

62. Steve Hom, March 2019.

63. Steve Hom, March 2019.

64. Steve Hom, March 2019.

65. Steve Hom, March 2019.

66. Steve Hom, March 2019.

67. Steve Hom, March 2019.

68. Donna Hom obituary, available at https://obits.cleveland.com/us/obituaries/cleveland/name/donna-hom-obituary?id=7866277, accessed April 3, 2023.

69. Ho Wah Restaurant, available at https://howahrestaurant.com/, accessed April 3, 2023.

70. Li Wah Restaurant, available at https://liwahrestaurant.com/about-us, accessed April 3, 2023.

71. Joe Fong, May 2018.

72. This is Fong's original language but refers to the population of African Americans, not African immigrants.

73. Steve Hom, March 2019.

74. Lisa Wong Interview 2, February 2018.

75. Lisa Wong Interview 2, February 2018.

76. Lisa Wong Interview 2, February 2018.

77. Joe Fong, May 2018.

78. Trieu 2023, 53–59.

79. Trieu 2023, 53.

80. See Dutka 2014, 124–127, and "Asia Plaza," available at https://asiaplazacleveland.com/, accessed April 17, 2023, for more on the history of Asia Plaza.

81. Steve Hom recalls that the store opened in the mid-1980s, but Dutka (2014, 124) states that John Louie "learned the grocery business working in his uncle's store while majoring in industrial design at Kent State University. In 1976, he founded Hall One Chinese Imports, Cleveland's first major Chinese grocery store, on Payne Avenue."

82. MidTown Cleveland 2020, 21.

83. Steve Hom, March 2019.

84. Dutka 2014, 124.

85. Dutka 2014, 125–126.

86. Steve Hom, March 2019.

87. Steve Hom, March 2019.

88. San Francisco's Japantown Center development is notable for its building in the post–World War II period in the city proper, see Oda 2018. Lung-Amam's 2017 work on suburban Silicon Valley notes that the Asian malls did not face difficulty in securing funding for development. However, notably, the City of Fremont and some of its residents expressed open contempt and attempted to prohibit the continued building of Asian malls in the city and instead focus on promoting "high quality" retail (115–134).

89. U.S. Census Bureau, "Historical Census Statistics."

90. Since that initial tenancy, CHN has undergone a name change (see Chapter 4) and "now they occupy the entire third floor, over half the second floor, and then they have some space on the first floor as well," Steve Hom, March 2019.

91. See, e.g., Lung-Amam 2017; Võ 2004; W. Cheng 2013; Aguilar San-Juan 2009; Fong 1994; Saito 1998.

92. Lung-Amam 2017, 99.

93. Lung-Amam 2017, 99.

94. Lung-Amam 2017, 106.

95. In her study of Silicon Valley Asian Malls 1970–2010, Lung-Amam maps not only the growth of the Asian American community but the shifting class, ethnicity, and neighborhood by examining the differentiation between the malls (2015, 22).

96. See, e.g., Qadeer 2016, 73–76; Lung-Amam 2015, 2017; Wood 2006.

97. There is a discrepancy here, as Steve Hom, who is the property manager of the building, indicated that the space is 70,000 sq. ft., and Dutka (2014) cites the space as 50,000 sq. ft. In this instance, I defer to Hom's expertise.

98. As of February 2023, Szechuan Café closed and Pho Sunshine is newly opened; for more information, see Douglas Trattner, 2023, "Now Open: Pho Sunshine Vietnamese Restaurant at Asia Plaza," *Cleveland Scene*, February 6, available at https://www.clevescene.com/food-drink/now-open-pho-sunshine-vietnamese-restaurant-at-asia-plaza-41364001, accessed April 6, 2023.

99. As of this writing, there is news of an Asian Mall under construction in Novi, Michigan, available at https://sakuranovi.com/, accessed May 11, 2023. Nick Manes, 2023, "Long-Planned 'Asian Village' Development in Novi Takes Big Steps Forward," *Crain's Detroit Business*, February 3, available at https://www.crainsdetroit.com/real-estate/long-planned-asian-village-development-novi-takes-big-steps-forward, accessed May 11, 2023. Additionally, there are a number of supermarkets and stores in various Asian strip malls in both Troy and Madison Heights, Michigan, see, e.g., Zheng, 2018.

100. The restaurant that Steve's mom opened in the 1970s, King Wah, is still open today. In 1979, Donna opened Ho Wah, another American Chinese restaurant about twenty miles east of King Wah, in an East Side suburb. King Wah is in Rocky River, and Ho Wah is in Beachwood.

101. Steve Hom, March 2019.

102. See Li Wah Restaurant, "About Us," available at https://liwahrestaurant.com/about-us and Cleveland.com; "Donna Cheung Hom Obituary," available at https://obits.cleveland.com/obituaries/cleveland/obituary.aspx?n=donna-cheung-hom&pid=197568667&fhid=4400, accessed July 1, 2024.

103. Zhou (2004, 40) writes, "An ethnic community provides a demand for goods and services that immigrant businesses are uniquely qualified to provide, because immigrant businessmen know the tastes and buying preferences brought from their homeland. The ethnic niches that provide culturally specific products in the ethnic community become the protected sector of ethnic economies."

104. Lisa Wong Interview 2, February 2018.

105. Dutka 2014, 134.

106. John Petkovic, 2011, "Cleveland's AsiaTown Becoming a Melting Pot for the Larger Community," *Plain Dealer*, March 25, available at https://www.cleveland.com/entertainment/2011/03/clevelands_asiatown_becoming_a.html, accessed July 1, 2024.

107. Lisa Wong, October 2016.

108. Although, a notable exception is the opening of the market-rate Mueller Lofts apartments in June 2018. Current information on leasing is available at https://themuellerlofts.com/.

109. Cohen 2003, 258–259.

CHAPTER 4

1. Joyce Huang Interview 3, March 2019. A note here that Ms. Huang's role at MidTown and in the Cleveland planning community, more generally, grew from 2017 to 2023. From 2017 to 2022, her work at MTC put her on the map in the city planning community. She began at MidTown as an "urban planner" and was promoted through the ranks of MTC to the director of planning and placemaking and then vice president of community development. Her efforts and successes in AsiaTown have proved beneficial for the community and the CDC. And, in January 2022, she was tapped to be the Cleveland city planning director by incoming mayor Justin Bibb. She proudly states that she is the first woman, the first Asian American, and the first mother to hold the position. The City Club of Cleveland, 2022, "A Fresh Perspective on City Planning, City Club in Public Square," June 28, available at https://www.cityclub.org/forums/2022/06/28/a-fresh-perspective-on-city-planning, accessed April 27, 2023. Steven Litt, 2022, Cleveland.com. "Cleveland Mayor Justin Bibb Taps Joyce Huang of MidTown Cleveland Inc. to Become New City Planning Director, Ricardo León as Strategist for Equity," January 20, available at https://www.cleveland.com/news/2022/01/cleveland-mayor-justin-bibb-taps-joyce-huang-of

-MidTown-cleveland-inc-to-become-new-city-planning-director-ricardo-leon-as-strat egist-for-equity.html, accessed April 27, 2023.

2. AsiaTown Advisory Committee Meeting Minutes, April 9, 2018.

3. The number of CDCs appears to be shrinking over time. I did not ask when I began this research for a precise number of CDCs. As of July 2020, there were twenty-seven, according to Christopher Roy, "Community Development Corporations," *Encyclopedia of Cleveland History*, Case Western Reserve University, available at https://case.edu/ech /articles/c/community-development-corporations#:~:text=Neighborhood%20block%20 clubs%2C%20sanctioned%20by,Kamm's%20Neighborhood%20to%20the%20west, accessed May 8, 2023. However, the website of Cleveland Neighborhood Progress lists only twenty-four, "Cleveland CDCs," available at http://www.clevelandnp.org/cleveland-cdcs/, accessed May 8, 2023.

4. AsiaTown Advisory Committee Meeting Minutes, October 9, 2017.

5. AsiaTown Advisory Committee Meeting Minutes, October 9, 2017.

6. AsiaTown Advisory Committee Meeting Minutes, October 9, 2017.

7. "AsiaTown Transportation and Streetscape Plan," December 2010, and "Greater AsiaTown Area Master Plan," October 30, 2013.

8. Lin 2011, 45–56.

9. U.S. Census Bureau, 2022.

10. Joyce Huang Interview 3, March 2019.

11. Asian Services in Action homepage, available at https://www.asiaohio.org/, accessed April 27, 2023.

12. In 2018, he announced his departure and intention to take a position in Seattle, his hometown. Liza Javier, 2019, "Meet Michael Byun, Executive Director of ACRS," May 23, available at https://iexaminer.org/meet-michael-byun-executive-director-of-acrs/, accessed April 27, 2023.

13. Zip code covering the AsiaTown neighborhood.

14. Michael Byun, May 2018.

15. At meetings with city planners, local planning professors, and other CDC personnel, people outside of the AsiaTown community validated and reinforced the narrative of invisibility that the Asian American community continuously communicated. A number of people were unaware that "AsiaTown" as a neighborhood existed and, beyond a few restaurants concentrated in the area, tended to be unaware of the residential community and other neighborhood businesses.

16. Chia-Min Chen, March 2019.

17. Cleveland Community Relations Board, available at https://www.clevelandohio .gov/CityofCleveland/Home/Government/CityAgencies/CommunityRelationsBoard, accessed May 1, 2023.

18. This is Chen's recounting of history, but cities throughout the country developed "community relations boards" through the mid-twentieth century. For example, Detroit had a Mayor's Interracial Committee, as early as 1943, as a response to the 1943 Detroit Riot, which many consider to be a race riot.

19. Chia-Min Chen, March 2019.

20. Chia-Min Chen, March 2019.

21. See, e.g., Ahmed 2012 for a discussion on the importance of the performative role of representation in institutional settings.

22. Chia-Min Chen, March 2019.

23. Chia-Min Chen, March 2019.

24. Chia-Min Chen, March 2019.

25. W. Cheng 2013, 157.

26. Lisa Wong Interview 2, February 2018.

27. Lisa Wong Interview 2, February 2018.

28. Snow and Leahy 1980, 463.

29. Federally, "the CDC can be traced to Robert Kennedy's 1966 tour of Bedford-Stuyvesant and the subsequent Special Impact Amendment to the Economic Opportunity Act," Stoecker 1997, 2.

30. Stoecker 1997, 4.

31. Levine 2017.

32. Yin 1998.

33. Dewar 2013.

34. Yin 1998, 143–144.

35. Stoecker 1997, 5.

36. See Montgomery 2020.

37. See, e.g., Akers, Béal, and Rousseau 2020; Safransky 2014.

38. Akers 2015.

39. Safransky 2023.

40. Yin 1998.

41. Federal money for community redevelopment funded the Hough Area Development Corporation (HADC), one of the first CDCs in the country in 1968. On the heels of the Hough Rebellion (see Chapter 2), the HADC "received an initial federal grant of $1.6 million to implement programs that focused on low-income housing and community-controlled enterprise" and continued to receive direct federal funding throughout its life cycle (Yin 1998, 40). In 1970, the Famicos Foundation was founded by Sister Henrietta Gorris in the Hough neighborhood (Yin 1998, 139). According to the contemporary Famicos CDC website, "Sister Henrietta Gorris, CSA, worked tirelessly with residents after the Hough riots to rebuild their home and their spirit. With the help of volunteers, Sr. Henrietta worked to provide essentials and helped residents with minor home repairs," available at https://famicos.org/history, accessed March 12, 2022. Early on, Famicos "identified housing as an issue fundamental to neighborhood revitalization" (Yin 1998, 140). HADC, over its lifetime from 1968 to 1984, "produced over 600 units of low-income housing, a major mixed-use community center, and a manufacturing subsidiary that employed as many as 100 people" (Yin 1998, 140). Yet, even with its accomplishments, in 1984, HADC shuttered after its federal funding ended.

42. Yin 1998.

43. Yin 1998; Stoecker 1997, 3.

44. Stoecker 1997; Yin 1998.

45. Kirkpatrick 2007.

46. Bratt and Rohe 2007.

47. Stoecker 1997, 5.

48. Joyce Huang, February 2018.

49. Joyce Huang Interview 3, March 2019.

50. See "AsiaTown Transportation and Streetscape Plan," December 2010; "Greater AsiaTown Area Master Plan," October 30, 2013.

51. St. Clair Superior, "About Us, History," available at https://www.stclairsuperior.org/about-us/#history-service, accessed July 1, 2024.

52. For their discussions on planning San Diego's Asian Pacific Historic Thematic District, see, e.g., Võ 2004; Saito 2009.

53. Lin 2011, 165–204.

54. Wilson 2015, 111–112.

55. Steve Hom, March 2019.

56. Robert L. Smith, 2007. "East Side Neighborhood Unveils New Name: AsiaTown." *Plain Dealer*, August 10, B2.

57. Detroit, another Rust Belt city, has worked hard to rebrand itself and its neighborhoods. See, e.g., Kinney 2018, 2017, 2016.

58. Joyce Huang Interview 3, March 2019.

59. W. Cheng 2013, 138.

60. ACS Demographic and Housing Estimates, 2016, zip code 44114, available at https://data.census.gov/table/ACSDP5Y2016.DP05?g=860XX00US44114.

61. Lisa Wong, October 2016.

62. Kim Scott, May 2018.

63. Michael Fleming, October 2016.

64. Dan DeRoos, 2019, "Super Popular Night Market Cleveland Makes Its Return This Summer," Cleveland 19 News, March 29, available at https://www.cleveland19.com/2019/03/29/super-popular-night-market-cleveland-makes-its-return-this-summer/, last accessed September 13, 2024.

65. Multiple interviewees asked for me to stop the recording and/or not directly attribute their critiques of the Night Market, even as they openly discussed multiple issues. During my interview with Michael Fleming, he was well aware of the multiple critiques being leveled at the event. This leads me to believe that community members were simultaneously making direct critiques to SCSDC and also did not want to go "on the record" with their criticism to preserve relationships with SCSDC.

66. The "staff" that Fleming refers to here is actually Joyce Huang who began as an unpaid volunteer. After the controversies, her role changed to a contract paid position, but, like many of the event vendors, she was never actually paid for her work.

67. Michael Fleming, October 2016.

68. MidTown Cleveland/AsiaTown is one of the "Strategic Investment Initiative" grants; more information is available at http://www.clevelandnp.org/cdcgrantmaking/, accessed May 8, 2023.

69. St. Clair Superior Development Corporation email blast, November 27, 2018.

70. Kim Palmer, 2023, "Cleveland CDC Shakeups Continue as St. Clair Superior Director Leaves," *Crain's Cleveland*, December 14, available at https://www.crainscleveland.com/politics-policy/terri-hamilton-brown-becomes-st-clair-superior-interim-director.

71. Kim Palmer, 2024, "St. Clair Superior Board Solidifies Leadership Positions," *Crain's Cleveland*, March 14, available at https://www.crainscleveland.com/politics-policy/terri-hamilton-brown-now-permanent-director-st-clari-cdc.

72. See the List of Interviews.

73. Kim Scott, May 2018.

74. Kim Scott, May 2018.

75. AsiaTown Discussion PDF presentation, attachment to minutes from December 3, 2018, meeting.

76. Joyce Huang Interview 3, March 2019.

77. Joyce Huang Interview 3, March 2019.

78. AsiaTown Advisory Committee Meeting Minutes, July 29, 2020. In an email sent to ATAC, Karis Tzeng announced that her last day at MTC would be March 6, 2024. By the time she left MTC, she had risen in the ranks to vice president of planning.

79. Announcement circulated to ATAC via email, August 23, 2019.

80. AsiaTown Advisory Committee Meeting Minutes, November 6, 2020.

81. AsiaTown Advisory Committee Meeting Minutes, February 5, 2020.

82. Võ's (2004) examination of San Diego's Asian Pacific Thematic Historic District discusses how, for some communities, because they do not have a historical tie to the neighborhood, a "connection must be created" (193–194).

83. *Crain's Cleveland Business*, 2018, "Radhika Reddy," available at https://www.crainscleveland.com/custom-content-notable-women-real-estate-2018/radhika-reddy, accessed April 20, 2021.

84. *Crain's Cleveland Business*, 2019, "Notable Women in Entrepreneurship Radhika Reddy," available at https://www.crainscleveland.com/awards/radhika-reddy-notable-women-entrepreneur-2019, accessed April 20, 2021.

85. *Crain's*, 2018, "Radhika Reddy."

86. *Crain's Cleveland Business*, 2014, "Women of Note 2014 Radhika Reddy," available at https://www.crainscleveland.com/awards/radhika-reddy, accessed April 20, 2021; Radhika Reddy, May 2018.

87. *Crain's*, 2014, "Women of Note."

88. See Kibria 1996.

89. Radhika Reddy, May 2018.

90. ACS Demographic and Housing Estimates, 2016.

91. Radhika Reddy, May 2018.

92. Radhika Reddy, May 2018.

93. Ed Carroll, 2019, "Dave's Markets Expands, in Good Hands for Five Generations," *Cleveland Jewish News*, March 21, available at https://www.clevelandjewishnews.com/news/local_news/dave-s-markets-expands-in-good-hands-for-five-generations/article_a8d1d320–4bdd-11e9-ba08-9b54b39be1bb.html, accessed July 1, 2024.

94. Cleveland Public Library Staff Writer, 2022, "The Library Is Bringing Family Fun Programs and Activities to You This Summer," Cleveland Public Library, June 14, available at https://cpl.org/the-library-is-bringing-family-fun-programs-and-activities-to-you-this-summer/, accessed July 1, 2024.

95. Radhika Reddy, May 2018.

96. Radhika Reddy, May 2018.

97. Cleveland hosted the 2016 Republican National Convention.

98. Radhika Reddy, May 2018.

99. Radhika Reddy, May 2018.

100. Gaston and Kennedy, in their study of the rapid change in Boston's Roxbury neighborhood in the 1980s, pointedly argued that the structure of capitalism relies on a process of disinvestment and reinvestment. This argument bears out again and again, as scholars of racial capitalism have continued to show over the subsequent forty years (1987, 180).

101. In September 2017, the CHN announced a rebranding name change to CHN Housing Partners. Throughout this chapter, I simply refer to the organization as CHN. At the time of my meeting with Rob Curry, the new name was used interchangeably with the former name. More information available at https://chnhousingpartners.org/cleveland-housing-network-now-chn-housing-partners/, accessed May 9, 2023.

102. We met in May 2018, and, in September 2018, he announced that he was stepping down, with nine months of lead time to completely transition leadership by June 30, 2019; more information available at https://chnhousingpartners.org/longtime-chn-executive

-director-rob-curry-announces-his-plan-to-step-down/. One week after the announcement CHN announced that Kevin Nowak would take over as the next executive director and the transition would be planned over the next nine months; more information available at https://chnhousingpartners.org/chn-board-names-kevin-nowak-as-chns-next -executive-director/, accessed May 9, 2023.

103. Akers, Béal, and Rousseau 2020.

104. Vince Grzegorek, 2018, "New Data Map Reminds Us Cleveland Is Hyper-Segregated," *Scene*, May 10, available at https://www.clevescene.com/news/new-data-map-re minds-us-cleveland-is-hyper-segregated-18297703.

105. Rob Curry, May 2018.

106. Rob Curry, May 2018.

107. Rob Curry, May 2018.

108. Kim Scott, May 2018.

109. Rob Curry, May 2018.

110. See, e.g., Sides 2004.

CHAPTER 5

1. Lisa Wong, October 2016.

2. This name, "Asian American and Pacific Islander Heritage Month" was the common usage at the time of research and is the official name used in the program booklets discussed in this chapter. However, the name itself has had various uses officially and unofficially since "Asian/Pacific Heritage Week" was introduced in 1977. Since then the name has changed to "Asian Pacific Heritage Month" (1990), "Asian American and Pacific Islander Heritage Month" (2009), "Asian American and Native Hawaiian/Pacific Islander Heritage Month" (2021), and "Asian American, Native Hawaiian, and Pacific Islander Heritage Month" (2022). Given the changing names and associated acronyms used to describe this month, there is a very wide range of names that the month is known as in government, media, and colloquial conversation. When I am quoting directly in this book I will use whatever the source states, and in all other cases I will use "Asian American and Pacific Islander Heritage Month," the official name during the period of research for this book. See Terry Tang, 2024, "Nearly 50 Years Later, Asian American and Pacific Islander Month Features Revelry and Racial Justice," *AP News*, May 1, available at https://apnews .com/article/asian-american-pacific-islander-native-hawaiian-month-634189f4094 791fd6c7f02f33d1e5597, accessed December 10, 2024 for a history of the name. See "A Proclamation on Asian American and Native Hawaiian/Pacific Islander Heritage Month 2021," issued by the White House, April 30, 2021, available at https://www.whitehouse .gov/briefing-room/presidential-actions/2021/04/30/a-proclamation-on-asian-american -and-native-hawaiian-pacific-islander-heritage-month-2021/, accessed December 10, 2024 and "A Proclamation on Asian American, Native Hawaiian, and Pacific Islander Heritage Month 202," issued by the White House, April 29, 2022, available at https://www .whitehouse.gov/briefing-room/presidential-actions/2022/04/29/a-proclamation-on -asian-american-native-hawaiian-and-pacific-islander-heritage-month-2022/.

3. Cuyahoga County, "2020 Census: Population by Race."

4. See, e.g., Yeh 2008; L. Kurashige 2002.

5. Yeh 2008, 8.

6. Yeh 2008, 9.

7. Yeh 2008, 11.

8. Yeh 2008; L. Kurashige 2002.

9. Tuan 1998.

10. Molina 2006, 6–11.

11. Molina 2006, 9.

12. This production relied on racial scripts that constructed Asians as disease-carrying bodies that engage in aberrant vice and sexual practices (see Anderson 1987; Shah 2001), which then provided a rationalization for their ghettoization in particular districts in the city, contributing to an ongoing discourse of their "un-fitness" for citizenship (see Molina 2006; Ngai 2004).

13. In this, Molina (like Chang 2010, as discussed in Chapter 1) offers up the idea that the *barrio* is a racial script produced relationally with the conception of the *ghetto*. Mexican Americans and Black Americans are not only racialized in the United States but these racializations impact the structures of space. Additionally, and crucially, the meanings of *barrio* and *ghetto* are both overlapping but have different connotations because of the ways in which racialization happens differently among racial groups. The production of the *barrio* relies on and adapts the racial script of the *ghetto*; although the spaces have been racialized differently, there are overlapping structures that produce both locations as segregated spaces (2014, 8).

14. Brooks 2009.

15. Chang 2010; Võ 2004; Aguilar San-Juan 2009.

16. Lung-Amam 2017; W. Cheng 2013.

17. Lisa Wong, October 2016, italicized to highlight her speech pattern.

18. See Trieu 2023.

19. Josephine Lee 2011, 2. See also Ahlgren 2018, on Asian American taiko drumming in Minnesota, in which she suggests that the cultural outreach that the Minneapolis-based Mu Daiko group engages in happens within the presumed whiteness of Minnesota. Ahlgren shows how Mu Daiko intercedes in the narrative of a white-only space by literally taking space and showing up.

20. Ahlgren 2018, 57.

21. Ahlgren 2018, 57.

22. Hawkins 2015.

23. hooks, 1992, 24.

24. Fincher et al. 2014, 44.

25. Dan Hansen, 2019, "Over 40,000 Attend 2019 Cleveland Asian Festival," June 14, available at https://clevelandasianfestival.org/2019/over-40000-attend-2019-cleveland -asian-festival/, accessed April 5, 2021.

26. Lisa Wong, October 2016.

27. Lisa Wong, October 2016.

28. Lisa Wong, October 2016.

29. Lisa Wong, October 2016.

30. Lisa Wong Interview 2, February 2018.

31. Lisa Wong, October 2016.

32. Lisa Wong, Interview 2, February 2018.

33. Lisa Wong, October 2016.

34. The 2020 CAF was on the books and planned but had to be canceled due to COVID-19. The 2021 CAF was held remotely and returned to its in-person format in 2022.

35. Cleveland Asian Festival, "11th Annual Cleveland Asian Festival, About," available at https://clevelandasianfestival.org/2020/home/about/.

36. Lisa Wong, October 2016.

37. Lisa Wong, October 2016.

38. Hawkins 2015, 116.

39. Hawkins 2015, 121.

40. Hawkins 2015, 116.

41. Lisa Wong, October 2016.

42. Lisa Wong, October 2016.

43. The performance stage schedules have varied within thirty to forty-five minutes over the two days and from year to year. CAF Program 2017, 2018, 2019, "Performance Schedule," 30–31.

44. Field notes and CAF website, available at https://clevelandasianfestival.org/2021/, accessed July 29, 2021.

45. Field notes and CAF.

46. Lisa Wong, October 2016.

47. Espiritu 2003.

48. The program covers from 2010 to 2012 all had a standard format and color palette with a slight change in the main visual component. Likewise, those in 2013–2015 continued the existing color palette and slightly shifted the visual orientation of the program but were standard across years. However, since 2016, there has been an annual poster design contest. The winner's design, in addition to a cash prize, is featured on all of that year's branding and marketing, including the program cover. As a result of the competition, the programs from 2016 onward are each distinct in style and color. All of the past CAF program covers can be viewed here: available at https://clevelandasianfestival.org/2019/get-involved/contest/poster-design-competition/, accessed August 5, 2021.

49. It is notable that Mayor Frank G. Jackson's message is exactly the same welcoming letter across all three years, except for the change in date. CAF 2017 program, 5; CAF 2018 program, 5; CAF 2019 program, 5.

50. CAF 2019 program, 5, 7.

51. Ahmed 2012, 54–60.

52. Ahmed 2012, 57, italics in the original.

53. CAF 2019 program, 46.

54. CAF 2019 program, 46.

55. In a google search for the title of the article and author it seems that the history itself comes from a modestly edited version found on a website called "Infoplease," available at https://www.infoplease.com/history/apa-heritage/asian-american-history, accessed August 9, 2021.

56. See, e.g., Hong 2020; Wu 2014.

57. CAF 2019 program, 47.

58. CAF 2019 program, 48.

59. The language of "Japanese internment" has been roundly critiqued and is deemed passé. Typically used is either "incarceration" or "concentration camp." See Japanese American National Museum, "Terminolgy and the Japanese American Experience," available at https://www.janm.org/sites/default/files/2020-11/janm-education-resources-enduring-communities-terminology.pdf, accessed November 18, 2021.

60. CAF 2019 program, 48.

61. CAF 2019 program, 44–45.

62. This category of "other Asian" is sizable, representing 2.4 million of the aforementioned 16.2 million.

63. CAF 2019 program, 44.

64. CAF 2019 program, 45.

65. As scholars have shown, data are not neutral. Biruk (2018) argues that "all data—even that verified as clean by demographers—are cooked by the processes and practices of production" (5). Even in situations where quantitative data is deemed to be "neutral" or that "numbers don't lie," Biruk reminds us that "activities of data collection not only produce numbers but shape personhood, sociality, and truth claims" (4). The pages themselves are directly credited from a *Diversity Inc. Best Practices* "Asian American and Pacific Islander Heritage Month Meeting in a Box" 2017 document. It is unclear where *Diversity Inc. Best Practices* draws its data from, but, given the information provided earlier and the "clients" it serves, it is likely based on census and advertising information. According to its website: *Diversity Inc. Best Practices,* "is a subscription website that offers insights, best practices and case studies on diversity and inclusion management. Corporations, nonprofits, academia and government/military organizations utilize content on the website to help evolve and gain support for their workplace diversity and inclusion initiatives," available at https://www.diversityincbestpractices.com/about-diversityinc -best-practices/, accessed August 6, 2021.

66. Park 2005.

67. The tour has not been part of the CAF since 2019. Due to COVID-19, the 2020 festival was canceled, and the 2021 festival was online. Both the 2022 and 2023 festivals were in person and a map and self-guided walking tour was included in the program booklet that discussed some of the elements of the trolley tour. When I volunteered at the 2023 festival as a greeter, a handful of visitors inquired about the absence of the trolley tour.

68. CAF, *Tour Guide Instructions and Script*, 2018, 3.

69. Trolley tour field notes, May 20, 2017.

70. After my first year as a tour guide in 2018, I was invited to participate as a volunteer in the same capacity for the 2019 CAF. However, I was unable to volunteer or even attend the 2019 festival as a result of an unavoidable scheduling conflict.

71. CAF field notes, May 18, 2018.

72. CAF field notes, May 18, 2018.

73. CAF field notes, May 18, 2018.

74. Michael Byun, May 2018.

75. Michael Byun, May 2018.

76. Michael Byun, May 2018.

77. See Finkel and Platt 2020.

78. Richards 2017.

79. Finkel and Platt 2020, 4.

80. Finkel and Platt 2020, 5. See, also, Hawkins 2015.

81. Duffy, Mair, and Waitt 2019.

82. L. Kurashige 2002.

83. In L. Kurashige's 2002 long historical view we can see the various roles and tensions of the festival leading up to and after the mass incarceration of the Japanese American community during World War II and then the changing role of the festival in the late twentieth century as a form of transnational Pacific Rim nodal connection. Kurashige's work shows that the economic project of placemaking is different on the scale of ethnic neighborhood than at the scale of city branding.

84. Lisa Wong, October 2016.

85. Lisa Wong, October 2016.

86. Field notes May 20, 2017.

87. CAF program book 2019, 2018, 2017, 34, in all three versions.

88. CAF program book 2019, 2018, 2017, 34, in all three versions.

89. CAF program book 2019, 2018, 2017, 34, in all three versions.

90. CAF program book 2019, 2018, 2017, 34, in all three versions.

91. Lisa Wong, October 2016.

92. Bentley 2010, 209.

93. Lisa Wong, October 2016.

94. Mannur 2005, 74.

95. Ku 2014, 63.

96. hooks 1992.

97. hooks 1992, 23.

98. Heap 2009. As L. Kurashige notes, the organizers of the Little Tokyo Nisei Week Festival, looking to capitalize on this trend, began to outreach to white people as a source of revenue and festival growth (2002, 43–47).

CONCLUSION

1. AsiaTown Interactive Map, available at http://midtown.landau.design/, accessed January 19, 2022.

2. MidTown Cleveland 2020, September 8. available at https://www.asiatowncleveland.org/imagine/, accessed May 18, 2023.

3. MidTown Cleveland 2020, "Imagine AsiaTown Visioning Report: We're Growing Home," November, available at https://www.asiatowncleveland.org/wp-content/uploads/Imagine-AsiaTown-Visioning-Report.pdf.

4. MidTown Cleveland 2020, "Imagine AsiaTown Visioning Report," 5, accessed January 19, 2022.

5. A note that the visioning process meetings occurred August to October 2020, during the COVID-19 pandemic and a virulent surge of anti-Asian racism throughout Cleveland and the country.

6. MidTown Cleveland 2020, "Imagine AsiaTown Visioning Report," 5.

7. MidTown Cleveland 2020, "Imagine AsiaTown Visioning Report," 5.

8. Betts 2020.

9. Mss 3788, "Federation for Community Planning," Container 16, Folder 389, the Western Reserve Historical Society.

10. Utah State University Digital Collections, Topaz Japanese American Relocation Center Digital Collection, "Central Utah Final Accountability Report," October 1945, p. 46, available at https://digital.lib.usu.edu/digital/collection/p16944coll135/search/searchterm/Central%20Utah%20Final%20Accountability%20Report/field/title/mode/exact/conn/and/order/title/ad/asc, accessed October 6, 2022.

11. George's father Toraichi was born on August 11, 1890, and his mother, Ishino, was born on September 27, 1893, both presumably in Japan as they are recorded as "A" for alien. Utah State University Digital Collections, Topaz Japanese American Relocation Center Digital Collection, "Central Utah Final Accountability Report," October 1945, p. 46, available at https://digital.lib.usu.edu/digital/collection/p16944coll135/search/searchterm/Central%20Utah%20Final%20Accountability%20Report/field/title/mode/exact/conn/and/order/title/ad/asc, accessed October 6, 2022.

12. George Inada letter, Mss 3788, "Federation for Community Planning," Container 16, Folder 389, the Western Reserve Historical Society.

13. Hartman 2019, xiii.

14. Hartman 2008, 12.

List of Interviews

Name	Date	Location	Position at Time of Interview
Lisa Wong and Tony Louie	October 10, 2016	Asia Plaza	President OCA/Cofounder CAF/Community member
Michael Fleming	October 11, 2016	Café 55	Executive director, St. Clair Superior CDC
Ashley Shaw	October 11, 2016	Flying Fig	Chief operating officer, Ohio City Inc. CDC
Mark Souther	October 11, 2016	Sung's House	CSU professor, urban history
Joyce Huang—tour	May 20, 2017	CAF AsiaTown Tour	CAF volunteer
Lisa Wong 2	February 17, 2018	Li Wah bar	President OCA/Cofounder CAF
Joyce Huang 1	February 18, 2018	KoKo Bakery	Urban planner, Midtown Cleveland Inc. CDC
Norm Krumholz	April 9, 2018	CSU office	CSU professor, urban studies, past City of Cleveland Planning Director
Dennis Keating	April 9, 2018	CSU office	CSU professor, urban studies
Luanne Bole-Becker	May 19, 2018	Rising Star Coffee	Producer, Faces of AsiaTown
Rob Curry	May 21, 2018	CHN, Housing Partners, Asia Plaza	Executive director CHN Housing Partners
Michael Byun	May 21, 2018	Tastebuds	Executive director ASIA Inc., ATAC member

(continued)

(*continued*)

Name	Date	Location	Position at Time of Interview
Joe Fong	May 21, 2018	Koko Bakery	AsiaTown resident, ATAC member
Kim Scott	May 22, 2018	City Hall	Planner, Cleveland City Planning Commission, ATAC member
Radhika Reddy	May 22, 2018	Ariel International Center	Partner, Ariel Ventures, ATAC member
Kate Durban and Kevin Nowak	May 23, 2018	CHN, Housing Partners, Asia Plaza	CHN Housing Partners Asst Director/Legal liaison
Michael Yap	May 23, 2018	Phoenix Coffee	Developer, ATAC member
Joyce Huang 2	May 23, 2018	Plum	Director of planning and placemaking, MidTown Cleveland Inc., ATAC member
Kathy Haka and Jean Waschtschenko	May 25, 2018	Asian Evergreen	Asian Evergreen, Service coordinator/Manager
Josh Rosen	June 13, 2018	Mueller Lofts	Partner, Sustainable Community Associates
Steve Hom	March 4, 2019	Wonton Gourmet and BBQ	Manager Asia Plaza, ATAC member
Joyce Huang 3	March 4, 2019	KoKo Bakery	Director of planning and placemaking, MidTown Cleveland Inc., ATAC member
Chia-Min Chen	March 4, 2019	Ariel International Center	Asian liaison, City of Cleveland, ATAC member
Karis Tzeng	September 14, 2022	LJ Shanghai	Vice president of planning/Director of AsiaTown initiatives, ATAC member

References

PRIMARY DOCUMENTS

Newspapers
Cleveland Plain Dealer
New York Times
Topaz Times

Community Documents
AsiaTown Advisory Committee Meeting Minutes.
"AsiaTown Transportation and Streetscape Plan: Uncovering an Emerging Neighborhood," December 2010.
Cleveland Asian Festival Program Books 2017, 2018, 2019.
"Federation for Community Planning." MS 3788. Western Reserve Historical Society.
"Greater AsiaTown Area Master Plan—Phase 1A, 1B and 1C." Draft report, October 30, 2013.
"The Hough Riots." Regional Church Planning Office. Report No. 43, July 1968. Available at http://web.ulib.csuohio.edu/hough/HoughRiots.pdf. Accessed December 16, 2021.
MidTown Cleveland. "'We're Growing Home': Imagine AsiaTown Visioning Report." November 2020.

Government Documents
Cuyahoga County Planning Commission. "2020 Census: Population by Race." Available at https://www.countyplanning.us/resources/census-data/decennial-census/2020-race/. Accessed April 26, 2024.
Executive Order 9066, February 19, 1942; General Records of the United States Government; Record Group 11; National Archives.

U.S. Department of the Interior. War Agency Liquidation Unit (formerly War Relocation Authority). 1947. "People in Motion: The Postwar Adjustment of the Evacuated Japanese Americans."

U.S. War Relocation Authority. 1946. "Great Lakes Area Final Overall Report."

Utah State University Digital Collections. 1945. Topaz Japanese American Relocation Center Digital Collection. "Central Utah Final Accountability Report," https://digital.lib.usu.edu/digital/collection/p16944coll135/search/searchterm/Central%20Utah%20Final%20Accountability%20Report/field/title/mode/exact/conn/and/order/title/ad/asc, accessed October 6, 2022.

ORAL HISTORIES, DENSHO DIGITAL ARCHIVE

Isao East Oshima Interview. Densho Digital Repository. Twin Cities JACL Collection, denshovh-oisao-01, June 17, 2009. Accessed December 5, 2022.

Yae Wada Interview. Densho Digital Repository. Densho Visual History Collection, ddr-densho-1000-476, April 12, 2019. Accessed December 5, 2022.

Yasu Koyamatsu Momii Interview. Densho Digital Repository. Densho Visual History Collection, denshovh-myasu-01, October 25, 2011. Accessed December 5, 2022.

SELECTED BIBLIOGRAPHY

Aguilar San-Juan, Karin. 2009. *Little Saigons: Staying Vietnamese in America*. Minneapolis: University of Minnesota Press.

Ahlgren, Angela. 2018. *Drumming Asian America: Taiko, Performance, and Cultural Politics*. Oxford: Oxford University Press.

Ahmed, Sara. 2012. *On Being Included: Racism and Diversity in Institutional Life*. Durham, NC: Duke University Press.

Akers, Joshua. 2015. "Emerging Market City." *Environment and Planning A: Economy and Space* 47 (9): 1842–1858.

Akers, Joshua, Vincent Béal, and Max Rousseau. 2020. "Redefining the City and Demolishing the Rest: The Techno-Green Fix in Postcrash Cleveland, Ohio." *Environment and Planning E: Nature and Space* 3 (1): 207–227.

Anderson, Kay J. 1987. "The Idea of Chinatown: The Power of Place and Institutional Practice in the Making of a Racial Category." *Annals of the Association of American Geographers* 77 (4): 580–598.

Aronson, Emily, and Robert B. Kent. 2008. "A Midwestern Chinatown? Cleveland, Ohio in North American Context, 1900–2005." *Journal of Cultural Geography* 25 (3): 305–329.

Babson, Steve. (1984) 1986. *Working Detroit: The Making of a Union Town*. Reprint, Detroit: Wayne State University Press.

Banh, Jenny, and Haiming Liu, eds. 2020. *American Chinese Restaurants: Society, Culture, and Consumption*. London: Routledge.

Bedoya, Roberto. 2014. "Spatial Justice: Rasquachification, Race and the City." *Creative Time Reports*, September 15, 2014. Available at https://creativetimereports.org/2014/09/15/spatial-justice-rasquachification-race-and-the-city/.

Bentley, Amy. 2010. "From Culinary Other to Mainstream America." In *Culinary Tourism*, edited by Lucy M. Long, 209–225. Lexington: University Press of Kentucky.

Betts, Victor. 2020. "Imagining Futures through the Archives." *American Studies Journal Dialogues*, July 1, 2020. Available at https://amsj.blog/2020/07/01/on-teaching-in-the-time-of-covid-19-imagining-futures-through-the-archives/.

Biruk, Crystal. 2018. *Cooking Data*. Durham, NC: Duke University Press.

Bow, Leslie. 2010. *Partly Colored: Asian Americans and Racial Anomaly in the Segregated South*. New York: New York University Press.

Boyle, Kevin. 2004. *Arc of Justice: A Saga of Race, Civil Rights, and Murder in the Jazz Age*. New York: Henry Holt.

Bratt, Rachel G., and William M. Rohe. 2007. "Challenges and Dilemmas Facing Community Development Corporations in the United States." *Community Development Journal* 42 (1): 63–78.

Brooks, Charlotte. 2000. "In the Twilight Zone between Black and White: Japanese American Resettlement and Community in Chicago, 1942–1945." *Journal of American History* 86 (4): 1655–1687.

———. 2009. *Alien Neighbors, Foreign Friends: Asian Americans, Housing, and the Transformation of the Urban California*. Chicago: University of Chicago Press.

———. 2019. *American Exodus: Second-Generation Chinese Americans in China, 1901–1949*. Oakland: University of California Press.

Chang, Yoonmee. 2010. *Writing the Ghetto: Class, Authorship, and the Asian American Ethnic Enclave*. New Brunswick, NJ: Rutgers University Press.

Chen, Yong. 2014. *Chop Suey, USA: The Story of Chinese Food in America*. New York: Columbia University Press.

Cheng, Cindy I-Fen. 2006. "Out of Chinatown and into the Suburbs: Chinese Americans and the Politics of Cultural Citizenship in Early Cold War America." *American Quarterly* 58, no. 4 (December): 1067–1090.

Cheng, Wendy. 2013. *The Changs Next Door to the Díazes: Remapping Race in Suburban California*. Minneapolis: University of Minnesota Press.

Cho, Lily. 2010. *Eating Chinese: Culture on the Menu in Small Town Canada*. Toronto: University of Toronto Press.

Choi, Anne Soon. 2016. "'La Choy Chinese Food Swings American?': Korean Immigrant Entrepreneurship and American Orientalism before World War II." *Cultural and Social History* 13 (4): 521–538.

Coe, Andrew. 2009. *Chop Suey: A Cultural History of Chinese Food in the United States*. Oxford: Oxford University Press.

Cohen, Lizabeth. 2003. *A Consumers' Republic: The Politics of Mass Consumption in Postwar America*. New York: Alfred A. Knopf.

Day, Iyko. 2016. *Alien Capital: Asian Racialization and the Logic of Settler Colonial Capitalism*. Durham, NC: Duke University Press.

Dewar, Margaret. 2013. "What Helps or Hinders Nonprofit Developers in Reusing Vacant, Abandoned, and Contaminated Property?" In *The City after Abandonment*, edited by Margaret Dewar and June Manning Thomas, 174–196. Philadelphia: University of Pennsylvania Press.

Dhingra, Pawan. 2012. *Life behind the Lobby: Indian American Motel Owners and the American Dream*. Palo Alto: Stanford University Press.

Duffy, Michelle, Judith Mair, and Gordon Waitt. 2019. "Addressing Community Diversity: The Role of the Festival Encounter." In *Accessibility, Inclusion, and Diversity in Critical Event Studies*, edited by Rebecca Finkel, Briony Sharp, and Majella Sweeney, 9–20. New York: Routledge.

Dunbar-Ortiz, Roxanne. 2021. *Not "A Nation of Immigrants": Settler Colonialism, White Supremacy, and a History of Erasure and Exclusion*. Boston: Beacon.

Dutka, Alan F. 2014. *AsiaTown Cleveland: From Tong Wars to Dim Sum*. Charleston, SC: History.

East Asian Resources in Ohio. 1981. Columbus: Ohio State University.

Espiritu, Yến Lê. 1992. *Asian American Panethnicity: Bridging Institutions and Identities.* Philadelphia: Temple University Press.

———. 2003. *Home Bound: Filipino American Lives across Cultures, Communities, and Countries.* Berkeley: University of California Press.

Espiritu, Yến Lê, and Michael Omi. 2000. "'Who Are You Calling Asian?': Shifting Identity Claims, Racial Classification, and the Census." In *Transforming Race Relations: A Public Policy Report,* edited by Paul Ong, 43–101. Los Angeles: LEAP and UCLA Asian American Studies Center.

Fajardo, Kale Bantigue. 2014. "Queering and Transing the Great Lakes: Filipino/a Tomboy Masculinities and Manhood across Waters." *GLQ: A Journal of Lesbian and Gay Studies* 20 (1–2): 115–140.

Fincher, Ruth, Kurt Iveson, Helga Leitner, and Valerie Preston. 2014. "Planning the Multicultural City: Celebrating Diversity or Reinforcing Difference?" *Progress in Planning* 92:1–55.

Finkel, Rebecca, and Louise Platt. 2020. "Cultural Festivals and the City." *Geography Compass* 14:1–12.

Fong, Timothy. 1994. *The First Suburban Chinatown: The Remaking of Monterey Park, California.* Philadelphia: Temple University Press.

Freund, David M. 2007. *Colored Property: State Policy and White Racial Politics in Suburban America.* Chicago: University of Chicago Press.

Frey, William, H. 2018. *Diversity Explosion: How New Racial Demographics Are Remaking America.* Washington, DC: Brookings Institution.

Fugita, Stephen. 1977. "The Japanese Americans." In Fugita et al. 1977, 53–120.

Fugita, Stephen, David Namkoong, Domingo Patawaran, and Suey Yee, eds. 1977. *Asian Americans and Their Communities of Cleveland.* Cleveland Ethnic Heritage Studies. Cleveland: Cleveland State University.

Gaston, Mauricio, and Marie Kennedy. 1987. "Capital Investment or Community Development? The Struggle for Land Control by Boston's Black and Latino Community." *Antipode* 19 (2): 178–209.

Gilmore, Ruth Wilson. 2002. "Fatal Couplings of Power and Difference: Notes on Racism and Geography." *Professional Geographer* 54 (1): 15–25.

Gupta-Carlson, Himanee. 2018. *Muncie, India(na): Middletown and Asian America.* Urbana: University of Illinois Press.

Hartman, Saidiya. 2008. "Venus in Two Acts." *Small Axe* 12 (2): 1–14.

———. 2019. *Wayward Lives, Beautiful Experiments: Intimate Histories of Social Upheaval.* New York: W. W. Norton.

Hawkins, Michael. 2015. "Ethnic Festivals, Cultural Tourism, and Pan-Ethnicity." In *Contemporary Ethnic Geographies,* 2nd ed., edited by Christopher A. Airriess, 115–138. Lanham, MD: Rowman and Littlefield.

Hayashi, Amy N. 2004. "Japanese American Resettlement: The Midwest and the Middle Atlantic States, 1942–1949." Ph.D. diss., Temple University, Philadelphia.

Heap, Chad. 2009. *Slumming: Sexual and Racial Encounters in American Nightlife, 1885–1940.* Chicago: University of Chicago Press.

Hong, Cathy Park. 2020. *Minor Feelings: An Asian American Reckoning.* New York: One World.

hooks, bell. 1992. *Black Looks.* Boston: South End.

Hsu, Madeline Y. 2015. *The Good Immigrants: How the Yellow Peril Became the Model Minority.* Princeton, NJ: Princeton University Press.

Jayasanker, Laresh. 2020. *Sameness in Diversity: Food and Globalization in Modern America*. Oakland: University of California Press.

Johnson, Susan Lee. 2009. "Domestic Life in the Diggings." In *American Studies: An Anthology*, edited by Janice A. Radway, Kevin K. Gaines, Barry Shank, and Penny Von Eschen, 135–144. Chichester, U.K.: Wiley-Blackwell.

Joshi, Khyati Y., and Jigna Desai, eds. 2013. *Asian Americans in Dixie: Race and Migration in the South*. Urbana: University of Illinois Press.

Kaplan, David H., and Wei Li. 2006. "Introduction: The Places of Ethnic Economies." In *Landscapes of the Ethnic Economy*, edited by David H. Kaplan and Wei Li, 1–14. Lanham, MD: Rowman and Littlefield.

Kibria, Nazli. 1996. "Not Asian, Black or White? Reflections of South Asian American Racial Identity." *Amerasia Journal* 22 (2): 77–86.

Kinney, Rebecca J. 2016. *Beautiful Wasteland: The Rise of Detroit as America's Postindustrial Frontier*. Minneapolis: University of Minnesota Press.

———. 2017. "Detroit Is Closer Than You Think." *Radical History Review* 129:164–176.

———. 2018. "'America's Great Comeback Story': The White Possessive in Detroit Tourism." *American Quarterly* 70 (4) (December): 777–806.

Kirkpatrick, L. Owen. 2007. "The Two 'Logics' of Community Development: Neighborhoods, Markets, and Community Development Corporations." *Politics and Society* 35 (2): 329–359.

Ku, Robert Ji-Song. 2014. *Dubious Gastronomy: The Cultural Politics of Eating Asian in the USA*. Honolulu: University of Hawai'i Press.

Kurashige, Lon. 2002. *Japanese American Celebration and Conflict: A History of Ethnic Identity and Festival, 1934–1990*. Berkeley: University of California Press.

Kurashige, Scott. 2007. *The Shifting Grounds of Race: Black and Japanese Americans in the Making of Multiethnic Los Angeles*. Princeton, NJ: Princeton University Press.

———. 2016. "Race, Space, and Place in Asian American Urban History." In *Oxford Handbook of Asian American History*, edited by David Y. Yoo and Eiichiro Azuma, 373–389. Oxford: Oxford University Press.

Kusmer, Kenneth. 1976. *A Ghetto Takes Shape: Black Cleveland, 1870–1930*. Urbana: University of Illinois Press.

Lackritz, Mark E. (1968) 2010. "The Hough Riots of 1966." *Cleveland Memory*, 50. Available at https://engagedscholarship.csuohio.edu/clevmembks/50.

Lee, Erika. 2009. "Asian American Studies in the Midwest: New Questions, Approaches, and Communities." *Journal of Asian American Studies* 12 (3): 247–273.

Lee, Jennifer 8. 2008. *The Fortune Cookie Chronicles: Adventures in the World of Chinese Food*. New York: Twelve.

Lee, Josephine. 2011. "Introduction." In *Asian American Plays for a New Generation*, edited by Josephine Lee, Don Eitel, and R. A. Shiomi, 1–10. Philadelphia: Temple University Press.

Lee, Robert G. 2009. "The Cold War Origins of the Model Minority Myth." In *Asian American Studies Now: A Critical Reader*, edited by Jean Yu-wen Shen Wu and Thomas C. Chen, 256–271. New Brunswick, NJ: Rutgers University Press.

Levine, Jeremy L. 2017. "The Paradox of Community Power: Cultural Processes and Elite Authority in Participatory Governance." *Social Forces* 95 (3): 1155–1179.

Li, Wei. 2009. *Ethnoburb: The New Ethnic Community in Urban America*. Honolulu: University of Hawai'i Press.

Lin, Jan. 1998. *Reconstructing Chinatown: Ethnic Enclave, Global Change*. Minneapolis: University of Minnesota Press.

———. 2011. *The Power of Urban Ethnic Places: Cultural Heritage and Community Life.* New York: Routledge.

Linehan, Thomas M. 1993. "Japanese American Resettlement in Cleveland." *Journal of Urban History* 20 (1): 54–80.

Ling, Huping. 2004. *Chinese St. Louis: From Enclave to Cultural Community.* Philadelphia: Temple University Press.

———. 2012. *Chinese Chicago: Race, Transnational Migration, and Community since 1870.* Palo Alto: Stanford University Press.

———. 2022. *Chinese Americans in the Heartland: Migration, Work, and Community.* New Brunswick, NJ: Rutgers University Press.

Lipsitz, George. 2011. *How Racism Takes Place.* Philadelphia: Temple University Press.

Liu, Haiming. 2015. *From Canton Restaurant to Panda Express: A History of Chinese Food in the United States.* New Brunswick, NJ: Rutgers University Press.

Lung-Amam, Willow S. 2015. "Malls of Meaning: Building Asian America in Silicon Valley Suburbia." *Journal of American Ethnic History* 34 (2): 18–53.

———. 2017. *Trespassers? Asian Americans and the Battle for Suburbia.* Oakland: University of California Press.

Mannur, Anita. 2005. "Model Minorities Can Cook: Fusion Cuisine in Asian America." In *East Main Street: Asian American Popular Culture*, edited by Shilpa Dave, Leilani Nashime, and Tasha G. Oren, 72–94. New York: New York University Press.

Melamed, Jodi. 2011. *Represent and Destroy: Rationalizing Violence in the New Racial Capitalism.* Minneapolis: University of Minnesota Press.

Mendelson, Anne. 2016. *Chow Chop Suey: Food and the Chinese American Journey.* New York: Columbia University Press.

Molina, Natalia. 2006. *Fit to Be Citizens? Public Health and Race in Los Angeles, 1879–1939.* Berkeley: University of California Press.

———. 2014. *How Race Is Made in America: Immigration, Citizenship, and the Historical Power of Racial Scripts.* Berkeley: University of California Press.

———. 2022. *A Place at the Nayarit: How a Mexican Restaurant Nourished a Community.* Berkeley: University of California Press.

Montgomery, Alesia. 2020. *Greening the Black Urban Regime: The Culture and Commerce of Sustainability in Detroit.* Detroit: Wayne State University Press.

Ngai, Mae. 2004. *Impossible Subjects: Illegal Aliens and the Making of Modern America.* Princeton, NJ: Princeton University Press.

Oda, Meredith. 2018. *The Gateway to the Pacific: Japanese Americans and the Remaking of San Francisco.* Chicago: University of Chicago Press.

Okihiro, Gary Y. 1999. *Storied Lives: Japanese American Students and World War II.* Seattle: University of Washington Press.

Omatsu, Glenn. 2009. "The 'Four Prisons' and the Movements of Liberation: Asian American Activism from the 1960s to the 1990s." In *Asian American Studies Now: A Critical Reader*, edited by Jean Yu-wen Shen Wu and Thomas C. Chen, 298–330. New Brunswick, NJ: Rutgers University Press.

Omi, Michael, and Howard Winant. 1994. *Racial Formation in the United States: From the 1960s to the 1990s.* New York: Routledge.

Padoongpatt, Mark. 2017. *Flavors of Empire: Food and the Making of Thai America.* Oakland: University of California Press.

Park, Lisa Sun-Hee. 2005. *Consuming Citizenship: Children of Asian Immigrant Entrepreneurs.* Palo Alto: Stanford University Press.

Pulido, Laura. 2006. *Black, Brown, Yellow, and Left: Radical Activism in Los Angeles*. Berkeley: University of California Press.

———. 2016. "Geographies and Race and Ethnicity II: Environmental Racism and Racial Capitalism." *Progress in Human Geography* 41 (4): 524–533.

Qadeer, Mohammad Abdul. 2016. *Multicultural Cities: Toronto, New York, and Los Angeles*. Toronto: University of Toronto Press.

Richards, Greg. 2017. "From Place Branding to Placemaking: The Roles of Events." *International Journal of Event and Festival Management* 8 (1): 8–23.

Safransky, Sara. 2014. "Greening the Urban Frontier: Race, Property, and Resettlement in Detroit." *Geoforum* 56:237–248.

———. 2023. *The City after Property: Abandonment and Repair in Postindustrial Detroit*. Durham, NC: Duke University Press.

Saito, Leland. 1998. *Race and Politics: Asian Americans, Latinos, and Whites in a Los Angeles Suburb*. Urbana: University of Illinois Press.

———. 2009. *The Politics of Exclusion: The Failure of Race Neutral Politics in Urban America*. Palo Alto: Stanford University Press.

Shah, Nayan. 2001. *Contagious Divides: Epidemics and Race in San Francisco's Chinatown*. Berkeley: University of California Press.

Sides, Josh. 2004. "Straight into Compton: American Dreams, Urban Nightmares, and the Metamorphosis of a Black Suburb." *American Quarterly* 56 (3): 583–605.

Snow, David A., and Peter J. Leahy. 1980. "The Making of a Black Slum-Ghetto: A Case Study of Neighborhood Transition." *Journal of Applied Behavioral Science* 16 (4): 459–481.

Souther, J. Mark. 2017. *Believing in Cleveland: Managing Decline in "The Best Location in the Nation."* Philadelphia: Temple University Press.

Stapleton, Darwin. 2020. *A History of University Circle in Cleveland*. Cleveland: MSL Academic Endeavors.

Stoecker, Randy. 1997. "The CDC Model of Urban Redevelopment: A Critique and an Alternative." *Journal of Urban Affairs* 19 (1): 1–22.

Stradling, David, and Richard Stradling. 2015. *Where the River Burned: Carl Stokes and the Struggle to Save Cleveland*. Ithaca, NY: Cornell University Press.

Sugrue, Thomas J. 1996. *The Origins of the Urban Crisis: Race and Inequality in Postwar Detroit*. Princeton, NJ: Princeton University Press.

Sumida, Stephen H. 1998. "East of California: Points of Origin in Asian American Studies." *Journal of Asian American Studies* 1 (1): 83–100.

Sussman, Marvin B., R. Clyde White, and Eleanor K. Caplan. 1959. *Hough, Cleveland, Ohio: A Study of Social Life and Change*. Cleveland: Press of Western Reserve University.

Tang, Eric. 2015. *Unsettled: Cambodian Refugees in the New York City Hyperghetto*. Philadelphia: Temple University Press.

Teaford, Jon. 1993. *Cities of the Heartland: The Rise and Fall of the Industrial Midwest*. Bloomington: Indiana University Press.

Thomas, June Manning. 1997. *Redevelopment and Race: Planning a Finer City in Postwar Detroit*. Baltimore: Johns Hopkins University Press.

Tighe, J. Rosie, and Stephanie Ryberg-Webster, eds. 2019. *Legacy Cities: Continuity and Change amid Decline and Renewal*. Pittsburgh: University of Pittsburgh Press.

Trieu, Monica Mong. 2023. *Fighting Invisibility: Asian Americans in the Midwest*. New Brunswick, NJ: Rutgers University Press.

Tuan, Mia. 1998. *Forever Foreigners or Honorary Whites? The Asian Ethnic Experience Today.* New Brunswick, NJ: Rutgers University Press.

U.S. Census Bureau. 2005. "Historical Census Statistics on Population Totals by Race, 1790 to 1990, and by Hispanic Origin, 1970 to 1990, for Large Cities and Other Urban Places in the United States." Working Paper No. POP-WP076, by Campbell Gibson and Kay Jung. Available at https://www.census.gov/library/working-papers/2005/demo/POP-twps0076.html.

———. 2022. "American Community Survey 5-Year Estimates Demographic and Housing." Available at https://data.census.gov/table/ACSDP5Y2022.DP05?g=860XX00US 44114.

Võ, Linda Trinh. 2004. *Mobilizing an Asian American Community.* Philadelphia: Temple University Press.

Wilkinson, Sook, and Victor Jew, eds. 2015. *Asian Americans in Michigan: Voices from the Midwest.* Detroit: Wayne State University Press.

Wilson, Kathryn E. 2015. *Ethnic Renewal in Philadelphia's Chinatown: Space, Place, and Struggle.* Philadelphia: Temple University Press.

Wood, Joseph S. 2006. "Making America at Eden Center." In *From Urban Enclave to Ethnic Suburb: New Asian Communities in Pacific Rim Countries,* edited by Wei Li, 23–40. Honolulu: University of Hawai'i Press.

Wu, Ellen D. 2014. *The Color of Success: Asian Americans and the Origins of the Model Minority.* Princeton, NJ: Princeton University Press.

———. 2015. "Deghettoizing Chinatown: Race and Space in Postwar America." In *Race and Retail: Consumption across the Color Line,* edited by Mia Bay and Ann Fabian, 141–162. New Brunswick, NJ: Rutgers University Press.

Yan, Nancy. 2013. "Negotiating Authenticity: Multiplicity, Anomalies, and Context in Chinese Restaurants." Ph.D. diss., Ohio State University, Columbus.

Yee, Suey. 1977. "Part One: The Chinese Americans." In Fugita et al. 1977, 8–51.

Yeh, Chiou-Ling. 2008. *Making an American Festival: Chinese New Year in San Francisco's Chinatown.* Berkeley: University of California Press.

Yin, Jordan S. 1998. "The Community Development Industry System: A Case Study of Politics and Institutions in Cleveland, 1967–1997." *Journal of Urban Affairs* 20 (2): 137–157.

Yorichi, Alex. 1942. "First Wedding Held." *Topaz Times,* November 17, 2.

Zhao, Xiaojian. 2002. *Remaking Chinese America: Immigration, Family, and Community, 1940–1965.* New Brunswick, NJ: Rutgers University Press.

Zheng, Mingzhe. 2018. "You Have to Learn to Adapt: A Sociolinguistic Study of Chinese Americans in the 'Asian City' of Southeast Michigan." Ph.D. diss., Linguistics, Michigan State University, East Lansing.

Zhou, Min. 2004. "The Role of the Enclave Economy in Immigrant Adaptation and Community Building: The Case of New York's Chinatown." In *Immigrant and Minority Entrepreneurship: The Continuous Rebirth of American Communities,* edited by John Sibley Butler and George Kozmetsky, 37–60. Westport, CT: Praeger.

Zicter, Andrew. 2020. "Making Up Creative Placemaking." *Journal of Planning Education and Research* 40 (3): 278–288.

Zuzindlak, Chelsea. 2015. "'Tell 'Em You're from Detroit': Chinese Americans in the Model City." In *Asian Americans in Michigan: Voices from the Midwest,* edited by Victor Jew and Sook Wilkinson, 50–69. Detroit: Wayne State University Press.

Index

Page numbers in *italics* represent images.

Rebecca Jo Kinney is an Associate Professor in the School of Cultural and Critical Studies at Bowling Green State University. She is the author of *Beautiful Wasteland: The Rise of Detroit as America's Postindustrial Frontier*, which won the 2018 Institute for Humanities Research Transdisciplinary Book Award as well as the Midwest Popular Culture and American Culture Association's Best Single Work.

Also in the series *Asian American History and Culture*: